A Year of
Assemblies Book 2

Redvers Brandling

Published in 1993 in Great Britain by:
Simon & Schuster Education

This edition published in 2000 by:
Stanley Thornes (Publishers) Ltd

Reprinted in 2003 by:
Nelson Thornes Ltd
Delta Place
27 Bath Road
CHELTENHAM
GL53 7TH
United Kingdom

03 04/ 10 9 8 7 6 5 4 3 2

A catalogue record for this book is available from the British Library

ISBN 0–7847–5835–6

Typeset by Florence Production Ltd, Stoodleigh, Devon
Printed and bound in Spain by Graphy Cems

Contents

Section A Complete assemblies

September

October

November

Acknowledgements

For many years the staff and children of Dewhurst St. Mary School, Cheshunt, were a receptive audience for material such as is contained in this book. They were also a source of both information and inspiration with their own presentations. I will always be grateful to them.

The material contained in *A Year of Assemblies Book 2*, originally made up part of the *Autumn*, *Spring* and *Summer* assembly books.

It should also be mentioned that some of the stories in these books have been used, heard and re-adapted several times in assemblies. In consequence their original sources are not remembered and if this has unwittingly caused the infringement of copyright, the author apologises and will correct this omission in future editions, if notified.

Introduction

The preparation of regular, effective assemblies is no easy task, but the rewards for good presentations are considerable. In examining this statement it is useful to look at some of the comments made in the Secretary of State's proposals in the review of the National Curriculum in England (QCA 1999). These comments highlight some consistent aims:

- 'to establish more explicit and coherent provision in the areas of personal, social . . . education and responsibility'

- 'develop pupils' knowledge and understanding of their role and responsibilities as active citizens in a modern democracy'

- 'equip them with the values, skills and knowledge to deal with the difficult moral and social questions they face'

- 'to be aware that people and other living things have needs, and that pupils have some responsibility in meeting them'

- 'to identify and show respect for differences and similarities between people'

- 'to recognise that family and friends care for each other'

Where better to achieve these aims than in a school assembly? In seeking to do so, and suggesting how they might be achieved, there still seems no better description of what is required than the list proposed in *Collective Worship for Schools in Hertfordshire*:

'In achieving this meaningful act . . . valid are . . . stories and readings, dance and drama, prayers/meditations, creative silence, songs/hymns/music, sacred/secular readings, artefacts and natural materials, children's contributions, visual aids.'

A Year of Assemblies Book 1 and *Book 2* seek to provide constructive and practical help for assemblies throughout the school year. Each book contains eighty ready-made assemblies. These are divided up into presentations for each month and they are 'instant' inasmuch as they provide an introduction, story and a suggested hymn and prayer as well as additional information for the teacher. It is also recommended that any pre-assembly reflection and preparation can add considerably to the material's potential.

Section A

Complete assemblies

September

1 Being different

Introduction

This is one of those stories which, when you listen to it, you think: 'Oh I would never have behaved like that'. But . . . could you be sure?

Story

Life was going on very much as usual on Planet Zemon. The space shuttles arrived from different galaxies, the living blocks maintained the same temperature as always, the automatic self-drive cars swayed round each other to get to their programmed destinations. Then, he arrived.

'I've never seen anything like him,' said RBT 1.

'Nor me,' answered WRBT 2.

'Where has he come from?'

'I've heard that somehow or other he's been transported through a time zone from a place called Earth.'

'Have you noticed the clothes he wears – disgusting – not at all like our all-in-one plastic coverings.'

'And food too – he doesn't like the computerised meal tablet bank. Keeps saying he'd like real bread and cornflakes, and something called chips.'

'Worst of all, when he was in the programmed environment he even seemed worried about that.'

'When they pressed "Summer Scene" to come up on the screen he said it wasn't the same as real trees and real grass.'

'Did you know that MEGA R had asked robots to invite this . . . person . . . into their homes? Well, I'm not going to.'

'Nor me. Indeed, if it was up to me I'd suspend him on Time Warp Island.'

'Yes, certainly get him away from us because he's . . . well . . . he's . . .'

'I know what you mean. We don't want him here. He's . . .'

'Different! That's what he is – different!'

'That's right. We don't want anybody who's different here.'

Information for the teacher

1 This may be a useful early-in-the-school-year assembly as, in the hands of a sensitive teacher, the material could be used to lead on to discussion of intolerance, in any of the many areas in which it is shown.

2 A useful calendar reference here might be the story of Roger Crab, who died on 11th September, 1680.
Crab was a soldier in Cromwell's army and then a successful business man in the field of selling hats. He suddenly decided to give up his affluent lifestyle; he gave away his shop and all his money and went to live in a wooden hut. Because he had chosen to be 'different' he was accused of being a wizard and tortured many times.

Hymn suggestion

Come and Praise Vol 1 'Black and white' No 67

Prayer

Lord, teach us to enjoy and appreciate the differences in people which make our world so interesting and varied. Help us always to be tolerant and understanding and never mean and narrow-minded. Amen.

2 A Maori heroine

Introduction

Sometimes we have to do something without any time to think. This morning's story is about someone who had to do just that – and how her courage and quick thinking saved many lives.

Story

'We're on the rocks!'
   The desperate cry came from a seaman on the deck of the small sailing ship. The 'Delaware' had sailed all the way from England to New Zealand in 1863. There had been no problems until 3rd September when the ship was caught in a terrible storm near Pepin's Island.

There, fighting the tremendous waves and howling wind, all seemed lost when the 'Delaware' struck submerged rocks a hundred yards off the coast.

The crunching, tearing sound of the rocks on the ship's bottom sent a chill of fear through Captain Baldwin. He knew it was only a matter of time before the sea pounded them to pieces.

'Sir, sir – on the shore – look!'

Another cry rang out from the deck. Baldwin peered through the spray to the distant beach. A group of Maoris stood there.

'Quick, get a line ready to throw,' shouted the captain. 'And you,' he went on to a passenger who he knew could speak the Maori language, 'tell them what we're doing.'

Try as they might however the crew couldn't get the safety line to reach the Maoris on shore. Time was running out fast. Then Huria Matenga, one of the Maori women, plunged into the raging seas and swam to a large rock near the ship.

'Now throw it,' she yelled above the turmoil.

This time the line reached her easily. Then, diving back into the sea, she swam once again to the shore. There the waiting Maoris pulled the line, and the heavy safety rope attached to it. In a few seconds the rope was made fast to a rock and the seamen began to swing along it to safety.

Soon, all but one of the crew were safe. Then the rope snapped and a huge wave swept the last man away. But for Huria's bravery nobody would have survived.

Information for the teacher

1   The 'Delaware' was 241 tons and made the passage from England under the command of Captain Robert Baldwin.

2   Huria Matenga was a very important Maori woman, being the chief of three tribes.

3   In recognition of their bravery Huria and the other Maoris were presented with watches and sums of money by the people of Nelson, on New Zealand's South Island.

4   This story could be added to a collection of 'heroes and hero-ines', the point being made to the children that such brave people come in all shapes, sizes, ages, etc.

Hymn suggestion

Come and Praise Vol 1 'Somebody greater' No 5

Prayer

Dear God, Let us give thanks for all those people, now and in the past, whose only thought has been to help others, regardless of the danger to themselves. Give us the strength of character to help other people wherever and whenever we can. Amen.

3 I'm sorry

Introduction

The title for this morning's story is 'I'm sorry.' These are two words which we often find very difficult to say!

Story

Hephaestus was believed by ancient people to be the god of fire, and also the god who looked after the month of September. Here is one of the stories about him.

Hephaestus was the son of Zeus and Hera. One day, after an argument between his parents, Hephaestus took the side of his mother. Zeus was so furious he threw his son out of Olympus, the home of the gods.

'I'm falling!' cried Hephaestus as he plunged through space for a whole day and night. Then, with a cry of pain, he landed on earth near Mount Etna. He was badly hurt, but when he recovered he used the great fires of the volcano to make things.

He built two golden robots who followed him around everywhere. Then, after a great deal of work, he made a spectacular golden throne.

'Now,' thought the still-dissatisfied Hephaestus, 'I'm going to get my own back on my mother. She let my father ban me from Olympus and she's never looked for me or tried to get me back. I'm going to send her this golden throne as a present.'

Now the point about this throne was that, although it looked magnificent, it was really a trap. Hidden springs meant that anybody who sat down in it would be trapped.

Eventually the throne reached Hera.

'It's wonderful,' she muttered to her servants, and sat down on the beautiful seat. Immediately hidden springs clamped shut over her. She couldn't move.

Try as they might the other gods couldn't release Hera. It was decided that the only thing to do was to bring Hephaestus back from earth. The gods knew it would be difficult to get him back so they tried all sorts of tricks, and flattery and false invitations.

Finally the god of wine, Bacchus, tricked Hephaestus into drinking some of his wine, and while the god of fire was sleeping he was taken back to Olympus.

Once there and awake again, he saw his mother trapped in the golden throne. As he did so, all his feelings of wanting to hurt her left him.

'I'm so terribly sorry,' he said, and rushed forward to release his mother from the cruel, hidden springs.

After that Zeus, Hera and Hephaestus were just delighted to be together again. All their disagreements were forgotten. But now Hephaestus had another home and soon he returned to earth to work again in his great forge at Mount Etna.

Information for the teacher

1 Although this is a very spectacular story of contrite behaviour, it could be compared with other examples within the children's own experience. A useful source for stories like this is *Greece and Rome Myths and Legends* by H A Guerber (Tiger Books International).

2 The Romans believed that September, because of its associations, was the month in which fires, volcanic eruptions and earthquakes were most likely to happen. This provides a good opportunity for a link with the Great Fire of London in 1666.

Hymn suggestion

Come and Praise Vol 1 'Light up the Fire' No 55

Prayer

Dear God, We are thinking this morning about how hard it is sometimes to say 'I'm sorry'. This is particularly difficult when somebody has done something unkind or hurtful to us first.

Give us the strength to realise that it is much better to be at peace with each other. Please help us in this way. Amen.

4 This month

Introduction

Every month of the year has interesting things about it. These can be very different. Let's think about September.

This month

September is an important month for everybody who works in a school! For children and grown-ups it is the beginning of the school year, a time of new classes and changes of teacher. It is a time of beginnings.

Outside of school it is a time of both beginnings and endings. Summer is ending and nature is getting ready for winter. The leaves on some trees are changing colour and others are already falling to the ground. Hedges and bushes have berries on them and birds who spend the winter here feast on these and grow fat in readiness for the hard times when it is cold and there is little food. People enjoy berries too, and blackberries collected from hedges make delicious jam.

There is a lot of activity in the sky with swallows and martins gathering in great flocks and preparing to fly off to warmer countries. If you get the chance to see any squirrels this month try and look closely at their tails. These are now getting thick and bushy so that their owners can wrap them round their bodies for extra warmth.

September is a month when we remember some great events of the past – the Great Fire of London (1666); the opening of Britain's first railway (1830); the start of the Second World War (1939).

Information for the teacher

1   As a follow-up to this assembly some outside observation would be helpful. Depending on localities and opportunities, the following natural things might be observed: horse chestnuts usually offer the first and most dramatic change in the colour of their leaves; leaves will already be falling from limes, and acorns from oaks.

Animals are getting their winter coats; birds are congregating; mushrooms and other fungi are beginning to appear; spiders can be found around the school buildings; daddy longlegs (craneflies) are prolific.

2   Two particularly appropriate September poems for use with primary children are: 'Friends' by Elizabeth Jennings, and 'Back to School' by John Walsh.

Hymn suggestion

Come and Praise Vol 1 'Autumn Days' No 4

Prayer

Dear God, Help us to use all our senses to appreciate the lovely month of September. Help us to be a good friend now that we are back at school. Help us to enjoy work and play during our school days.

5 A woman at sea

Introduction

In times past there have been quite a few jobs which men thought women couldn't do – until a woman proved them wrong! This morning's story starts with a little girl who was interested in engines.

Story

'Victoria, where have you been? You're filthy!'

'It's all right, Mum, I've just been taking that old car engine to bits.'

Victoria Drummond's mother looked at the grease and oil which covered her daughter's hands. No matter how she tried she could never keep her little girl away from engines, tools, oil and grease.

'I don't know what we're going to do with you,' gasped Mrs Drummond.

But Victoria certainly knew what she wanted to do with herself. As she grew older she became even more interested in engines and when she was nineteen she began to study to become a ship's engineer. When she passed her exams she was the first woman ever to qualify for this job. But there were still difficulties . . .

'We don't want a woman on our ship.'

'She'll never be able to do all that heavy work.'

'Women are unlucky on ships.'

These were the sort of comments Victoria heard, but she wouldn't give up. Finally she got a job on a ship going from England to Australia, and she proved to be so good that ships were always glad to have her after this.

During this time the Second World War broke out and one day Victoria was in the engine room of a ship when it was hit by a bomb from an enemy plane. For a time it seemed as if the ship might sink, so Victoria ordered all the men from the engine room to go on deck where they would be safer. They didn't want to leave her, but she insisted.

More damage took place to the ship and Victoria fought with the controls as broken pipes fired jets of scalding steam all round her. So hot was the steam that she would have been blinded or very badly burned if she had got in its way. Finally she managed to get things under control and the enemy planes flew away. Her engine room crew rushed back to help their chief.

'You're safe, Miss Drummond,' they cheered.

'But for you the ship would have gone down!'

'That's enough of that,' said the modest Victoria. 'Come on now – back to work.'

But more people were to hear of Victoria's bravery. When the ship docked back in England she was invited to Buckingham Palace to receive a medal from the king. Many people were pleased that a little girl had once loved engines as her favourite toys!

Information for the teacher

1   Victoria Drummond was the daughter of Captain Malcolm Drummond, who was a groom-in-waiting to Queen Victoria. The queen was her godmother.

2   She was recognised as a qualified sea-going Second Engineer in 1924.

3   In 1926 she became the first woman in the world to hold a Chief Engineer's ticket.

4   Victoria took part in the Dunkirk evacuation in 1940, and the action described in the story above took place in mid-Atlantic when her ship was attacked by a German Condor plane.

5   She was the first woman ever to be awarded the Lloyd's War Medal for bravery at sea. The September link is with the beginning of World War Two in September, 1939.

Hymn suggestion

Come and Praise Vol 2 'O let us spread the pollen of peace' No 145

Prayer

Let us appreciate the talents which have been given to us. Let us have the wisdom to see opportunities to use these talents. Let us have the sensitivity to use them always for the good of others.

6 The Victoria Cross

Introduction

There are many different kinds of courage. The Victoria Cross is the highest medal this country awards for courage in wartime. This is the story of how one young man won it.

Story

It was 15th September, 1940 and a Hampden bomber of the Royal Air Force was flying on a mission over Belgium in the early part of the Second World War. The pilot of the bomber was Flying Officer Connor and the wireless operator was Sergeant John Hannah.

'We are nearing the target.' The pilot alerted his crew over the intercommunication system.

'Keep a look out for . . .'

Flying Officer Connor couldn't finish the sentence because there was a terrific explosion in the plane. It had been hit by a shell. With engines screaming and flames already licking through the fuselage, the bomber dived earthwards as the pilot fought to regain control.

Finally Flying Officer Connor managed to get the plane levelled out but he knew they were in serious danger.

'Pilot to crew, pilot to crew,' he called over the intercom. 'I don't think I can get her back – bale out, bale out!'

The navigator and the rear gunner immediately put on their parachutes and jumped out of the plane. Sergeant John Hannah, however, looked at the raging flames and thought: 'If I bale out, the pilot will never get out in time. He'll be killed . . . but if I try to put the fire out . . .'

'Sir,' John's voice sounded in Flying Officer Connor's ears.

'What are you doing still on board? I told you to bale out,' replied the anxious pilot.

'I'm going to have a try at putting the fire out,' said John quietly.

Connor didn't say anything, but turning his head to look round he was horrified. Behind him was a wall of flames and the heat beat on his face.

Meanwhile John had started work with the fire extinguishers. There were great holes in the sides and floor of the plane and rounds of ammunition for the guns which lay on the floor kept exploding in the flames and flying in all directions. The metal doors in the plane had buckled and melted and the electrical equipment was on fire.

Refusing to be discouraged by the terrifying scene, John kept using one extinguisher after another to fight the flames, despite being almost suffocated by smoke and fumes. As he did so the plane juddered and sank lower and lower in the sky as it struggled homewards.

Finally, with the airfield in sight Flying Officer Connor felt a hand on his shoulder. 'Fire's out, sir,' said John in his quiet way.

Connor couldn't believe what his young, 18-year-old wireless operator had achieved, but he hadn't time to comment – the landing strip was coming up ahead.

Minutes later the cruelly damaged bomber landed. John jumped to the ground as if returning from a routine mission.

The next day, however, the plane was examined by experts. They could hardly believe what they saw. It seemed impossible that any aircraft could reach home after such damage had been suffered.

That it had done so, and the life of Flying Officer Connor had been saved, was due entirely to the courage of the young wireless operator. Sergeant John Hannah was awarded the Victoria Cross for his bravery.

Information for the teacher

1   The Victoria Cross was instituted in 1856. The medals used to be made from the metal of guns captured in the Crimea.

2   The Hampden bomber in this story was attacking German barges moored at Antwerp.

3   This assembly/story might be linked with a visit to somewhere like the Imperial War Museum, Lambeth Road, London SE1 6HZ, www.iwm.org.uk or its counterpart at RAF Duxford.

Hymn suggestion

Come and Praise Vol 1 'When a knight won his spurs' No 50

Prayer

Let us think this morning about some words from the Bible. Listen to them carefully: 'Prepare yourself for testing. Set a straight course, be resolute. Do not lose your head in time of disaster' (Ecclesiasticus 2, 1–2).

7 At the fair

Introduction

If somebody said to you, 'Let's go to the Fair', you would be pleased and probably excited. You would think of flashing lights, music, rides on roundabouts and dodgems, funny or interesting sideshows. But fairs weren't always like this.

Story

Matt kept bending the fingers of his left hand. When he did this the pain in his arm eased a bit and he could almost bend it properly.

'Well, I wonder who is going to pick us this time?' said Josiah, who stood next to Matt, shuffling in the cool autumn air.

Along with Matt and Josiah stood rows and rows of other men. They had all come to the Mop Fair on Michaelmas Day to offer themselves for hire for the coming year.

'I hope somebody does,' muttered Matt, as much to himself as Josiah.

He knew that the farmers picked only the strongest looking men to work on their farms for the year. And if you didn't get picked you didn't have any work . . . so you didn't eat and neither did your family.

Matt pulled his shoulders back and tried to look fit and keen to work. A ruddy-faced farmer stopped in front of him and Josiah: 'You two,' he said, 'done plenty of farm work?'

Josiah nodded. 'We certainly have. You won't find two better workers than us, boss.'

'Hmm, I wonder,' answered the farmer. Then shooting out his hand he grasped the muscles in Matt's left arm. Pain shot through Matt's arm like a stab of quick burning fire. Somehow he managed not to flinch.

'We can do anything those young'uns can do,' he managed to blurt out through gritted teeth.

Without a job he couldn't feed Martha and the children, and that didn't bear thinking about.

'Right,' said the farmer, making up his mind. 'Start tomorrow. You know the wages.'

Matt felt relief surge through him. He had a job for another year. Then the worry started again. How much longer would his arm last out? Could he stand the pain? Would anybody find out about it?

Information for the teacher

1 On the day after Michaelmas (29th September), every year after 1351 and the Statute of Labourers, agricultural labourers paraded with their implements at market towns all over the country. Each hoped to be hired for the coming year. After the hiring procedures a 'Mop Fair' was held.

2 Obviously Michaelmas (St Michael's Day) was a very important occasion in earlier years too. St Michael was often portrayed as a warrior with a spear, who killed Lucifer the rebel angel.

3 The eating of goose was a tradition on Michaelmas Day. One reason for furthering this was due to the fact that Queen Elizabeth I was eating goose when news of the great victory over the Spanish Armada was brought to her. She was so pleased that she said from that point on she would always eat goose on that particular day.

Hymn suggestion

Come and Praise Vol 2 'Michaelmas Daisies' No 137

Prayer

Dear God, Help us to appreciate how fortunate we are to live in this present day, when there are fewer hardships than in days gone by.

Please help those less fortunate people in other parts of the world for whom hardship, lack of work, education and food still make life very difficult. Amen.

October

8 On the roads

Introduction

Every day people are killed or injured on our roads. We must, at all times, be careful in traffic. Sometimes, however, when an accident does occur it is someone's bravery which saves lives.

Story

On an October day in a Hornsey courtroom a group of people were being praised for their courage.

'Without your bravery this man would have died,' said the coroner, Dr Vanezis.

He was talking about the road accident, from which Mr Shane Fowler was saved. Mr Fowler was in a Renault 21 car which crashed at a road junction in Enfield and burst into flames.

Keith Dear and his wife were out walking at the time. The terrible noise of the skid and the crunching of metal were followed by the whoosh of flame as the car caught fire.

'Come on,' shouted Mr Dear to his wife, 'we've got to get the driver out of there.'

The two of them ran towards the burning car. At the same time other pedestrians were racing to help too. All of them ignored the fact that the car, which was now lying on its side, could explode at any minute.

'Let's get it upright,' someone shouted.

'It's the only way we'll get him out.'

'Come on, all together – heave!'

Despite the pain of burnt hands and the choking smoke the group got the car back on its wheels.

'He's strapped in,' shouted Mr Dear.

'That's all right,' cried another voice, 'I've got a pocket knife. Let me through and I'll cut the seat belt straps.'

Moving forward as he spoke, the man with the knife began to saw frantically at the unconscious driver's seat belt. After what seemed an age the belt parted and the group found another difficulty – the car door was jammed and wouldn't open.

'We'll have to drag him through this open window,' said Mr Dear. As gently as they could, the rescuers eased the injured man from his car. Because he was unconscious and couldn't help, he was a dead weight and it was very difficult to get him through such a small space.

Whilst this struggle was going on the sound of an ambulance could be heard in the distance. Another pedestrian had rushed to call this.

By now Mr Fowler lay on the pavement.

'Come on, we can't let him stay here – this thing could go up any minute,' shouted Mr Dear. It was the first time anybody had mentioned the danger of an explosion.

As tenderly as possible, Mr Fowler was carried away from the scene of the crash. Soon the ambulance and the fire brigade arrived and experts took over. The rescuers quietly went home.

Later, when they had all been gathered together to hear Dr Vanezis's congratulations, they heard about how badly injured Mr Fowler had been.

With eight broken ribs, severe bruising and shock, he had had to stay in hospital for four weeks. Without the courage and quick action of Mr Dear and the others Mr Fowler would certainly have died.

Information for the teacher

1 Newspapers are a virtually inexhaustible source of stories like this. This one takes a positive approach, but sometimes a negative approach detailing the carelessness or irresponsibility of some road user is equally useful in getting a road safety message across to the children.

2 'Selflessness' is a useful theme into which this story would fit; there are many examples of people risking their lives for others. These could vary from those for whom it is a regular task – firemen, lifeboat crew members, industrial rescue workers, etc. to casual bystanders who act with courage and foresight as this group of people did.

3 An obvious Biblical link here is with the Good Samaritan (Luke 10).

4 A useful address in connection with this theme:

The Royal Society for the Prevention of Accidents,
Edgbaston Park, 353 Bristol Road, Edgbaston,
Birmingham B5 7ST, www.rospa.com

Hymn suggestion

Come and Praise Vol 2 'I was lying in the roadway' No 88

Prayer

Dear God, Please give us the wisdom and care to use our roads well so that we don't endanger ourselves or others. Help us to remember the rules of the road so that we might do this.

Let us also give thanks for all those people who help so bravely when accidents do take place. Amen.

9 Saved by a horse

Introduction

Sometimes on special occasions in London, horses can be seen pulling along carriages. Some of the most famous of these are the magnificent Whitbread shire horses. This is a story about one of them.

Story

'Come on there my beauties – giddup!'

Charlie Gardener had driven drays pulled by Whitbread shire horses for many years. On a brisk October morning in 1953 things were a little different because he had a new horse partnering his old friend Gracie.

'Come on Gracie – show him how it's done,' chuckled Charlie.

Between the shafts of the dray Gracie felt her master's tug on the reins and knew he would look after them in the busy London traffic.

For a time all went well, and then Gracie felt the reins go slack – and Charlie's encouragement and instruction could no longer be heard.

The horses of course had no idea that Charlie had collapsed unconscious in his seat. Seriously ill as he was, the reins dangled loosely in his hands and the horses and their mighty wagon were out of control in the hectic traffic.

Gracie, however, sensed that something was wrong – and she wasn't one of the famous Whitbread shire horses for nothing! Keeping a steady pace and making her companion follow suit, she clattered through the streets to the destination she knew best – the stables in Garrett Street.

Eventually Gracie turned into the narrow side street out of the main hustle and bustle. Then, as soon as she had stopped, she began to neigh, stamp her feet and throw her head about. Hearing this most unusual behaviour the stablemen rushed out – and saw Charlie slumped, apparently lifeless, in his seat.

Quickly they lifted the sick man down and he was rushed to hospital. Thankfully he made a full recovery and when he returned to Garrett Street it was with many an extra lump of sugar for Gracie.

'There can't be too many men who can say their life was saved by a horse,' he chuckled, patting Gracie's head.

Information for the teacher

1 Whitbread's shire horses have been pulling drays through the streets of London for over two hundred years. There are still stables in Garrett Street.

2 There are plenty of Biblical references to horses. When the Persians wanted to honour a man he was royally dressed and led through the streets on horseback (Esther 6, 9–11). Horses in Biblical times wore no shoes, were driven with bit and bridle and they often wore bells. The horses of rich men were decorated with handwoven material.

Hymn suggestion

Come and Praise Vol 1 'All creatures of our God and King' No 7

Prayer

Dear God, Help us in our responsibilities towards animals. Teach us to care for them properly and make us aware of their needs. Help us to value the pleasure, and often help, which they give us. Amen.

10 One autumn afternoon

Introduction

Sometimes, and unexpectedly, we meet wild creatures. Usually they dash away very quickly but in the passage which follows, a girl tells of her unusual meeting in a wood.

Story

My mum works at a field studies centre. This is a classroom in a beautiful wood. One day in the autumn half-term she let me go to work with her. While she was busy in her office I went for a walk in the wood.

It was late in the afternoon and the sun was shining through the trees in lovely shafts of light. I followed the path which went past the dining room and the camp fire bowl. There were squirrels everywhere and some of them were cheeky enough to come right up to my feet.

Without really thinking where I was going, my feet took me down the steep path to the brook. This wasn't flowing very quickly and when I looked up and around from its banks I could see a thin carpet of coloured leaves with, here and there, brightly patterned fungi poking upwards.

I must have been at the brook for about two minutes when I heard a rustling noise. The hairs on the back of my head seemed to stand on end and I felt as if I was a statue. What could it be?

Then, on the other side of the brook, a beautiful deer came into view. When it reached the water it bent its head to drink. I could see everything about it – its smooth brown coat and long legs; its small and pointed feet. Then, as I stood frozen to the spot, it lifted its head and looked straight at me. It didn't seem afraid or hurried.

For what seemed an age I stared at the deer and it stared back at me with huge brown eyes which seemed kind and gentle. Then suddenly, there was the cracking of twigs as the caretaker's dog chased some far-off rabbit. The deer turned, and raising its front legs in a twisting, bounding motion it moved away as quickly and smoothly as it had come.

I still stood there. The slanting sun's rays were fading now and the whole wood was growing dark quickly. I had a strange feeling of peace ... almost as if I was special for a moment ... and then ...

'Elizabeth – where are you?'

It was my mother's voice. Suddenly I wanted to tell her my secret.

(by Elizabeth, aged 11)

Information for the teacher

1   The deer which Elizabeth saw in a Hertford wood was a Muntjak.

2   Animal camouflage could be discussed here as it is one reason why so much wildlife is not easy to see.

3   The rapport which can exist between man and animal is a subject which could be followed up in connection with this piece.

Hymn suggestion

Come and Praise Vol 1 'All things bright and beautiful' No 3

Prayer

Let us think this morning about all those creatures of field and wood for whom the coming of winter means a time of hardship. We pray that the autumn allows them to prepare for this time.

11 The rich and the poor

Introduction

Look at this coin (*hold up a 50p coin*). October 14th is its birthday. In 1969 it first began to be used in Britain.

Money is very useful but lots of it does not necessarily bring happiness. This morning's story is about a rich man and a poor man, and what happens to them both.

Story

Abdul was a rich man and Ali was a poor one. They lived near each other and Abdul was very jealous of his neighbour. This was because Ali was cheerful and kind and people liked him. Abdul was mean and surly and people kept away from him.

'Why should Ali be so popular?' thought the mean Abdul. 'I'll fix him once and for all.'

Abdul went to the shop where Ali worked.

'That Ali – he's no good,' he said to the shopkeeper. 'You want to get rid of him.'

'Oh no, he's a good worker,' replied the shopkeeper. 'I . . .'

'Who is your best customer? Who supplies you with your finest cloth? Who owns the building this shop is in?'

When the shopkeeper heard Abdul asking these questions he knew he hadn't a chance. Abdul could ruin him. 'All right,' he said sadly. 'Ali goes tomorrow.'

So Ali lost his job, but he didn't know why he had lost it. A few days later he spent the last of his savings on a bowl of food for his family. He was taking this home when he slipped and bowl and food flew into the mud.

'Ah well,' thought Ali, 'something's bound to turn up.'

Cleaning the bowl, he stuck it on his head, and wandered down to the docks. Seeing some sailors loading a ship he stopped to help them.

'You're a good worker,' said one of the sailors. 'Why don't you come with us on this trip? One of the crew is sick. Pay's not bad.'

'Right,' said Ali.

He sent a message home and set sail. However, disaster struck when the ship was out at sea. A sudden storm blew up and a gigantic wave swept Ali overboard. After struggling in the sea for hours he was washed up on an island. Some natives helped him and he was taken before the chief.

'You had a lucky escape,' said the chief after listening to Ali's story, 'but tell me – why do you wear that thing on your head?'

Ali was puzzled – then he remembered he was still wearing the wooden food bowl stuck on his head.

'Oh,' he said, without really thinking, 'it's a special hat to keep your head cool.'

'Really?' remarked the chief. 'Well, it's always hot here on this island – can I try it?'

'Certainly, certainly,' said Ali kindly, and put the bowl on the chief's head. It was a perfect fit.

The chief walked round in the sun for about ten minutes.

'It's marvellous!' he said. 'Fantastic! It keeps your head really cool. I'd like to buy it from you.'

'No, no,' said Ali, 'have it as a gift. It will be my pleasure.'

The chief nodded gratefully. 'I couldn't take it for nothing. Please accept these in exchange.'

He snapped his fingers and a servant gave Ali a bag. It was full of precious stones, of which the island had thousands.

Soon after a boat was found to take Ali home. There he sold the precious stones for enough money to last him for the rest of his life. His family was delighted.

Abdul heard them celebrating.

'What could he have to celebrate?' he thought, and marched down the hill to find out.

Now Ali had no idea that it was Abdul who had caused him to lose his job. When he saw his neighbour, he called to him to come in. Over a glass of wine he told Abdul the whole story.

That night Abdul could hardly contain his excitement. If this stupid chief could give Ali a fortune for a wooden bowl, what might he give to somebody who brought him some real presents?

Next morning Abdul got to work. He sold off lots of his goods and bought some marvellous presents for the island chief. Then he hired a ship and crew and set sail. A few days later he stood before the chief.

'Your highness,' he said, 'people far and wide have heard of your great wisdom. As I was passing your island I felt it would be a privilege if I could offer you some humble gifts.'

At a signal, Abdul's men brought fabulous clothes, silks, satins, goblets, wonderful food – and laid them before the chief.

The chief was astounded.

Finally, after looking at all that lay before him, he spoke. 'Truly you are an amazingly generous man,' he said. 'I cannot accept these gifts without giving you something in return. You shall have our greatest treasure.'

Abdul, with head bowed, could hardly contain himself. 'This must be something really special,' he thought.

The chief clapped his hands and a large basket was brought to him. Lifting the lid the chief reached inside and with a kind smile handed over to Abdul Ali's wooden food bowl. (Adapted from an Egyptian folk tale.)

Information for the teacher

1   This is one of many stories which, by their use in assemblies, seek to indicate to children the way to better relationships between human beings. Such stories can be acted as well as told.

2   Other good sources for similar material are tales of Anansi, Brer Rabbit and Nasr-ud-Din.

3   Useful Bible references about greed include: Mark 10, 17–30; Luke 12, 13–21; Mark 12, 41–44.

Hymn suggestion

Come and Praise Vol 1 'Think of a world without any flowers' No 17

Prayer

Let us pray this morning that we are neither greedy for more for ourselves nor envious of those who seem to have more than we do.

Let us remember that there is always someone worse off than we are.

Let us pray that those people in need may be given hope and encouragement. Amen.

12 Confucius

Introduction

Many people think that a certain Chinese man was the wisest person who ever lived. His name was Confucius and he was born over two thousand years ago.

Story

The music teacher looked up at the very tall, awkward young man.

'Very well, Confucius, if you want to learn the zither I will try to teach you.'

So Confucius began to learn to play the stringed instrument. But whatever the teacher told him to do the sound somehow didn't seem to come out right.

After listening to his pupil practise a piece for what seemed like the twentieth time the teacher lost his patience. 'Perhaps you're not cut out to play a musical instrument,' he said. 'You should try something else.'

'No, no,' replied Confucius. 'It doesn't sound right yet because I've got to master each aspect of the music.'

'What do you mean?' asked the teacher.

'Well first of all there is the tune itself, then there is the rhythm, then there is the atmosphere of the music, and the mood the man who wrote the music wanted me to feel.'

'But that terrible noise you're making,' went on the irritated teacher, 'how can that possibly help you to get all those things right?'

'Because I've got to be patient,' replied Confucius. 'All this practice sounds awful but I am gradually mastering all those things I mentioned.'

'Humph,' muttered the teacher and stamped off, leaving his pupil to it.

A few more days went by and the teacher happened to be passing the room where Confucius did his practising. From it came the most beautiful sounds. The teacher was astonished.

'It can't be . . .' he mumbled to himself.

Stepping through the doorway he saw Confucius's fingers stroking a wonderful melody from the zither.

'Now it all fits together,' smiled the wisest of men.

Information for the teacher

1 Confucius (Kung Fu Tzu) was born in Shandong (Shantung) to poor parents. He never achieved any high office and was self-taught. His philosophy has had a tremendous and long-lasting influence.

2 Physically Confucius was exceptionally tall, awkward and unprepossessing in appearance – another example of 'the worth lying within'.

3 The keynote of Confucius's teaching is *reciprocity*: behave to others as you would like them to behave to you.

Hymn suggestion

Come and Praise Vol 1 'The wise may bring their learning' No 64

Prayer

Our prayers this morning are based on the thoughts and words of Confucius. He said that we should use our eyes and ears to help us learn; we should use our face to show kindness and our manners to show respect. Our words should be true and our dealings with other people should always be fair.

13 Akiba

Introduction

Do you sometimes find work at school hard? Is there a subject you never really seem to understand? This morning's story is about a man who found school work very hard indeed.

Story

Akiba fought to keep his eyes open. But the harder he tried the heavier his eyelids seemed to be.

'Oh, what's the use?' he thought. 'I'm just too tired for this reading business; after all, I do work all day.'

Akiba lived in Palestine and was a shepherd. He was tough and strong but he had never had the chance to learn to read and write. Then he met the beautiful Rachel.

Suddenly life changed and after a few weeks Akiba asked Rachel to marry him. Now Rachel came from a family where there were many books, and she knew what wonderful treasures they were.

'I will marry you, Akiba,' she said, 'on one condition.'

'What's that?' asked the poor shepherd.

'I know you've had a hard life,' went on Rachel, 'but I think it would be marvellous for you if you learned to read.'

'But . . . I'm nearly forty!' gasped the shepherd.

However, Rachel wouldn't change her mind until Akiba agreed. So after the wedding he went to see a rabbi. The rabbi agreed to teach Akiba to read. His lessons would be after his long days out in the fields with his sheep.

Akiba found it incredibly hard; he was always tired, he couldn't stay awake, and he just couldn't remember all the letters and sounds. So he decided he couldn't go on.

The day after having made his decision, he was out in the open air looking after his sheep when he came to a spring in the mountains. For some time he stood gazing at the little waterfall as it cascaded down on to the rock beneath. Then he looked even more closely at the rock and noticed the groove that had been worn in it by the water hitting it day after day after day. Akiba had a sudden thought.

'It's like reading,' he muttered to himself. 'If I keep on, and on, and on, like the waterfall, eventually *I will* be able to read.'

So Akiba went back to the rabbi and, putting his tiredness aside, he tried with even more determination. This time, not only did he learn to read, but he also began the journey which was to make him a very famous rabbi himself.

Information for the teacher

1   Akiba, after learning to read at forty, ultimately became one of the foremost authorities on the Torah (the Jewish law). He lived during the Roman occupation of Palestine and was executed in his nineties for refusing to obey an order from the Romans which forbade the study of the Torah.

2   This story could be linked with the Jewish festival of Simchat Torah (the Rejoicing of the Law) which takes place on 23rd of Tishri, a link with October.

3   A useful address here is:

The Jewish Education Bureau, 8 Westcombe Avenue,
Leeds LS8 2BS.

Hymn suggestion

Come and Praise Vol 2 'You can build a wall' No 91

Let us think this morning about the quality of determination. Without it we cannot succeed when things get difficult. Let us remember that in everybody's life there are good times and bad times and to deal with the last of these we often need determination and persistence.

We pray that we might be given the strength of character to be determined in times of difficulty.

November

14 The determined friends

Introduction

One of the best things about having a really good friend is knowing that he, or she, will always help you if you are in trouble.

Story

The sun was burning down. The four men were desperately hot and their shoulders ached from carrying the fifth man, who lay on a stretcher.

'Not long now,' said Timothy.

'No,' agreed Philip. 'I can just about see the houses of Capernaum from here.'

'We'll soon be there, old friend,' went on John, as he leaned forward to wipe the sweat from the brow of the sick man who lay on the stretcher.

Timothy, John, Philip and Thomas were four of a group of five close friends. The fifth friend, Abraham, was ill and the others were concerned about him. Timothy had heard that there was this man called Jesus, who was travelling round the countryside and doing wonderful things for sick people. He had suggested to the others that they carry Abraham to the nearby town of Capernaum which Jesus was visiting. He was sure Jesus would be able to help Abraham. After several hours of walking in the scorching heat they were nearly there.

'Look,' said Philip, 'he must be in that house over on the right. There's a huge crowd of people gathered round it.'

'It could be tricky getting through that lot,' muttered John doubtfully.

'We'll manage!' was Thomas's firm and confident answer.

Eventually the group reached the huge crowd gathered round one of Capernaum's larger houses.

'You can't get through here,' somebody shouted to the four stretcher bearers.

'Well just let us try, will you?' urged Timothy as the four friends struggled with the stretcher.

After half an hour of pushing and squeezing the group reached the door leading into the house. Then they finally came to a halt. The passage and room inside the house were absolutely packed with people standing shoulder to shoulder. It was impossible for even one more person to squeeze in, never mind four men with a stretcher.

Gasping with the efforts they had made the four disappointed men heard the voice of Jesus from inside the house. Abraham lay motionless on the stretcher. Suddenly Philip began gazing at the flight of open steps which led up to the roof of the house.

'I've got an idea!' he said suddenly. 'Come on, up here.'

As the friends eased the stretcher up the steps Philip explained: 'Right, now listen. These steps will take us up to the roof. The roof itself is only made of sticks and dried mud – so it will be easy to make a hole in it, and repair it afterwards. Once we have made a hole we can take the cords off our tunics. If we tie one to each of the four corners of the stretcher we can lower it through the hole – down to Jesus who will be underneath.'

A few minutes later the people crowded into the large room wondered what was happening when bits of the roof began to drop down. A very short time later the stretcher appeared and began to come down towards Jesus – the determined friends had succeeded!

Information for the teacher

1   1st November is All Saints Day, when people who gave much, or all, for the benefit of others are especially remembered.
The idea of 'four good friends' could be perpetuated by the story of the four Christian stone masons who together refused to carve a pagan statue for the Emperor Diocletian. He had them put to death for their refusal and the Feast Day in their memory is 8th November.

On 22nd November, in 1906, the international distress call 'Mayday' was universally accepted. It comes from the French *m'aider* or 'Help me.'

2   Teachers may wish to go on and finish this story from its Biblical origins. For those wishing to do so the source is: Mark 2, 1–12.

Hymn suggestion

Come and Praise Vol 1 'A man for all the people' No 27

Prayer

Dear God, Give us the determination to overcome disappointment and discouragement by your guidance and example. Teach us to value friendship and be grateful for the love and care of our friends. Amen.

15 This month

Introduction

No sun, no moon,
No morn, no noon,
No dawn, no dusk, no proper time of day . . .
. . . November.   (Thomas Hood)

This month

The whole of Thomas Hood's poem about November paints it as a gloomy, dark month with little good about it.

This, however, is not true. Whilst the trees which are not evergreens will have shed most of their leaves, this gives us an opportunity to see birds much more closely. There are plenty of birds still about too. Few of them are singing but the robin is an exception and his song can be heard frequently.

Flocks of birds are much easier to spot and groups of magpies and starlings are common at this time of the year. Squirrels are still about on milder days and when they are hungry. Woods are carpeted in leaves of the most lovely colours still and there are plenty of fungi on show.

Despite the fogs and mists of the month other things to look for are Old Man's Beard, and juniper, an evergreen shrub.

The Anglo-Saxons had two names for November, these were Winmonath and Blodmonath. The first was because cold winds often blew at this time; the second meant 'blood month' because this was the time when cattle were killed to provide winter food.

There are lots of weather predictions associated with November. For instance, if the wind is in the south-west on St Martin's Day (11th), it is supposed to stay there right through to Candlemas in February and make sure we have a mild winter.

So despite its miserable reputation November is still a month with lots of interest in the natural world around us.

Information for the teacher

1 Balancing the rather restricted activity of being outside in November is a whole list of things useful for children's interest – Guy Fawkes' Day; the Lord Mayor of London's Show; Armistice Day; St Cecilia's Day (22nd), (Cecilia is the patron saint of music); St Catherine's Day (25th). Catherine was a Christian girl who in the fourth century refused to give up her religion.

2 A useful piece of information which could be projected in a 'working together' theme and linked to this assembly, concerns starlings. Large flocks of them can be seen flying over the countryside at this time of the year. The birds at the rear who are feeding then fly over the birds ahead of them to scan the ground below. The process is continually repeated so that there are always some of the birds searching for food below, and no ground is therefore neglected.

Hymn suggestion

Come and Praise Vol 1 'Think of a world without any flowers' No 17

Prayer

Let us think this morning about those countries where the climate causes distress to people. Let us pray that all people might have sufficient warmth, food and homes to be comfortable. Amen.

16 Not so useless

Introduction

All of us like to laugh – but none of us likes to be laughed at. This morning's story starts with some cruel laughter.

Story

The lion, the elephant and the tiger all roared with laughter. The sound, rumbling from their deep chests, shook the leaves on the trees.

'You're useless,' growled the lion, 'you can't do anything.'

Anansi, the spider, listened to the laughter with bowed head.

'It's true,' twittered the birds flying overhead, 'you can't fight, fly, swim ...'

'... even run fast,' murmured the deer.

Anansi looked round at all the other animals in the forest and began to speak.

'I'm not useless, I'll ...'

'You'll what?' snarled the tiger.

'I'll ... I'll ... capture the snake. That'll show you who is useless!'

For a moment there was silence. Nobody laughed or joked about the snake – they were too scared of him. Then there was a chorus of catcalls from the animals.

'Capture the snake? Impossible.'

'He'll finish you off in the flick of an eyelid.'

'Bah!'

'Prove it.'

An hour later Anansi was alone. What had he let himself in for? He had no idea how he was going to capture the snake – or had he?

The next day Anansi sat outside the snake's house. When the bushes parted and the snake came sliding out Anansi shivered at the sight of the long, strong, cold-eyed creature. The snake ignored Anansi, went in search of food and returned home.

The same thing happened for the next few days. Eventually the snake stopped and fixed Anansi with his cold, cruel eyes.

'Every morning when I come out you are sitting there watching me, Anansi. It's beginning to annoy me, and when I get annoyed somebody had better watch out!'

'Oh the last thing I want to do is annoy you, Mr Snake,' said Anansi respectfully. 'No, no, certainly not, but ... well ... you see ...'

'Come on – out with it.'

'Well, the animals have been arguing about who is the longest creature in the forest. Of course I said it was you but the others all reckon the crocodile is . . .'

'I am the longest,' replied the snake curtly.

'Of course, of course, no doubt, I know,' stuttered Anansi, 'but it's proving it, you see. I've been plucking up courage to ask you.'

'Ask me what?'

'Well – could I possibly measure you, Mr Snake?'

'How are you going to do that?'

'Look at this bamboo pole, Mr Snake.' Anansi pointed to the pole lying on the ground. 'If you lie beside it I can mark off your measurements.'

The snake sighed and gave Anansi a baleful look.

'All right – if it will prove to those fools who is the longest.'

The snake stretched out alongside the bamboo pole. Anansi fussed around the pole, pushing it closer to the snake's body.

'Oh dear.'

'What's the matter?'

'Well when you press your head against the pole your tail moves away.'

'Tie my tail to the end then.'

Quickly Anansi tied the snake's tail firmly to the bamboo. 'Now, Mr Snake, could you really stretch out please?'

Keen now to be measured at his longest, the snake stretched fully, closing his eyes with the effort.

Anansi, scarcely able to breathe at his daring, snapped a rope round the snake's head and, in a flash, tied him to the bamboo. Two more pieces of rope secured his body in the middle.

No sooner had the snake been captured in this way than a passing bird saw him. News flashed round the forest in minutes.

The snake was captured! Anansi had done it. From that day on Anansi was never considered useless again.

Information for the teacher

1   Anansi is a cultural hero in West Africa. There are legions of stories about how his trickery more than compensates for his lack of strength. His fame is equally great in the West Indies.

For teachers seeking original assembly material then *African Myths and Legends* by K. Arnott (Oxford University Press) is a useful collection. Many of the stories emphasise such qualities as a sense of justice, patience and endurance.

2   The 3rd November is National Day in Dominica, West Indies and Panama.

Hymn suggestion

Come and Praise Vol 1 'All creatures of our God and King' No 7

Prayer

Dear God, Let us enjoy the pleasure of laughter together. Teach us to laugh with people and not at them. Help us to value the qualities and talents of everyone we know. Amen.

17 A life-saving swim

Introduction

If we look carefully enough at our daily papers we can usually find stories of very brave people. One November day all the papers told the following story.

Story

'I can't hold her much longer – we're going in.'

The pilot of the twin-engined Piper Seneca plane called out desperately to his passengers as he struggled with the controls. Using all his skill he managed to level the plane out before it hit the sea with a bone-shattering crash.

'OK – everybody out – as quickly as possible!' shouted pilot Brad Youngberg. Surprisingly no one was hurt and as their aircraft sank they kicked around in the water.

'Right,' spluttered Brad. 'I'm sure somebody must have seen us go in.'

But he was wrong, and soon he and the others, Dan Tuckfield, Delano Hicks, Ira and Dorothy Bloom, realised that their situation was desperate.

They had crashed off the coast of Florida in the USA, and twenty-five miles away the resort of Cat Cay was their nearest land. They had no dinghy or raft and their only hope was to swim the twenty-five miles.

It was then that Dan Tuckfield began organising things.

'You two,' he said to Brad and Delano, who were good swimmers, 'get going. I'll help the others.'

So Dan began to swim to the shore. Dorothy Bloom couldn't swim so Dan carried her on his back. Ira was such a poor swimmer that he had to hang on to Dan by a strap.

For hour after hour the small party struggled through the sea. As they did so tiger sharks hovered nearby, waiting to pounce.

All through the night the survivors swam on, with Dan doing the swimming for three people. When morning came the Blooms could go on no longer. They had both swallowed a lot of salt water and one after the other they died and slipped beneath the waves.

Don, Brad and Delano had now been swimming for more than twenty-four hours and Dan could see that the other two were almost ready to give up too.

'Don't stop,' he gasped. 'You must ... *must* ... keep going.'

Agonisingly slowly the land got nearer.

'Listen,' Dan called, 'I'm going to swim ahead and get help. All you've got to do is stay afloat until help arrives.'

With the last drop of his remaining strength Dan struck out strongly for the shore. When he reached it he staggered to the road where he saw a man walking. Hardly able to speak he gasped out his plea for help.

Soon a helicopter was roaring out to sea to pick up the other two exhausted men. Without Dan's courage and determination they would certainly have died too. He had swum the full twenty-five miles and it had taken him thirty-eight hours to do it.

'I'm sorry I couldn't save the other two,' he said later.

Information for the teacher

1   This story appeared on 16th November 1991. The party had been flying from Fort Lauderdale to the Bahamas when the crash occurred.

2   There is a natural link between this story and the other November feature 'Cold and Alone'. Both emphasise qualities of determination and resourcefulness.

3   An appropriate quotation from the Bible might be: 'A faithful friend is a secure shelter' (Ecclesiasticus 6, 14).

Hymn suggestion

Come and Praise Vol 1 'The journey of life' No 45

Prayer

Let us bow our heads and think this morning about those people who, by their courage, determination, strength and skill, save the lives of others. Let us pray that in time of need we might have the same qualities to help ourselves and others. Amen.

18 The star

Introduction

Do you sometimes wish you were a bit better at ... sport ... maths ... writing stories ... playing the recorder ... lots of things in fact! If so, this morning's story should interest you.

Story

Dee was fed up. No matter what the class did she always seemed to be the worst at it. Her maths always seemed to end up in a muddle, she could mess things up on the computer every time she touched it, and even when she was paint monitor she broke a couple of jars.

Despite this Mrs Jones never lost patience with her and had even put on her report things like ... 'keeps trying hard ... is always cheerful'.

'Ah,' thought Dee to herself, 'that's all right but wouldn't it be nice to be good at something?'

In November the Music and Drama Club at Highfield Primary School began rehearsals for its autumn term production. Dee had been in the club for a year. At the last show she had had the job of drawing the curtain – and somehow managed to get it stuck halfway across the stage at the end of the first act, just as the scene shifters came on.

'Dee.'

A voice broke into Dee's daydreams. It was the Thursday when casting was taking place at the Club.

'Yes, miss?'

'Well – will you do it please?' asked Mrs Jones.

'Er ...'

'Come on, wake up Dee. Louise was supposed to play the police-woman but the family has moved away suddenly. Will you take her part please?'

Dee reached for the paper in a daze, blushing as she did so. She'd never been asked to read a part before.

Slowly the words came into focus on the paper in front of her. She saw that her part wasn't a very big one, but 'Policewoman' did appear about half a dozen times down the page. Already Martin Scott was reading and it was nearly up to her first piece.

As she waited to read, thoughts chased through Dee's head. 'A policewoman wouldn't speak like me,' she thought. 'She would have a firm, loud voice – with an accent a bit different to mine.'

Suddenly it was Dee's turn to read. A voice which she hardly recognised as coming from herself began to say the lines. It was almost as if she *was* the policewoman . . .

The reading went on. As Dee read she saw some of the other children looking at her with odd expressions on their faces. When she had a funny bit to read they laughed as if it was the world's greatest joke. Finally the reading was finished. There was a long silence.

'Well,' said Mrs Jones at last, 'that was well read. And Dee – we'd no idea you were such a star. You'll bring the house down with a performance like that on the night – very well done!'

Dee could feel herself blushing but at the same time it seemed to be just about the very best moment in her whole life.

Information for the teacher

1   Teachers might like to compare this homespun story with the real-life experiences of the actress Susan Hampshire, who has achieved success despite the fact that she is dyslexic.

2   Many schools start productions for Christmas in November and often unexpected talents are revealed in the process. Local knowledge could aid discussion and reflection here.

3   'Theatrical' anniversaries in November which might be used as linking material could include: Jerome Kern (died 11th November 1945); the BBC began daily broadcasting in this month in 1922; Clark Gable died (16th November 1960); Mickey Mouse first appeared on 18th November 1928; 18th November 1836 was the birthday of W.S. Gilbert of Gilbert and Sullivan fame; the world's longest running play (*The Mousetrap*) began its London run on 25th November 1952.

4   Another relevant link with November is the fact that Miss Allen and Miss Harburn became the first policewomen in England on 27th November 1914.

Hymn suggestion

Come and Praise Vol 1 'Lord of the Dance' No 22

Prayer

In our prayers this morning let us think about some words of others: 'All that we are is the result of our thoughts.' (Buddha)

'May we get happiness from life and pass it on to other folk.'

'Let us be thankful for those people who entertain us and make us laugh.'

19 How can I help?

Introduction

Sometimes we meet people who seem to be good at everything. They often make us feel that it would be impossible for us ever to do anything which would help them in any way. This morning's story, however, might make us think a little bit more about this.

Story

Jamie and Michael were friends. They lived next door to each other and spent all their spare time together. Jamie was small and an accident as a baby had left him with a limp. He didn't see very well either and wore thick spectacles.

Michael, on the other hand, was not only good at work in school, but he was also a star footballer, swimmer and runner too. He never ever showed off and the two boys got on very well together ... but Jamie had secret thoughts.

'If only I could be just a little bit better than Michael at *something*. He must think I would never be able to help him if he got into any kind of trouble.'

One weekend Mr and Mrs Oakwood, Jamie's parents, were loaned a cottage by the sea. Because it was November nobody else wanted it and the Oakwoods thought it would be fun to get out of town.

'I'll tell you what,' said Mr Oakwood, 'if his Mum and Dad agree, you can bring Michael along.'

'That's great!' piped Jamie, with a big grin on his face.

They all got to the cottage on Friday night and after lighting the fire they had a smashing meal of hamburgers. On Saturday they did some walking and some fishing from the little pier, and the boys searched the sands for mystery finds.

On Sunday morning Michael asked if he could go to the paper shop in the village nearby to buy a small present for his mother. Jamie would normally have gone with him but all the exercise on Saturday had made his bad leg ache.

'Stay here,' said Michael, 'and we'll do something together when I get back. It'll only take me about an hour to get there and back.'

Michael went off and after about three-quarters of an hour a sudden change came over the weather. The air turned very damp and a thick mist rolled in from the sea. Soon it was impossible to see more than three or four paces from the front door.

'Oh dear,' said Mrs Oakwood, knowing how isolated the cottage was. 'I'm so worried about Michael. He'll never be able to find his way back.'

'Well,' said Jamie, looking at his watch, 'he must be on his way home now.'

'But you can't see a thing,' said his mother.

Jamie thought for a moment.

'I know,' he said, 'our secret cry.'

'What?' asked his mother, looking puzzled as well as worried now.

'We have a secret cry that only the two of us know,' went on Michael. 'If I go to the gate and keep shouting our secret signal he'll know it's me and he'll head for the sound.'

Putting on a thick coat Jamie took up position.

'Coooo . . . aaaa . . . oooooo.'

There was silence at first, then suddenly, from far off came an answering cry.

'Coooo . . . aaaa . . . oooooo.'

For what seemed a long time Jamie kept calling out – regularly and slowing. From time to time Michael replied and each time his voice seemed to be nearer and less nervous.

Finally there was a clatter as he arrived at the front gate. Coming up the path he flung his arms round Jamie.

'Thanks, Jamie, that was great. I was dead scared out there and then I heard our secret cry. I knew you'd guide me home after that.'

Information for the teacher

1   This is one of those stories which can be kept up a teacher's sleeve until conditions are appropriate for its use. As November is traditionally the season of 'mists and mellow fruitfulness' a suitable opportunity is likely during this long, dark month.

2   There are two parallel themes in this story: friendship and following a sign. Both could be related to religious events. The story of David and Jonathan (Samuel 1, 1–42) provides useful material for discussions on friendship.
    The leaving of drawings of a fish to show that there were Christians surviving the early days of persecution is an example of the help and inspiration of a sign.

3   Another useful link is with the Jewish Shema. This prayer is traditionally kept by many Jewish families in a mezuzah, a small box attached to the main doorpost of the house.
    The link with this assembly is that the Hebrew word 'Shema' actually means 'Hear', and this in turn is the first word of the Shema: 'Hear, O Israel, The Lord our God is one Lord.' (Deuteronomy 6, 4)

Hymn suggestion

Come and Praise Vol 2 'A still small voice' No 96

Prayer

Let us learn to listen; to value advice and guidance.
Let us learn to listen to those who are much wiser than we are.
Let us learn to listen; in order that we might learn.

20 Cold and alone

Introduction

Some days during November are very cold. Fortunately, because we have warm houses and good food, we can often enjoy cold days. But what if it was much colder . . . and we were alone . . . without food . . . and lost . . .

Story

Richard Byrd had a job to do. He was alone in a one man meteorological station in the Antarctic. Here, amidst the bitter, freezing wastes near the South Pole, he had to study and report on weather conditions.

With everything going well this would have been a terribly lonely and difficult task, but right from the start there was a serious problem. It was vital to keep warm, but from first lighting it, Richard found that the stove he had brought with him had leaking joints. This meant that when it was alight deadly fumes seeped out into any enclosed space.

'I've got a problem here,' Richard said to himself. 'If I stay in here with the stove on I'll poison myself; if I put the stove out I'll die of cold, and I've got no materials to mend the stove.'

Although it was possible for a rescue party to reach him this would take several days. He came to a decision.

'I'll stick it out,' he thought. 'I'll leave the stove on but every night I'll open the door of this little shack and I'll take a walk to clear my head.'

So began a nightmare existence. As the days went on Richard felt the effects of the fumes more severely. Every night he was forced to walk outside in the bitter weather. Here, in howling gales and impenetrable darkness, he staggered round in deep snow trying to clear his head. So easy was it to get lost within seconds in the swirling snow, that Richard had to stick bamboo poles with flags on them into the snow every few yards. In this way he could always retrace his footsteps back to the safety of his camp.

For weeks Richard kept up his work under these awful circumstances, but gradually the radio operators back at base camp realised from his radio messages that something was wrong. As a result of this a rescue party was sent out to relieve him.

Information for the teacher

1 The November link is that it was in the winter of 1934 that Admiral Richard Byrd undertook his meteorological task. He was already famous, having been the first man to fly to the North Pole (in 1926) and to the South Pole. The date of the latter achievement marks another November link because it was on the 28th of this month in 1929 that this flight was made.

2 The theme of this story – when we may be called upon to show courage and determination alone – could be broadened into

considering other situations requiring these qualities. These might include: times of serious personal illness; new situations, such as moving to a new home, school, area, country; unexpected responsibilities due to family illness, etc.

3 The difficulties which great religious leaders faced alone is another tangent which may be pursued.

Hymn suggestion

Come and Praise Vol 1 'One more step' No 47

Prayer

Dear God, Please give us the strength to face difficulties and hardships when we are alone. Help us to avoid panic and confusion and to be calm and resourceful. Give us the determination to keep on trying at all times.

December

21 You go first

Introduction

None of us much likes the kind of person who thinks they are cleverer than everybody else. One of the most satisfying things about this morning's story is that somebody in it is finally caught out.

Story

There was once a king who was lazy and foolish. He was easily flattered and he would always listen to advice which he wanted to hear. Now it happened that this king had a chief minister who was cunning and sly.

'Your majesty, rely on me,' he would say. 'I'll never let you down and wherever you go, I'll go too.'

This suited the lazy king because it meant he didn't have to think very much – he could just ask his minister for advice wherever he was.

One night the two men were walking near the palace. In the distance foxes were howling.

'Why are those foxes making such a noise, minister?' asked the king.

'Ah, well,' said the minister, thinking quickly, 'they are probably cold, and they know if someone as great as you hears them he will do something to help.'

'Oh,' replied the king, 'will I? Well . . .'

'Perhaps you will allow me to take some money from the royal treasury to buy the foxes some blankets?' said the crafty minister.

'It's the least we can do,' said the king. 'Please see to it.'

The minister drew the money out of the treasury and kept it all for himself, of course. When the foxes howled again he told the king they were saying thank you.

A week later the two men were out walking again when a boar shot out from a bush and startled the king.

'What was that?' he cried.

'An elephant, your majesty,' replied the minister.

'An elephant?' gasped the king. 'Well it didn't look like an elephant to me. Are you sure?'

'Definitely, your majesty,' said the crafty minister. 'You see it is so small because the man in charge of your elephants is lazy and doesn't do his job properly.'

'Disgraceful,' said the king. 'Have him dismissed at once – and take some money from the royal treasury so that the royal elephants are better cared for.'

So the minister got richer.

A week later the two men were out walking again. The same boar was disturbed and dashed out again.

'What . . .' cried the king, 'that elephant, look it's no bigger than it was before, but . . .'

'No, no, your majesty, that isn't an elephant, it's a mouse,' said the minister.

'A mouse?'

'Certainly – it just shows you how careless the royal cook is when mice from the kitchen grow as big as that.'

'Indeed!' cried the king. 'Have the man hanged.'

That night the minister went to see the royal cook and told him that he would be hanged unless . . . The cook got the idea and promised to pay the minister a lot of money if he would save him. The two of them made a plan.

Soon the day set for the hanging arrived. Everybody gathered in the courtyard to see it take place. Then just as the hangman was preparing the noose the minister rushed up to the king.

'Your majesty, your majesty – I've just found out that anybody hanged at this time will be forgiven everything they have done wrong and go straight to live in splendour with the gods. This man shouldn't get away with that.'

'Agreed, agreed,' said the king, 'but ... but if anyone who is hanged now goes straight to live in splendour with the gods, why don't you and I go?'

'But ... but ...' began the minister, for once at a loss for words at this unexpected turn of events.

'And you, my friend,' went on the king, 'have given me such good advice that I insist you go first. Hangman, see to it.'

Now you can imagine how popular the minister was at court! Within seconds he was seized and hanged before he could say anything else. Then the people told the king the truth about his minister and from that day on he became a much more sensible and caring ruler.

Information for the teacher

1   The teacher might reflect with the children on the ability of some people to tell wonderful stories. There are some notable anniversaries in December to provide an historical link to this theme: Robert Louis Stevenson died on 5th December 1894; Wilhelm Grimm (of the Grimm brothers) died on 16th December 1859; Emily Brontë died on 19th December 1848; Beatrix Potter died on 22nd December 1943 and Rudyard Kipling was born on 30th December 1865.

2   All the major religions use stories to make significant points, and those people who are self-seeking at the expense of others are regularly castigated. Examples from the Bible include: The prodigal son (Luke 10, 30–36); the king and the governor (Matthew 18, 23–24); the rich man and Lazarus (Matthew 22, 11–13).

Hymn suggestion

Come and Praise Vol 1 'A man for all the people' No 27

Prayer

Dear God, Teach us to use our intelligence for the good, and not the harm, of other people. Teach us the value of unselfishness. Make us worthy of your teaching. Amen.

22 Justice is done

Introduction

This morning's story is about a cruel king who thought he was much cleverer than anybody else. But was he?

Story

Azab was a king – and a cruel and cunning one. He had a prisoner in the dark and dirty cells beneath his palace. This was a young man called Rachid.

Rachid had come to Azab to ask for greater justice for the people; for an equal share of money for the crops; for less severe taxes. Azab's answer had been to throw Rachid into prison – but he was worried.

'That Rachid means trouble,' thought Azab. 'If I let him go he'll stir the people up; if I keep him in prison there might be even more trouble. I must think of a plan to sort him out.'

For over a week the cunning king thought and plotted, and then he came up with a brilliant idea. After another week he was ready to put it into practice.

In the great courtyard a group of people gathered together. There was Azab, his ministers and a squad of his best soldiers. Opposite them was a group of important local leaders, all friends and allies of Rachid. Between the two groups stood a table and on the table was a box.

When everybody was in place, Azab clapped his hands and two soldiers appeared, marching a still-chained Rachid between them. Kicking up spurts of dust with their feet, they reached the table and stopped in front of it.

'Now, my friends,' said Azab, looking at the group of his enemies. There was a mumble of annoyance and disagreement from them. 'I'm going to show you what a fair person I am,' went on the king. 'You see this box here . . .'

At this everybody followed the king's pointing finger with their eyes, and stared at the box.

'It's got two small balls inside it. One of them says *Innocent* on it; one of them says *Guilty*. Now this man Rachid here is imprisoned for plotting against me, but I'm going to give him a chance.

He is going to be blindfolded. Then he must put his hand in the box and pull out a ball. If it says *Innocent*, he and every other prisoner in my cells can go free today.

If, however, it says *Guilty* then he and every other prisoner will have their sentences doubled.'

As Rachid listened to the king's words he realised how sly and cunning his opponent was. He was absolutely certain that both balls had *Guilty* on them, but he would only be allowed to look at the one he chose. That meant that not only would his prison sentence be doubled, but so would that of every other prisoner. Then, they and their friends would start hating him and forget the evil ways of Azab. He looked at the king's smirking face and knew he was right.

'The blindfold,' ordered Azab, and the soldiers immediately bound a cloth tightly round Rachid's head. He then felt his hand pushed into the box and his fingers closed round one of the balls.

Then, before anybody could stop him, Rachid crammed the ball into his mouth and swallowed it. Tearing off his blindfold he shouted out so that everybody could hear.

'I have chosen my ball and swallowed it – the ball that is left will therefore show what my choice was.'

Before he could be stopped one of the guards picked up the other ball and called out: 'It says *Guilty* on here.'

At once there was a tremendous cheer from the people gathered in the courtyard. Azab's face was like thunder. He had been caught out by his own trick.

Information for the teacher

1   A useful anniversary link here is with 12th December. This was the date on which Robert Browning died in 1889. His 'Pied Piper' can be allied to this story in that both carry the same message of a promise being made which is never meant to be kept. Retribution follows as a result.

2   When this story is being told to the children it is interesting to leave out the ending initially and ask them if they can see a way out of Rachid's dilemma. Another story where the same ploy can be adopted is when Solomon is asked to decide which of the two arguing women is the real mother of the baby. (1 Kings 3, 16–28)

Hymn suggestion

Come and Praise Vol 1 'The wise may bring their learning' No 64

Prayer

Let us think this morning of fairness. How often we say, 'It's not fair,' when we are disappointed, don't get what we want, are not chosen for something when we think we should be.

Let us remember that there are many people in the world for whom life must seem really unfair.

Let us think this morning of fairness.

23 The Tom Eadie Story

Introduction

You could probably all write quite a bit about the subject 'A good friend'. There is an old saying: 'A friend in need is a friend indeed.' This morning's story shows exactly what this means.

Story

It was 17th December 1927 and the bitter winter wind lashed the white-topped waves into a frenzy. Ploughing through the swirling, icy sea off the east coast of America, the USS 'Falcon' battled to reach its destination.

This was the spot where a submarine had sunk. The 'Falcon' was to send down divers to see if there were any survivors.

'This is the worst diving weather I've ever seen,' said Tom Eadie, one of the two experienced deep sea divers on board.

'I couldn't agree more,' replied Fred Michels, his long-time partner. 'The pressure will be terrible down there.'

'Well, we've got to do it,' went on Tom. 'We've got to find out if anybody's alive in that sub.'

Some hours later Tom was over the side of the 'Falcon' and descending rapidly under the weight of his heavy diving suit. Currents pulled him savagely from side to side and it was difficult for him to see through the wave-swept mud.

By good navigation, however, the 'Falcon' had arrived in an excellent position. Despite the difficulties Tom saw the sunken submarine directly beneath him. Within minutes he was able to tap the conning tower and other parts of the craft. There were no answering taps as Tom went over every part of the submarine again and again.

'It doesn't seem hopeful,' he radioed to the surface.

'OK,' came the reply. 'Come up for a break. Fred will relieve you.'

Minutes later Tom was back aboard the 'Falcon' trying to get some warmth into his freezing limbs. He had hardly even begun to warm up when an urgent message flashed up from Fred: 'Cutters needed – cutters needed.'

In an instant Tom realised what had happened. His friend had got tangled up in the submarine's wreckage. Unless help could be got to him quickly, he had no hope of survival. Without even waiting to get his three pairs of warm underwear on Tom got back into his diving suit and, equipped with wire cutters, was soon plunging into the depths again.

When he reached Fred he found things worse than he expected. Hopelessly entangled in a mass of equipment the trapped diver was already unconscious and icy water had leaked into the body of his cut suit.

'Send down a hacksaw – quickly.' Tom flashed a message to the surface.

He had realised that the cutters were useless. As soon as the hacksaw was lowered to him Tom began to cut through the bent piece of iron which had his friend most securely held. Having forgotten his gloves in the rush, and with his own suit torn and leaking and his ears and hands aching unbearably, Tom sawed carefully in the freezing gloom.

Ten minutes ... twenty ... thirty ... forty ...

'There's no hope now,' muttered one of the anxious crew on the deck above. 'It's been too long.'

Just then there came another telephone message from below. 'Get me up!'

Down below Tom had finally sawn through the iron bar and, released from its grip, the unconscious Fred in his buoyant suit drifted up to the surface.

Unable to see where Fred had gone Tom was hauled up. Once back on board the 'Falcon' he was rushed to the decompression chamber where attendants began work on his freezing and battered body.

'I just lost him,' mumbled Tom. 'One minute he was there – the next he was gone.'

Just at that moment the still-unconscious and stiff body of Fred was passed into the chamber. He had been spotted floating on the surface and quickly rescued.

Both men made a full recovery, and for his courage and determination in rescuing his friend Tom Eadie was awarded the United States Congressional Medal of Honour.

Information for the teacher

1   This Atlantic adventure was necessitated by a collision between the US destroyer 'Paulding' and Submarine 'S4'. The latter sank immediately on impact. The submarine was raised three months later but there were no survivors.

2   The subject of courage at sea offers many follow-up possibilities. Useful addresses in this context are:

Royal National Lifeboat Institution, West Quay Road, Poole, Dorset BH15 1HZ, www.rnli.org.uk

Royal Life Saving Society, River House, High Street, Broom, Alcester, Warwickshire

Mission to Seamen, St Michael Paternoster Road, College Hill, London EC4R 2RL, www.missionstoseamen.org

Hymn suggestion

Come and Praise Vol 1 'He who would valiant be' No 44

Prayer

Let us pray this morning for those who earn their living on or under the sea. Keep them safe from accidents and storms. Let us give thanks for modern inventions which make their difficult work easier.

24 Julianne's story

Introduction

Christmas is a time of journeys. Mary and Joseph had to make a long journey before Jesus was born. Today lots of people travel by car, train, ship and aeroplane to be with families and friends at Christmas.

This morning's story is about a journey that didn't work out as it should have done.

Story

Julianne was excited. What would her father buy her for Christmas?

'I'm sure it will be something to do with animals,' she thought to herself. Her father was a zoologist and seemed to know everything about animals.

'Anyway, I'll find out soon,' she thought, as the announcement to board the plane came over the loud speakers. Julianne was making the four hundred and seventy-five mile trip from Lima to Pucallpa in Peru to be home for Christmas.

A few minutes later, along with ninety-one other passengers, Julianne was fastening her seat belt as the plane prepared for take-off.

'We hope you enjoy your flight,' announced the captain, and after a normal take-off, the plane climbed above the dense jungle.

As Julianne gazed down at the thick carpet of green below she seemed to hear her father's voice giving her a piece of his always wise advice: 'If you ever get lost in the jungle – look for a stream and follow it. That way you're sure to be rescued eventually.'

Julianne's thoughts were interrupted by the captain's voice again. 'Ladies and gentlemen, would you return to your seats and fasten your seat belts please. We have some bad weather ahead and it may get a little bumpy – nothing to worry about.'

As Julianne tightened her seat belt the plane began to lurch sickeningly, lightning flashed past the windows and rain hammered on the fuselage. Suddenly there was a bigger bump than any that had gone before and the plane began to fall.

People started screaming, the luggage racks crashed open and bags fell in every direction. The lights suddenly went out and there was a tremendous roaring noise. Terrified, Julianne gripped the arms of her seat and felt rain beating on her – she was no longer in the plane!

What happened next Julianne never knew because she fainted. When she woke up she was still strapped in her seat but it was lying on its side. Around her she could feel grass and she could hear frogs croaking. But how could this be? She fell into a deep, exhausted sleep.

When Julianne awoke the next time it was morning. Looking round she saw that she was still strapped in her seat, which was lying on the ground in dense jungle. Quickly she realised what had happened.

'The plane must have crashed – or somehow I fell out. Perhaps there are other people around. I must look.'

A terrible feeling of panic swept over her. She was cut and bruised and when she tried to stand up shooting pains surged through her foot. She broke a branch off a tree to use as a crutch – and then saw a little, gaily-wrapped parcel lying near her. 'It must have come from the plane too,' she muttered. Opening it she found inside some toys, a piece of Christmas cake and some sweets.

A large tear ran down her cheek as she looked at the little toys and realised that it was Christmas Day.

Then, shaking her head determinedly, she put the cake and sweets in a pocket of her torn dress and straightened up. Now she must do what her father had always said – 'Find a stream'.

So began a nightmare journey for Julianne. Existing only on the cake and sweets she staggered through the jungle looking for a stream. Savage mosquitoes attacked her constantly; poisonous snakes slithered across her path and beautifully coloured and juicy-looking berries tempted her to taste their poison.

After a few days she found a stream.

'Now I'll be safe,' she thought, falling by the water and gulping refreshing mouthfuls.

But it was not to be. Day after day she fought her way along the stream, terrified of alligators, and getting weaker and weaker. By now one of her eyes wouldn't open, the pain in her injured foot was almost unbearable and she couldn't lift one of her arms. But this brave and determined girl just wouldn't give up – and then she saw it! Moored in a clearing by the stream was a boat, and further into the clearing stood a small hut.

With a hoarse cry Julianne staggered to the hut and pushed open the door. It was empty. Tears of disappointment coursed down her face and she slumped to the floor.

Now, however, her ordeal was nearly over. Within hours a party of Indian hunters found her and soon she was on her way to hospital and safety.

Information for the teacher

1 The girl's name was Julianne Koepcke. She was a passenger on a plane flying over the Peruvian jungle from Lima to Pucallpa in December 1971.

 The plane ran into a violent storm at 10,000 feet and broke up in mid-air. By a miracle Julianne fell to the ground in her seat and survived. Her courage and determination kept her alive in the jungle for ten days, with only the cake and sweets to sustain her. She was seventeen years old at the time.

2 The 'difficult journeys' theme could incorporate that of Mary and Joseph; for Bible reference see Luke, chapter 2.

3 Another theme which may be pursued in relation to Julianne's story is the one of being alone and surviving only by courage, determination and initiative. There are plenty of examples of

this – Robinson Crusoe, round-the-world sailors, Polar explorers, etc. Such stories appear regularly in newspapers.

Hymn suggestion

Come and Praise Vol 2 'Give us hope Lord' No 87

Prayer

In our prayers this morning let us think of times when:

We have to make decisions alone because we face worrying and difficult situations.

We have to be brave because of illness or things happening which we don't really understand.

We have to rely only on ourselves.

Let us pray that we have the courage to face these situations.

25 Season of goodwill

Introduction

When we think of Christmas in the British Isles it is usually with very pleasant thoughts – our family and friends, people being kind and generous to each other. We like to think of it as the season of goodwill. For children in other parts of the world, it is sometimes rather different.

Season of goodwill

Peru is a country in South America where there is desperate poverty. A visit there shows how this affects young children.

In 1992 the school attendance figures in Lima, the capital, were down by fifty per cent because so many children were taking time off to earn money, or because their parents couldn't pay fees, or both.

Although by law children are not supposed to work until they are fourteen, nobody seems to pay much attention to this rule. In Lima the streets are full of children as young as six who are trying to earn money. They do this in a number of ways.

Some sell small things like bubble gum or biros. One way of doing this is to wait until cars stop at red lights and then rush up to them and try and make a sale to their owners. This is obviously very dangerous and there have been many accidents as a result.

Other children try to sell their services – they will clean anything from shoes to cars for very small sums of money. Often when they go home there is not enough food and their homes are broken-down, overcrowded shacks.

The children who do go to school don't have a particularly happy time either. School buildings are often in desperate need of repair and there are never enough books to go round. Worst of all, most state schools do not even have toilets.

Fortunately some people are trying to help. The Save the Children organisation is working hard in Peru to help these unfortunate children.

Information for the teacher

1 Save the Children, Mary Datchelor House, 17 Grove Lane, London SE5 8RD, www.oneworld.org/scf is a useful address to link with this assembly. This organisation estimates that there are some twenty-five million children in need through war, famine and poverty.

2 This concern with children would allow this material to be linked to an anniversary on 9th December. Arthur Pearson died on this date in 1921. As a philanthropist he raised funds for poor London children to enjoy outings into the countryside. He later founded St Dunstan's Home for the Blind.

3 This is an assembly obviously best suited for use with older children in the primary school. A Bible reading which might be used with it is Luke 21, 1–4:

> He looked up and saw the rich people dropping their gifts into the chest of the temple treasury; and he noticed a poor woman putting in two tiny coins. 'I tell you this,' he said, 'this poor widow has given more than any of them; for those others who have given had more than enough, but she, with less than enough, has given all she had to live on.'

Hymn suggestion

Come and Praise Vol 1 'Father hear the prayer we offer' No 48

Prayer

Father, Hear the prayer we offer – for those children who must work rather than go to school, and who suffer in so many other ways. As Christmas approaches give them hope, and let the kindness of those who wish to help be effective. Amen.

26 Kindness at Christmas

Introduction

Christmas is a time when people make special efforts to be kind to each other. There are many stories from all over the world which show this. Here is one of them.

Story

One Christmas Eve, long ago in Germany, a poor widow sat looking at her bare Christmas tree in her small hut. Her children were sound asleep in their beds, and she wished desperately that she could have afforded some decorations to put on the tree for them.

'It's no use,' she sighed, 'but at least I can make it clean and tidy.'

So she swept all round the tree, plumped up the branches and arranged it as attractively as she could. Then, wiping a tear from her tired eyes, she too fell asleep in the simple room.

No sooner was the widow asleep than a strange thing began to happen. Spiders appeared out of the woodwork and started to spin webs. These webs were draped over the Christmas tree from top to bottom and from side to side. Their work done, the spiders once more disappeared from view.

Then, an even stranger thing happened. For a moment it seemed that Jesus was actually in the hut with the poor woman and her children. Whilst this was happening, the tiny tree began to glow. Slowly the dull threads of the spider's webs changed colour, until they became a beautiful, gleaming silver, glowing in the darkness of the hut.

As the first pale light of dawn shone through the hut window on Christmas morning, the widow and her children awoke. There were cries of delight as they saw the wonderful tree standing in all its glory in the corner.

'This is going to be a wonderful Christmas,' whispered the widow in amazement and joy.

From that time on, Christmas trees were often decorated with silver tinsel.

Information for the teacher

1 Another traditional German story on a similar theme is about a simple woodcutter and his family. Tired and poor, they hear a knock on their door on Christmas Eve.

Despite having barely enough for their own needs they welcome the boy who has knocked on the door. He is invited in and made welcome.

Next morning everybody is awakened by the singing of a choir of angels. The family has in fact given shelter to the Christ Child.

Hymn suggestion

Come and Praise Vol 2 'I want to see your baby boy' No 117

Prayer

Dear God, At this and every Christmas help us to understand the true meaning of kindness. Amen.

27 Maria

Introduction

Getting presents is fun – and so is giving them. This morning's story is about a little girl who had absolutely nothing to give, or so she thought.

Story

The weather was warm – as it usually was in this part of the world on Christmas Eve. It was just as well because the clothes Maria wore were little more than rags and could certainly not have kept her warm.

She stood on the edge of a graveyard watching people going to church on Christmas Eve. Each person who went into church carried a little box or parcel. Maria knew that these were presents which would be placed on a table next to the crib in the church.

'I wish I had a present I could give to the baby Jesus,' muttered Maria to herself.

At that moment a beautifully-dressed lady passed by. She was wearing a vivid red dress and she carried a gold-covered box in both hands. Maria looked at her shoes which gleamed with polish and were expensive and smart. Then the little girl looked down at her own feet. There were no shoes on them and they were dirty, with broken nails telling of many journeys through stony, dusty ground.

A tear slid down Maria's cheek and dropped on to one of her feet. It sparkled there for a minute in the moonlight and then was gone as quickly as it had come.

'I wish I had a present I could give to baby Jesus,' Maria murmured again.

It was then that Maria seemed to hear the voice in her head.

'Look behind you,' it said.

A little bit frightened, Maria turned and looked behind her. It wasn't a very pretty sight. The graveyard was not well cared-for and the gravestones were surrounded by a sea of weeds.

The little girl sighed. What was there to look at here? Then she heard the voice again.

'Pick some of the weeds.'

Looking at the tangle of dusty, miserable-looking weeds, she wondered why anybody would want to pick a bunch of them.

'Maria – pick a bunch of weeds.'

There was the voice in her head again. Turning her back on the stream of people going into church, the little girl knelt by the nearest gravestone and began to gather some of the weeds in her hands. When she had collected a large bunch she stood up and turned to face the church again.

'Now take the weeds into the church and put them beside the crib as a present for Jesus.'

For a moment Maria hesitated. How could she possibly put this pile of dirty, unwanted weeds beside all the other lovely presents? But somehow her feet seemed to move her towards the church door without her being able to stop them.

Soon she was passing through the great door. People looked curiously at her. Then she was moving down the long aisle towards the crib. As she did so a feeling of tremendous joy began to swell up within her. The other people in the church all seemed to be turning to stare at her, and as they did so their faces lit up with astonishment and wonder.

As Maria walked something incredibly beautiful was happening to the weeds. With each step she took, the leaves at the top of every weed stem turned into a brilliant, lovely red. When she reached the crib their vivid colour made all the other presents look quite drab.

Carefully Maria laid her flowers down. She still felt happy and joyful in a way she had never felt before. Not only had she been able to give a present to the baby Jesus, but it was also a present more beautiful than she could ever have dreamed of.

Information for the teacher

1   This story is based on the old Mexican folk tale of how the first poinsettias came into being. They are still sometimes known as fire flowers.

2   Some comment on other plants associated with Christmas might occur in connection with this story.

Holly featured in the Roman Festival of Saturnalia. People exchanged sprigs of it then because it symbolised eternal friendship. The fact that it bears fruit in winter was another reason why it was considered sacred.

Straw is significant in that in Middle Eastern countries at the time of Jesus' birth, mangers were made of clay or stone. The way of making them warmer and more comfortable was to line them with straw.

There are many legends associated with mistletoe. It was thought at one time to cure illnesses, and if a soldier saw some mistletoe in a wood he would immediately cease from using his weapons for the rest of that day.

In the Norse legends, Loki used mistletoe to kill Baldur. After Baldur returned to life the gods agreed that mistletoe should never hurt anyone again. Thus it became the symbol of love.

Tree worship was pagan in origin but St Boniface is credited with being the person who told his followers that the fir tree would be 'the Christmas tree'. In the sixteenth century its church steeple shape was used by Martin Luther to display candles.

Queen Victoria's husband, Prince Albert, introduced the Christmas tree to England in 1841.

Hymn suggestion

Come and Praise Vol 2 'The holly and the ivy' No 119

Prayer

Dear God, Let us give thanks at Christmas for all the beautiful trees and plants of the world. Let us admire this beauty and value our natural world. Help us to care at all times for our environment. Amen.

January

28 Home Sweet Home?

Introduction

Let's suppose that you've had 'one of those days' at school – you've had an argument with your best friend, got your maths all wrong, you got drenched on the way home, you're freezing … where do you most want to be? Now listen to this morning's story.

Story

Geoff was excited. He had been away for the weekend with a party from school. They had been at a computer centre and it had been great, right from the Friday night when they got there. He'd missed home though, and now the coach was turning down the familiar street he thought how glad he would be to be back.

'Anybody want to get out here?' called out the coach driver.

'Yes, please,' replied Mr Clarke. 'This is your place, isn't it, Geoff?'

'Yes, sir,' answered Geoff, looking to see if there were any lights on in the flat on the second floor.

The bus stopped and Geoff dragged his haversack off the step and slung it over his shoulder.

'Bye, Geoff,' called one or two of his friends, and Mr Clarke gave him a friendly wave.

'I can't wait to tell them all about it,' thought Geoff as he pushed through the front door and began to climb up the stairs to his flat. When he reached the landing he pressed the switch and the lights came on over the staircase. He noticed that the door to his flat – number 4 – was standing slightly open.

'Funny,' he thought, and pushed it open.

'I'm home,' he called in a loud voice. 'I'm …'

It was then that he got his first shock. The front room was empty – no furniture, no carpet, no TV, and all the pictures gone from the walls.

'Mum —' Geoff called out, in a faltering voice. 'Mum … Dad …'

Dropping his bags on the floor, he charged through the flat like a madman. 'Mum … Dad … MUM! DAD!'

The flat was empty. There was no sign of his mother or father. Everything else had gone too. Even the fridge was empty.

Geoff thought he was having some horrible nightmare. He couldn't believe what he saw around him. He was hungry and thirsty and lonely, and his home – had gone.

Information for the teacher

1 On occasion, assemblies which come under the banner of 'Causes for Concern' are extremely effective. This is one of them and it is based on the true story of Frank, an American boy who returned to his home in New York after a trip and found just this situation. He had to survive living on the streets.

2 Frank's mother and stepfather had simply fallen on hard times and left him while he was away at camp. He had no inkling such a thing was going to happen.

3 It is estimated that 2,000–3,000 young people sleep rough in central London every night, many through no fault of their own.

4 The poignancy of this story is emphasised by the following comment by a child of refugee parents who were still with her: 'Yes, we have a home, but no house to put round it.'

Hymn suggestion

Come and Praise Vol 2 'Sad, puzzled eyes' No 74

Prayer

Dear God,
Let us think this morning of those children who, wherever they are in the world, are without a home and all that means. Let us think of those children who are lonely and abandoned. Let us pray that they do not lose hope and find the love that everyone needs. Amen.

29 Good value?

Introduction

What do you think is the greatest treasure you have? (*You may seek answers if you wish.*) Sometimes what seems a treasure to one person is certainly not to another. This morning's story really makes us think about 'good value'.

Story

Ali was fat. He was also very rich and very boastful. He had got rich by leading his camels from town to town and selling rich silks, ebony, coral, rubies and fine-quality linen clothes. He had grown fat sitting beside open fires in towns like Damascus and Jerusalem, boasting about the quality of his goods and how much money he made on every trip.

Ali liked talking, but he wasn't so good at listening. He certainly didn't want to listen to another merchant telling everybody about how rich and successful *he* was. But that's what happened.

Ali's arrival in a desert town had coincided with the arrival of Achmed. Now, Achmed wasn't fat, but in every other respect he was like Ali – rich, hard-working and boastful.

The group of listeners who had gathered around the blazing fire listened with a mixture of awe, interest and disbelief as the two merchants held forth.

'Best trip I ever had to old Jerusalem,' said Ali loudly. 'Bought a sack of coloured silk from Damascus and I couldn't sell it fast enough. I was up half the night counting the money I made on that trip.'

Achmed gave a superior smile. 'Silk, bales of silk, bah! That's not really a money-earner. What you want is precious stones. Now there's a chance for a real profit . . .'

Ali interrupted. 'Oh, I've carried plenty of precious stones in my time too. But of course only the biggest and the best.'

The crowd round the fire gasped as Ali reached into the folds of his cloak and brought out a huge pearl. The firelight sparkled as Ali twisted it round in his fingers. 'A merchant who has a load of pearls like this with him has nothing to worry about, nothing at all. His future is guaranteed.'

Achmed was just about to go one better when a small and rather poor looking man at the back of the group spoke, in a harsh, cutting voice.

'Rubbish,' he said.

Everyone turned to look at him: Ali and Achmed eyed him indignantly; everyone else waited with expectation.

'I was once a merchant like you two, with one of the biggest camel trains ever seen on the desert. Richer and richer I got and, on one final trip, I decided to make myself more money than I could ever have imagined. My father and brothers decided to join me on the trip. We filled all the camel bags with jewels and precious stones. Everything else was abandoned so we could travel fast and light.

'We were a day out on our journey when the worst sandstorm in living memory blew up in the desert. In minutes we were lost. We struck camp, intending to get back to our route when everything had blown over – but it didn't. We had hundreds of precious stones, but no food or water. Gradually my father and two brothers died, and then the servants, and then the camels.

'How I survived I don't know, but a search party came across me more dead than alive – and I've never been the same man since.'

Sweeping his cloak round his skeleton-like frame, the speaker got up and left the fireside group. There was silence. What Ali and Achmed had to say didn't seem important any more.

Information for the teacher

1   An ancient city's gate was one of its focal points. Here was a market place, and here justice was meted out and jobs sought and given. (Bible references: Matthew 20, 3; Ruth 4.)

2   Linen was a very prized material in the East, being both fresher and cleaner than wool. Clothes of purple and scarlet were particularly expensive because the dye for these could only be obtained from the juices of a shellfish caught near the Phoenician port of Tyre.

3   The great caravan routes ranged over the Sinai desert, alongside the Dead Sea, and from Egypt through the passes of Mount Carmel.

4   Camels are mentioned frequently in the Bible. (Genesis; Exodus; 1 Kings 10 refers to the Queen of Sheba's camel train of gifts to Solomon; 11 Kings 8, 9 refers to the forty-camel train of gifts for Elisha.) Camels were very valuable because they were durable and cheap to feed. They would even eat thistles. Reaching maturity at sixteen years, they lived to an old age.

5   There are two useful calendar links with this story. The 6th is the date linked with the journey of the Magi. On the 24th the 'value' angle could be developed. It was on this date in 1848 that gold was first discovered in California, leading to the Gold Rush and many tragedies.

Hymn suggestion

Come and Praise Vol 1 'The best gift' No 59

Prayer

Let us think this morning about the value of things. How precious is food to the starving and water to the thirsty; a home to those who have none; a friend to those who are lonely.

Let us have the sense to value the really important things in life and always to appreciate our own good fortune.

30 The prince

Introduction

We all want people to like us. When they don't, however, we tend to say things like: 'What's the matter with him?' Perhaps we ought to say: 'What's the matter with me?' This morning's story tells of a prince long ago . . .

Story

Father and son stood in an upper room in the palace. For as far as they could see, in every direction, was land which they ruled because they were a king and a prince.

'Look well, my son,' said the king, brushing a tired hand across his forehead. 'I am an old man and I will soon be dead. Then you will be king.'

'Yes, father,' said the prince worriedly. He knew his father was a wise and caring king who was loved by his thousands of loyal subjects. 'But,' he went on, 'the people know you. They know you are just and have tried to improve their lives. They admire your wisdom and respect your decisions. How can I even hope to get them on my side, like you?'

'Think about it,' said the old king quietly. 'Think about it.'

The prince did think about it. When he had done this he decided that the only way to get the respect of his subjects was for them to know who he was.

He sent for the commander of the army.

'Prepare a troop of your finest soldiers,' he said. 'I am going to ride with them throughout the length and breadth of the land. Then the people will see what their new king looks like.'

A special troop of soldiers was drawn up. They were the pick of the army – big, fierce looking, well armed and warlike. When they rode, the sound of their horses' hooves was like rolls of thunder. The prince set off with his soldiers.

Things didn't work out as he had planned. When the people in villages and towns saw the clouds of dust and the galloping horsemen, they were frightened. They didn't bother to wait to see what it was all about. Instead they fled, and hid, until the soldiers moved on. The prince was distraught.

'Father,' he said when he returned home, 'I can't get to know your subjects. They run away before I can even see them, never mind talk to them.' He explained to the wise old king what he had done.

The king nodded. 'But you want to win their confidence, not destroy it. Think, my son, think.'

So the prince thought long and hard again. Then he came to a decision. Working day and night, he called learned men from the farthest parts of the kingdom and learnt to be a doctor. Then he set out again.

Wherever he travelled this time he gave freely of his time and skills. His reputation went before him and soon, on arriving at a new town, he would find a meal and a bed waiting for him. He got to know the problems of many of his people and he spoke with thousands of them.

Finally, the old king died and the young prince became the new king. After a brief period of sadness there was great rejoicing. The people felt that they knew their new ruler and that he would rule with wisdom, care and concern. They were right.

Information for the teacher

1   A useful calendar link with the medical side of this story is with Marie Curie who was born on 7th November 1867. Born Maria Sklodovska in Warsaw, she went to Paris to study when she was twenty-four. There she met and married Pierre Curie, a scientist. They discovered that radium was of great value in curing certain diseases. Pierre died in 1906, Marie in 1934 – from the effects of the radioactive substance which had helped so many other people.

2   The 'wisdom' aspect of the story could be expanded to include such people as Solomon, Confucius, Socrates, the Buddha, Guru Nanak. In all cases, reflection on the 'wisdom' aspect would involve comparisons between the characters and their situations.

3   Another useful anniversary is 24th January – the feast day of St Francis de Sales. A brilliant and wealthy scholar, he was expected to become a senator in the French Parliament. Instead

he gave up these ambitions and became a priest. As such he always had time for individuals and those in need. He became Bishop of Geneva and died in 1622.

Hymn suggestion

Come and Praise Vol 1 'The wise may bring their learning' No 64

Prayer

Let us pray this morning that those people who are important in guiding our lives are given the wisdom and concern to do it well. Let us give thanks for those people in the past who have set such fine examples of caring for others.

31 St Nathalan

Introduction

Have you ever done something wrong at home and known that your father and mother have been annoyed at you? (*Pause for answers.*) Have you known, even though they haven't said anything, when they have forgiven you? (*Pause for responses.*) This morning's story is about a man who found he'd been forgiven in a most amazing way.

Story

St Nathalan was a man who felt that helping others was the most important thing in his life. At one time a terrible famine swept over the land where he was living. People were starving and desperate.

'What can we do?'

'How can we survive?'

'Don't worry,' said Nathalan. 'I'm sure we'll get a crop if we sow some of that fine sand this spring.'

'Sand? Sand?!'

'You must be mad. How can we get a crop from sand?'

'You'll see,' said Nathalan, and he got busy with his sowing.

Sure enough, at harvest time a rich crop rose from the ground just waiting to be collected in. Then disaster struck. A terrible storm raged over the countryside and destroyed the entire crop.

Nathalan was flabbergasted – and completely lost his temper. For days he cursed everything and everybody and behaved very badly. Then, as suddenly as it had started, his bad temper left him. When it did he felt more ashamed than he had ever been in his life before.

'After the way I behaved, how can I possibly claim to be helpful to people?' he thought. 'Well, I'm going to try to do all the good I can – but I'm going to give myself a reminder never to lose my temper again.'

Thus Nathalan did a drastic thing. He locked a heavy chain around one of his ankles. This was painful and made it difficult for him to walk. Once the chain was in place he took the key of the lock to the top of a cliff and hurled it far out to sea. He would never see it again and the chain would be locked on his leg forever to remind him of his weakness.

Nathalan then set out on a pilgrimage to Rome. Trying to do good whenever he could, he reached the city absolutely tired out. Desperately hungry, he bought a fish in the market place. He went out into the countryside and built a little fire.

'I'm certainly ready for my supper,' he said to himself, as he cooked the fish on the fire. 'It looks as if it will be very tasty.'

The fish was soon ready and he started to slice it open with his sharp knife: almost at once the knife hit something sharp in the fish's body. Mystified, Nathalan prized it open carefully and . . .

He could hardly believe his eyes. There, lying inside the fish, was a key.

Nathalan closed his eyes and said a prayer. He knew, before even trying it, that it was the key which would unlock his chain.

He had been forgiven.

Information for the teacher

1   St Nathalan's feast day is on 8th January. If the 'food/crops' aspect of the story is developed, there are two other useful anniversaries: on the same date in 1940 food rationing was introduced in Britain; on 12th January 1948 Britain's first supermarket opened.

2   Some discussion could be generated about how forgiveness can be shown, and children's experiences could be related here. A useful reference to supplement the discussion might include the King and the Governor (Matthew 18, 23–34).

3   Fish play an important role in the Bible: the disciples who were fishermen; the feeding of the five thousand (Matthew 14, 19–20); Jonah and the whale (Jonah 1, 1–17).

The sign of the fish was used by early Christians as a secret sign. This was because the letters of the Greek word for 'fish' (pronounced 'icthus') are the first letters of the words meaning 'Jesus Christ, Son of God, Saviour'.

Hymn suggestion

Come and Praise Vol 1 'Water of life' No 2

Prayer

Let us pray this morning that we can control ourselves and not lose our tempers. In thinking about this, let us listen to the following words:

> Think of the body as a chariot
> Think of thoughts as the driver
> Think of the senses as the horses.
>
> He who has no understanding,
> Whose mind is not held firm,
> Whose senses are uncontrolled,
> Is like a vicious horse out of the control of its driver.
>
> He who has understanding,
> Whose mind is held firm,
> Whose senses are held under control,
> Is like a good horse in the hands of a firm driver.
>   (Adapted from the *Katha Upanishad.*)

32 It will be all right

Introduction

Often, when we are tempted to do something we shouldn't, we try to make it easier for ourselves by saying, 'It will be all right.' This morning's story is a reminder about this saying.

Story

January is often a very cold, frosty, icy month. In Britain, in years gone by, it was often colder than it is now. The January of 1867 was absolutely freezing. Snow lay thickly on the streets of London, icicles hung from rooftops and windows and a brilliant blue sky covered the city.

On the 15th of the month crowds of people began to gather at Regent's Park. Snowball fights broke out and a few daring young men began to slide and skate on the ice of the lake.

'Look at them,' cried a young woman in the crowd, 'they're having fun – let's go and join them.'

'That's a good idea.'

'Great! Come on, hurry up.'

Not everyone was quite so enthusiastic and a few people muttered doubts.

'How do we know the ice is strong enough?'

'Aren't there too many on it already?'

'I'm sure it will crack.'

But the crowds of fun-seeking people ignored the doubters. 'It'll be all right,' they cried. 'The worst that can happen is you'll slip over and get your clothes wet!'

Crowds more piled on to the ice and the sounds of laughter echoed through the cold, crisp air. Then, above the laughter, a different sound was heard – a shrill cry of fear. Suddenly the air was filled with shrieks of panic and screaming. The ice had broken!

As wedges of ice broke and tipped their terrified occupants into the freezing water, there was a mad scramble to get to the safety of the banks. But as the crowd moved this way and that further platforms of ice cracked and broke. People who tried to pull friends out found themselves slipping into the water. Whole families crashed screaming through the ice.

Eventually the terrible scene calmed down. The lake, which had looked before like a glistening white sheet, was now a mass of broken ice platforms bobbing on the bitter water. Beneath the surface lay many of the skaters, drowned within minutes.

It hadn't been 'all right'.

Information for the teacher

1   Another of the severest winters recorded in Britain began on 13th January 1881. January was the month of mediaeval Frost Fairs which were held in many European cities. As well as the trading aspect of these there was entertainment such as bull and bear baiting. The latter obviously offers some further discussion material in an RE context.

2   Another possible development from this story is that disasters often throw up heroes or heroines. There are plenty of examples from the past but up-to-date newspaper cuttings will also soon build up into very useful modern source material.

3   The following poem was written by a nine-year-old girl. It captures the essence of the two sides of winter.

> Winter is a beautiful time of the year.
> But is it?
> Frost glistens.
> Ice sparkles dazzling white.
> This is the beauty of winter.
> But the beauty is just a covering,
> To a cold miserable world.
> Dark and dull,
> That starves the animals
> Who dare to come out in winter.

Hymn suggestion

Come and Praise Vol 2 'Lay my white cloak' No 112

Prayer

Let us think this morning about those words: 'It will be all right.' Let us pray that we might be given the wisdom, determination and strength of character to decide for ourselves whether something is 'all right' or not.

Let us pray that we may be given the strength to resist temptation, when we know deep down that what we are being tempted to do is wrong.

33 Be prepared

Introduction

Cubs, Brownies, Scouts and Guides all know how important it is to 'be prepared'. This morning's story is a reminder of the sort of thing that can happen when we are not prepared.

Story

'It's fantastic!'

'It'll be great, won't it?'

'Fancy us being chosen like this.'

The ten girls all crowded round each other. They were thrilled with the news. Cliff Crosby, the great singer, was coming back to his home village to get married and they had been chosen to form a 'passage of light' when he arrived.

To do this each of the girls had been given an oil lamp and when Cliff arrived photographers were to be there taking pictures of him going into the house with the girls' oil lamps lighting his way.

'We'd better get our lamps ready for when he comes,' said Julie. 'We'd better have them all lit so we are ready.'

'Will we have enough oil?' asked Sally.

'I've bought some spare oil,' said Mehnaz.

'So have I.'

'I haven't.'

As a result of their talking, the girls found that five of them had brought some spare oil for their lamps and five hadn't bothered.

'It doesn't matter,' said Jayna, one of the girls who hadn't brought any spare oil. 'He'll be here soon anyway.'

It was then that the telephone rang. It was Cliff's agent. 'There's going to be a delay, girls – but he'll be there some time this afternoon.'

Time began to drag and some of the girls fell asleep. They were awakened by the shrill ringing of the telephone. Sally answered it. At once the girls were awake and getting their oil lamps ready – but now there was a problem.

Because of the delay several of the lamps had gone out. Those girls who had brought extra oil to be prepared for such a happening quickly filled up their lamps and got them going again. The girls who hadn't brought spare oil panicked.

'Quick, lend me some of yours.'

'Oh come on, just a drop.'

'Why didn't we think to bring some spare?'

'Hurry, we'll have to go down to the shops and get some.'

So the five girls without oil dashed out of the house and headed for the shops. No sooner had they disappeared than a fleet of cars swept into the street.

Cliff and his agent got out of the first car, while newspaper reporters and TV cameramen jumped out of those behind.

'Right, let's get this romantic picture.'

'Cliff going into his old house . . .'

'. . . with the way being lit by some old oil lamps.'

Cliff's agent grinned at the girls. 'These pictures will be in newspapers all over the world,' he said. 'And think of the folks who'll see this on TV tonight.'

So the girls who were prepared were caught up in all the excitement – they must have been photographed forty times! When the other girls returned – the ones who hadn't bothered to bring any spare oil – the street was empty. They had missed everything.

Information for the teacher

1   This adaptation of the well-known Bible story of the Foolish Maidens could be used in conjunction with two others. The first is the story of the two men who built houses – the wise one on firm ground, the foolish one on sand.
These stories could then be contrasted with an example of how Jesus told his followers about the way they should listen carefully and heed what they had been told. The example could be of the Sower and the Seed.

The Bible references for all three stories are:

> The Foolish Maidens: Matthew 25, 1–11
> The Builders: Matthew 7, 24–27
> The Sower and the Seed: Mark 4, 3–8

2   Two useful calendar references for this story are 17th January which is St Anthony's Day, and 5th January which is the birth-date of Robert Morrison in 1782.
Anthony lived between 250 and 350 years after the time of Jesus. He became a hermit but such was his reputation for giving wise advice that people travelled from great distances to seek it from him.
Robert Morrison gave guidance in a different way. A missionary to China, he risked his life to get copies of the Bible in Chinese into the country.

Hymn suggestion

Come and Praise Vol 1 'The wise may bring the learning' No 64

Prayer

Christians believe that our lives can be guided by advice given in the Bible.
Listen to the words of a Christian prayer:

> Lord of the loving heart,
> May mine be loving too;
> Lord of the gentle hands,
> May mine be gentle too;
> Lord of the willing feet,
> May mine be willing too;

So may I grow more like to Thee,
In all I say and do.
Amen.

34 Our daily bread

Introduction

I expect that all of us in assembly this morning had at least some bread yesterday. Bread is one of the commonest of the foods we eat. But what do we really know about it?

Story

We know that, about five thousand years ago, when the pyramids were being built, priests and officers in Egypt were paid part of their wages in loaves of bread. The Romans were so keen to make sure that people buying bread were not cheated that they set up bakeries in public places and had them carefully inspected and guarded.

The Greeks were so keen to keep bread free of germs that they made all bakers wear masks, and in Turkey any baker who failed to give proper value in his loaves was tortured.

The Great Fire of London in 1666 was supposed to have started in a baker's shop in Pudding Lane. As a result of this bakers were forbidden to use straw overnight on their oven fires so that the same thing would not happen again. During the 1800s some bakers were thought to add the chemical alum to their loaves to make them whiter and therefore more tempting to customers. Two lines from the story of 'Jack and the Beanstalk' also had a very sinister meaning at this time:

Be he alive or be he dead,
I'll grind his bones to make my bread.

It was actually thought that one baker ground human bones to use as an ingredient in his bread.

In France, the great revolution which took place there in 1789 happened partly because although there was plenty of bread to buy people were so poor that they couldn't afford it.

So you see, when we get our sliced, pre-wrapped, hygienic loaf of bread from the supermarkets these days we are looking at something that has a very ancient and interesting history.

Information for the teacher

1 'Bread' has been a popular RE theme and the Bible abounds in references to it. In Bible lands it was an essential food and was made from wheat or barley ground with mortar and pestle.
Bread features in such stories as the feeding of the five thousand (Mark 6, 31–46); it was always a popular gift and was often used in quotations – 'Man shall not live by bread alone' (Matthew 4, 4). The symbolism of bread reaches its highest point in the Holy Communion service.

2 One possible calendar link is that John Howard died on 20th January 1790. He was Sheriff of Bradford and it was mainly owing to his efforts that laws were passed to make sure that prisoners had adequate food and living conditions.
Robert Burns was born on 25th January 1759. The poet's birthday is celebrated annually by Scots all over the world. No celebrations would be complete without the traditional eating of the haggis. A description of this – sheep's liver and heart, suet, oatmeal, served in the sheep's stomach and boiled for three hours – could contrast with the basic plain fare of bread.

Hymn suggestion

Come and Praise Vol 2 'Bread for the world' No 75

Prayer

Let us bow our heads and think about the words: 'Our Father, Give us this day our daily bread.'
Let us give thanks for the treasure of food.
Let us pray that those who haven't enough are given both hope and help. Amen.

35 Is it worth it?

Introduction

Think about your school building for a minute. How long has it been built? Can you imagine what the area was like before it was built? How long did it take to build? Who was involved in building it?

This morning's story is about a building – one of the world's most famous. The same sort of questions could be asked about it.

Story

If you went to your local travel agents you could probably get a brochure advertising a holiday in China. This might suggest a visit to the Great Wall of China because every year thousands of people walk short distances along it. You certainly couldn't walk along all of it in a short package holiday – it is 2,400 kilometres in length, and ten metres high. Two questions you might ask about this wall are Why was it built? and Was it worth it?

About two thousand years ago the Emperor Shih Huang Ti decided a wall was needed to keep enemies out of his country.

'Get it organised,' he said to his chief ministers.

'But your majesty,' they replied, 'who will want to work in such a hard and lonely place? How can we possibly get enough men to do the job?'

'Start by emptying the prisons. Get every prisoner we've got in the country and send him up to the north to work on the wall.'

'Yes, sir, but . . .'

'Move the army up there too. They can look after the prisoners and work on the wall as well.'

So began ten years of misery for thousands of people. Fearful that they might have to labour themselves, the overseers drove the workers with terrible cruelty. Hundreds of thousands laboured under severe weather conditions with the most primitive of tools and with practically nothing in the way of comfort when they weren't actually working. Not surprisingly, all sorts of diseases broke out and all were overworked in the rush to get the wall completed. Thousands of men died while working on the wall – but work never stopped. As a man died, his body was thrown into the rubble and the wall built on top of him.

There is an old legend which says that a man died for every stone in the Great Wall of China – you can imagine how many deaths this must have meant in 2,400 kilometres!

Information for the teacher

1 This assembly is obviously best suited for upper juniors and could provoke discussions on values, and an appreciation of how fortunate we are to live today when building can take place without such cruelty and loss of life.

'Building' is a theme which, in itself, can expand into a variety of RE considerations – foundations, co-operation, quality, purpose, etc. 'Barriers' is another useful theme.

2 A useful calendar connection with this story is the Chinese New Year. Located in late January or early February this goes through a cycle – for instance, 2000 is the year of the Dragon, 2001 the year of the Snake then subsequently Horse, Sheep, Monkey, Rooster, Dog, Pig, Rat, Ox, Tiger, Rabbit and then back to Dragon again.
Chinese New Year is basically a family festival when houses are decorated and presents exchanged. Processions are held in the streets and 'Kung Hei Fat Choy' is the New Year Greeting.

3 A useful Biblical link with this story is a comparison with the Tower of Babel. In this story God was displeased with His people and decided to teach them a lesson. They were in the process of building a huge tower when God caused the workmen to suddenly start speaking different languages – as a result the project ended in confusion. (The word 'babel' has thus come to mean 'a scene of noise and confusion'.) Biblical reference: Genesis 11.

Hymn suggestion

Come and Praise Vol 2 'You can build a wall' No 91

Prayer

Let us think this morning of the many lessons people have learned through history. Let us give thanks for modern technology and a greater awareness of the needs of all people.

February

36 What's inside?

Introduction

You will certainly know the person standing next to you in assembly this morning. But if you didn't, and you looked carefully at him or her, you would see face, eyes, hair, clothes – but you wouldn't know what he or she was like 'inside'.

Story

If you go to London and walk along by the river on the Thames Embankment you come to a rather strange monument. It is made of weather-beaten stone and points towards the sky like a long stone finger. This is Cleopatra's Needle, and it has an interesting history.

Cleopatra was an Egyptian Queen who lived hundreds of years ago and this monument once stood in Egypt. When it was brought to England it was found that inside it someone had put lots of souvenirs of the time when it was built. Things like children's dolls and ladies' jewellery were discovered.

The monument was then brought on a long, adventurous journey by sea to England. When it arrived there was a lot of discussion by the experts who had to decide what to do with it.

'We must put it up in an important position.'

'We want as many people as possible to see it.'

'What about putting something inside it too?'

'How do you mean?'

'Well, if it's ever moved, or opened up again, the people who move it will be able to see the sort of things we use today in our time.'

'What a good idea.'

It was decided to put the monument up beside the River Thames where it now stands. Inside it were put some children's toys, a few mirrors, a telephone directory, a number of newspapers, some photographs of ladies of the day showing fashions, and a packet of razor blades.

So, when you are in London, try and go to see Cleopatra's Needle and as you look at it think of the treasures which are inside it.

In a way it's a bit like people – what we look at and see certainly doesn't tell us about the treasures that lie inside.

Information for the teacher

1   Cleopatra lived from 69 to 30 BC. The obelisk which is Cleopatra's Needle stands 68 feet high and once stood at Heliopolis. It was brought to England in the nineteenth century and therefore its inner contents already reflect another bygone era.

2   This theme of 'what lies within' is very evocatively told in the story of Caedmon. Caedmon, a poor cowherd, was at a farmhouse party. The guests sat in a circle and a harp was passed from one to another. Each guest sang and played when the harp reached him.

Caedmon had a terrible voice so before the harp reached him he slipped off and went to bed. He dreamed that a stranger came and told him 'to sing God's praises'. Knowing he couldn't sing, Caedmon was mystified. He sought advice at the great monastery at Whitby. There it was found that after reading passages from the Bible he could immediately rephrase them into wonderful poetry.

So Caedmon began to 'sing God's praises' and spent the rest of his life in the monastery rewriting sections of the Bible in language people could understand and enjoy.

3   For those in a position to do so, a visit to see Cleopatra's Needle would be an excellent follow-up to this story. February would be a good month for such an urban visit.

Hymn suggestion

There is something to be said for using two hymns in this assembly. This would depend on how the presenter has developed the theme, but the two suggestions are:

Come and Praise Vol 2 'In the bustle of the city' No 101
Come and Praise Vol 1 'Song of Caedmon' No 13

Prayer

Dear God,
Let us think this morning about what makes us ugly: telling lies, being rude, acting in a jealous, selfish, cruel or thoughtless way.

Let us think about what makes us beautiful: always being ready with a kind word, thinking the best of people, caring about the thoughts and feelings of others.

Help us to be beautiful, inside. Amen.

37 This month

Introduction

February is always the shortest month of the year but there are many interesting things about it – both indoors and outside.

This month

Many people think one of the best things about February is that flowers start appearing after the long winter. These include the small white flowers which are called snowdrops. They are a sign of hope for the spring which is now a little nearer, but they are also called the 'flowers of hope' for another reason. An old story is that when Adam and Eve were sent out of the Garden of Eden an angel turned a snowflake into this flower to give them some hope for the future. Crocus buds can also be seen pushing up during this month.

It is worth keeping an eye on trees in February. The hazel starts to have a furry appearance because of its catkins and high up in tall trees there is a lot of activity going on. Rooks in particular are busy getting their nests ready. Sometimes they do this by repairing old ones and sometimes they pull the old ones to pieces and start again on new ones. The sounds of birds singing can begin during February and most probably it will be the voices of blackbirds or thrushes which you hear.

Indoors in February, the 2nd is a special day. This was the day on which Mary took the baby Jesus to be blessed at the temple. To remember this candles are lit in churches and blessed for the whole year. This date is known as Candlemas.

Pancake Day is one all children enjoy. It came into being because people once used up all their eggs and fat on this day. This was because it was just before a time called Lent – when people did without certain foods for forty days to remind themselves of Jesus's life.

All Scouts, Guides, Brownies and Cubs will know that 22nd February is a special time for them, called Thinking Day.

Finally, if at any time during this month you are having beans for lunch, have a closer look at them. They probably don't look very special but if you were Japanese you could enjoy having them this month. This is because in February Japanese people throw beans at each other – this is supposed to send winter away!

Information for the teacher

1   Carrying beans as protection against demons and witches is a long-held folk tradition in many cultures. A man with a bean ready in his mouth was considered to be well prepared if he met a witch – he simply spat the bean at her.

2   In the time when Jesus was born it was the custom of every Jewish mother to take her first male child to the temple forty days after he was born. The child was then presented to the Lord and the mother was blessed. Candlemas is therefore the fortieth day after Christmas.

3   Pancake Day – Shrove Tuesday – is the forty-first day before Easter and the day before Ash Wednesday, which begins Lent. In days when there was more revelry and feasting before Lent the day before Shrove Tuesday was known as Collop Monday – when large pieces of fried meat were eaten.

Hymn suggestion

Come and Praise Vol 1 'At the name of Jesus' No 58

Prayer

Let us give thanks this morning for time. Let us learn to enjoy each month and know about it as it comes round during the year.

Let us make the most of every minute, hour, day, week and month of our lives.

38 Pass it on

Introduction

Have you ever thought about how the way you behave affects other people? This morning's story might act as a reminder.

Story

It was a cold February Monday morning and Jason got out of bed feeling really down in the dumps. He'd been moved in class to sit next to the new kid; he was sure he wouldn't be in the football team after Friday night's practice; and it seemed they were going to have that miserable supply teacher again.

By the time he'd lost a button off his shirt and found that Julie had been using his toothbrush, he was even more tetchy.

'Come on, Jason, hurry up or you'll be late.'

'Hmm.'

'Come on, eat your breakfast.'

'Leave off, Mum.'

On his way to school Jason passed a line of shop windows. The shops weren't open yet and as he looked at his reflection one of the most miserable faces he'd ever seen stared back at him. Window after window showed the same unhappy face until, as the last window came up, Jason spread his mouth wide and the reflection came to life with his smile. A woman was passing in the opposite direction and as soon as Jason smiled, she not only smiled back but she bade him a cheerful 'Good Morning'.

Immediately he felt better. Some of the gloom seemed to lift, and the first person he bumped into in the playground was the new kid – who looked nervous.

Seeing Jason's smile the new kid came up to him. 'Jason ... I just wanted to say ... I'm glad Mrs Watts moved you to sit beside me ... I'm really glad.'

Jason slapped the new kid on the back and they moved into line together as the whistle went. Mr Clarke, the teacher in charge of games, was on duty and as the classes filed in he took Jason by the arm.

'Football,' he said. 'You don't need me to tell you that you didn't play well in Friday's practice. So Alex is going to be in the team for the next match ... but keep trying – your turn is sure to come again.'

When Jason smiled and nodded his head Mr Clarke slapped him on the back.

'I knew you would take it like the real sportsman you are. Well done.'

In a funny sort of way, Jason felt as if he'd scored the winning goal rather than been dropped from the team.

After assembly the class bustled into their room as usual. They already knew Mrs Watts was away on a course and when the supply teacher came in the first person she looked at was Jason.

Jason smiled, and said, 'Good morning, Miss.'

The supply teacher nodded, and then said, 'I've got some really interesting old newspapers for you to look at this morning.'

And they *were* interesting too! In fact the whole day seemed to go with a real swing.

That afternoon, as Jason walked home, he paused at the shop windows again.

'Funny', he thought, 'that smile seemed to make all the difference.'

Information for the teacher

1   In pursuing the idea of the value of a smile, these are some relevant February anniversaries: P G Wodehouse, creator of Bertie Wooster and Jeeves, died on 14th February 1975; David Garrick, one of England's greatest actors who played many roles in comedy, was born on 19th February 1717; Baron Münchhausen, teller of fantastic and amusing tales, died on 22nd February 1797.

2   A little poetic licence could be used with the following quotation: 'Every day, and in every way, I am becoming better and better.' Originally designed as an auto-suggestion catch-phrase by the French psychotherapist Emile Coué, it could be linked to this assembly story and ensuing work.

Another useful phrase in this context is one coined by Sir Wilfred Grenfell: 'It's not what you have that matters. It's what you do with what you have.'

Hymn suggestion

Come and Praise Vol 2 'You shall go out with joy' No 98

Prayer

Dear God,

Help us to be the sort of person other people are pleased to meet. May we smile more than we frown; may we encourage more than we criticise; may we look for good points rather than bad points. Amen.

39 We need a king!

Introduction

Sometimes, we complain about certain things in our lives: 'I wish I could stay up later to watch TV . . . I wish I didn't have to go outside on cold playtimes . . . I wish my brother didn't sleep in the same room as me' . . . and so on.

This morning's story will give those who complain something to think about.

Story

'We need a king! . . . We need a king! . . . We need a king!' The frog chorus croaked over the ponds and lakes. They had had a long meeting and decided that they were as important as anyone else, so . . .

'We need a king . . . we need a king!'

High above, the gods heard the croaking.

'What's all that about?'

'It's those frogs – they want a king.'

'But why? They've always lived peacefully together until now.'

'You know how it is – somebody starts to complain and before you know where you are . . .'

'I know – "We need a king".'

The gods thought about how helpful the frogs had previously been to each other, and how peaceful they had been. Perhaps this problem could be solved easily. So, one of the god's messengers arranged for a big log to be thrown into the lake.

'Your king has arrived,' he called, as the log hit the lake with an enormous splash.

The frogs were impressed. Their new king was very big. He didn't say a lot but he looked very powerful.

For a few days the frogs kept away from the king, until two of them swam close, and dared each other to jump on his back. One frog took a deep breath and leaped up onto the log.

When nothing happened other frogs jumped on the log too. Soon they were calling out again.

'Our king's useless.'

'He can't even move.'

'He's not a proper king at all.'

'We need a king . . . we need a king . . . we need a king!'

Once again the gods heard the cry and this time they decided the frogs needed a proper lesson.

Later that day a stork flew to the edge of the large lake and called out.

'Frogs – I am your new king, and I want to see my subjects. Show yourselves.'

'That's better,' thought the frogs. 'A proper king who gives orders and looks important.'

So from every bit of rock and mud and water the frogs came out to acknowledge their king.

No sooner did he see them than the stork swept forward and began eating frogs as fast as his huge beak could cram them in.

The frogs were terrified. They dodged away to safety, shivering with fear.

'Oh – if only we had been satisfied,' said one of them.

Information for the teacher

1   This well-known fable has virtually limitless possibilities for adaptation and improvisation. It is the sort of material which can also be very simply dramatised for assembly purposes.

2   A possible calendar link for this story is 12th February, when Charles Darwin, the naturalist, was born.

3 This story, with its mixture of foolishness and wisdom, could be linked very appropriately to an anonymous verse which emphasises the same qualities via a 'creature' source:

> The wise old owl sat high in an oak,
> And the more he heard the less he spoke,
> The less he spoke the more he heard,
> So why can't we be like that wise old bird?

Hymn suggestion

Come and Praise Vol 1 'He's got the whole world' No 19

Prayer

Dear God,

Help us to remember that no life is perfect and that we will all suffer disappointments. Teach us to value the good things in our lives and help us to try and show how much we appreciate these. Amen.

40 Teamwork

Introduction

February is a month when the weather can change quickly – and dangerously. A day which has been bright and sunny can change into a night of freezing fog – something to beware of if you are on a long-distance walk.

Story

'It's a bit scary!'

'Yeah – I'll be glad when we're home.'

'I can't even see Michael.'

'He's moved up ahead, he wants to be ...'

A shrill scream stopped the conversation. It tore through the mist and sleet high up in the hills of the Peak District National Park, where the boy scouts had gone for their hike. The scoutmaster pushed past the tired boys and dashed ahead to where the scream had come from. Following him, the boys helped him search, but it was no use – fourteen-year-old Michael Parsons had simply disappeared.

The party had set off for their hike that morning, 17th February, but the bad weather had closed in before they could get home. The dense fog had them all worried, even before Michael's disappearance.

'Come on, lads,' said the scoutmaster. 'I know we're on the right track and I know that where it meets the road there's a telephone box. We must get help.'

A short while later, to the boys' great relief, the party reached the road. The call for help brought an immediate response. Soon the scouts were met by a police car. In it were Inspector Guest of the local police, and Mr Heardman, an expert on the local area.

'Right,' said Inspector Guest. 'The local mountain rescue team have been called out, the Land-Rover radio truck and ambulance is on its way. But we must know where to search.'

'But it was so foggy, we don't know whereabouts on the trail Michael was lost,' said one of the boys.

'Think carefully,' said Mr Heardman to the scoutmaster. 'There are several danger spots on that route. Think carefully about any other sounds you heard.'

'Well,' said the scoutmaster doubtfully, 'we heard Michael's scream, then the sounds of him falling and stones scattering . . . and I think I also heard water . . . and there was a lot of ice and snow about.'

Mr Heardman thought carefully for a minute.

'That sounds to me like Kinder Downfall,' he said. 'There's always water there, and snow and ice when it's cold. That's the place to start the search.'

Leaving the scouts in safe hands, the rescue team set off to search for Michael. Wary of the dangers of thick mist, ice and snow, the team reached the rocky wall of Kinder Downfall and began their inch-by-inch torchlight search in the bitter winter night.

They were almost ready to give up when the torch of Derek Figg suddenly picked out a crumpled figure on a ledge.

'He's here! Careful, he needs help.'

'Coming.'

'Get the stretcher forward.'

'Keep your torch on him, Derek.'

The well-drilled team moved swiftly into action and soon Michael was being stretchered to safety.

Later, from the warmth and safety of his hospital bed, Michael told his story.

'I just slipped over the side,' he said, 'hit my head and blacked out. When I came to I couldn't stand on one leg, and one of my arms was just dangling . . . I must have passed out again.'

Inspector Guest told how Michael had not uttered one sound despite the terrible pain he must have been in during his rescue.

'He's a brave lad,' said the policeman.

But the 'brave lad', and his parents, knew that without the expert local knowledge of Mr Heardman, and the skill and courage of the mountain rescue team, he would never have survived.

Information for the teacher

1   The party had set out from the village of Hayfield in Derbyshire for their expedition, in 1957. Their difficulties started during the afternoon of 17th February, and Michael was not found until 5.15 am on the morning of 18th February.

Hymn suggestion

Come and Praise Vol 1 'Lost and found' No 57

Prayer

Let us pray this morning for those brave people who help when there are accidents on land, at sea or in the air.

Let us give thanks for the qualities of trust, reliance and courage which enable people to work so successfully in rescue teams.

41 The man whom everybody liked

Introduction

Is there anybody you know whom everybody likes? If so, then this person must have very special qualities – like the man this morning's story is about.

Story

George Peabody was born in a little town in the United States of America. The town was called South Danvers and George was born on 18th February 1795.

The Peabody family was very poor and by the time he was eleven years old George was already working for a grocer in town. Obviously he had had very little time to go to school.

As George grew older, he joined another man called Elisha Riggs and they opened a store selling general goods. Business was good.

George was a hard worker, and when Elisha died George opened other shops all over the country and became rich.

'I'm not bothered about big houses and fancy clothes,' thought George to himself, 'but I would like to make sure other folks can benefit from my good fortune.'

So George set off alone on horseback to visit Red Indians who were considered highly dangerous by other people. Like everybody else, the Indians trusted George. He sold them useful goods at fair prices and went out of his way to be of help if they were in any kind of trouble.

George went on helping people, giving money away and being a friend to all. His fame spread right across the United States.

One day George had an idea. 'My ancestors came from England. I wonder what it's like there?' he thought. 'Well, there's only one way to find out – I'll go.'

When George arrived in London in 1837, he had two equally strong feelings. He loved the city, the bustle of the streets, the friendliness – but he hated the slums in which desperately poor people lived miserable lives.

'Hmm – this looks like something I should help with,' he thought.

George began to use his money to find areas where he could build flats to house the thousands of poor people who were living in dreadful hovels. He hired the best architects he could find to design the flats and he made sure the rents to live in them were as low as they possibly could be. His name and his actions were like magic to thousands of desperately poor Londoners.

'We're going to have a proper flat.'

'It's really got a toilet in it.'

'And there are shops on the ground floor.'

'And we can dry our clothes on the roof.'

'He's a marvellous man.'

And so he was. By 1919 over 23,000 people were living in Peabody homes and George was admired by everybody – from Queen Victoria to the poorest man in the street. When a statue of George was built and unveiled in central London the streets were packed with cheering crowds saying their own Thank You to him.

Information for the teacher

1   When George Peabody died on 4th November 1869 he had given away over two million pounds to charitable causes – a staggering sum even by today's standards.

In his latter years he spent time in both London and the USA and gave donations to Harvard, Yale, and for the education of black people in America.

He died in England; his funeral service was held in Westminster Abbey and his body was taken back to the USA. The town of South Danvers, Massachusetts, was renamed Peabody.

2   This story could be linked to those of other philanthropists – Lord Nuffield, the Cadbury family, Dr Barnardo, Leonard Cheshire, Sue Ryder, etc.

3   'To give and not to count the cost' is a theme which pervades all religious teachings. There are therefore several appropriate quotations to supplement this story.

Regarding George Peabody himself, Ecclesiasticus 44, 1–2, is appropriate: 'Let us now sing the praises of famous men; the heroes of our nation's history.'

Other 'giving' references could include:

'The beggar was given a horse. He did not want a horse, only a meal.' (Japanese proverb)

'When you help people, don't let your right hand know what your left hand is doing: help people without others noticing it.' (Matthew 6, 2–3)

'He is best loved who does most good to other creatures.' (Islamic saying)

'Give as generously as you can and share people's sorrows.' (Adapted from Ecclesiasticus 4)

'Take a real interest in ordinary people.' (From a letter from St Paul to the Christians in Rome)

Hymn suggestion

Come and Praise Vol 2 'You shall go out with joy' No 98

Prayer

Dear God,

In thanking you for those people who help us, let us remember, and think about, some words from the Bible: 'Let us never tire of doing good, for if we do not slacken our efforts we shall in due time reap our harvest. Therefore, as opportunity offers, let us work for the good of all.' Amen.

(The quotation used in this prayer is from Galatians 6, 9–10.)

42 In a garden in Medina

Introduction

When we are very tired we tend to think things like: When can I get a drink? When can I have something to eat? I wish I could have a rest.

You'll notice that 'I' is used a lot here. This morning's story makes us think about this.

Story

In the days when Muhammad the Prophet (pbuh) was a camel driver, lots of the long, hot journeys across the desert ended in Medina. Here there was a beautifully cool, shady garden and it was one of the first places the camel drivers headed for to get a refreshing drink and a rest.

One day Muhammad had finished a trip, and he took his camel to the garden in Medina. Making sure that his trusty animal was well fed and watered, he then made his way towards a large group of fellow camel drivers. The conversation was much the same as always.

'Did you have a good trip, Ahmad?'

'Yes, no trouble, and the cloth sold very well.'

'Did you hear about poor Abu Bakr?'

'No, what was that?'

'His camel went lame twenty miles from the city.'

'Oh that's . . .'

Suddenly, above the chatter of the drivers, Muhammad heard another noise. It was the gasping, throaty noise of a camel in great distress. Leaving the group, Muhammad moved to where a second lot of camels had been tethered. Most of them were comfortable in the shade, but one poor beast had been left out in the full blast of the scorching sun. Worse still, one look was sufficient to tell Muhammad that the creature was very old, had certainly not been given a drink and was in great discomfort and distress. The prophet hurried back to the camel drivers.

'Stop,' he commanded above their conversation.

Surprised, and a little alarmed, the drivers stopped talking and looked at Muhammad.

'What's wrong?' asked one of them, worriedly.

'You are all comfortable here,' said Muhammad. 'You are among friends, have eaten and drunk and are contented. One of you has left a camel out there – miserable, unfed, uncomfortable and distressed. Whoever it is should be ashamed.'

A young camel driver got to his feet, his head bowed.

'I'm sorry, Muhammad. It is my camel. I was so tired and thirsty that I . . . well, I was going to as soon as I . . . I just . . .'

'Stop wasting time and go and see to your animal,' said Muhammad. 'You would do well to remember that God places animals in our care. To neglect them or to be cruel to them is to insult God.'

Information for the teacher

1   The sensitive teacher will need always to be aware of the current year's Muslim calendar, which is not only based on the lunar year but also on sightings of the moon rather than on reckonings.

2   Muhammad believed in one God, Allah. He was a man who liked to be alone and when he was forty the Archangel Gabriel appeared before him and began to teach Muhammad God's message for the world. This message was ultimately written down in the Qur'an. Gabriel's appearance to Muhammad is celebrated during Ramadan, at the festival of Lailat-ul-Qadr, meaning 'The Night of Power'.

3   Hadith is the name given to the sayings and deeds of Muhammad which help Muslims understand more about Islam. One of these sayings is very appropriate for this assembly story: 'None of you believes until he wishes for his brother what he wishes for himself.'

Hymn suggestion

Come and Praise Vol 2 'All the animals' No 80

Prayer

Let us bow our heads this morning and listen to some of the words of the Prophet Muhammad:

'Forgive him who does you wrong; do good to him who does you wrong; always speak the truth even if it is against you.'

Let us keep silent for a little while to think about these words.

March

43 Guard my treasure

Introduction

'Honesty is the best policy' is a very old saying but it is a good one to follow – as this morning's story shows.

Story

'It's such a shame – but the truth is, I can't really trust him'.

As he said these words to himself, Giovanni the rich merchant looked out of one of the windows of his fine house. Down below in the garden Alfredo played with the family dog.

Alfredo had called on Giovanni many months ago.

'I'm down on my luck,' he said. 'Could you give me some work? You'll find I am a very good worker.'

Feeling sorry for the nice looking young man, Giovanni had taken him in. Alfredo did indeed prove an excellent worker and in no time at all he was Giovanni's right-hand man. He ran the estate, paid the workers, bought and sold fine cloth, and did it all with a smile on his face.

But Giovanni hadn't got to be a rich man by being foolish. He soon found out that a bale of the finest cloth had 'disappeared'; some of the workers complained about not getting their proper wages; odd valuable items were no longer to be seen about the house.

'None of these things happened before Alfredo came,' thought Giovanni sadly. 'I'm sure he's stealing from me – so we shall have to see.'

That night Giovanni asked Alfredo to join him for the evening meal.

'Alfredo,' started the merchant seriously, 'I have to go away on business for a few days and I need to be sure that everything is safe at home. I'm going to put my most precious jewels and possessions in a large chest. Will you look after it for me while I am away?'

'Of course, Giovanni,' replied the handsome Alfredo, with one of his most charming smiles. 'It will be a pleasure. You can sleep well at night knowing everything is safe with me.'

Two days later two servants carried a large and very heavy chest into Alfredo's room. Behind them Giovanni and Alfredo walked along in deep conversation.

'Guard it well,' said Giovanni. 'My fortune lies in that chest.'

As he spoke, he pointed to the large box which was sealed with two large seals.

'Don't worry,' replied Alfredo. 'It will be locked in my room and neither I nor anybody else will touch it until you get back.'

Giovanni went on his way. A little over a week went by and then one hot and sunny morning he and his fellow horseman were seen approaching the house up the long and dusty driveway.

'Alfredo! It's good to see you again,' said Giovanni. 'That was a very successful trip. How has everything been here?'

'All right.'

'You don't sound very happy,' replied Giovanni glancing at the surly looking Alfredo. 'What's the matter?'

For a moment, Alfredo said nothing. Then his irritation and impatience got the better of him.

'It's you ... you said you trusted me. You told me you were leaving all your riches in my care. But that chest was just full of heavy stones. It was ...' Alfredo stopped. He had realised his mistake – but it was too late.

Information for the teacher

1   Useful calendar references for this story could be the deaths of the Wesley brothers, both of whom died in March. Both were great advocates of Christian virtues and John, who died on 2nd March 1791, not only founded Methodism but was a pioneer in 'taking Christianity to the people'.

Charles Wesley died on 29th March 1788 and is mostly remembered for his hymns. He believed that the words of hymns should be as simple and honest as possible so that they would appeal to ordinary people.

2   'Honesty' is a theme which can be used to incorporate folk stories of all cultures, and modern, true-life stories as well. There are plenty of thought-provoking sayings which are relevant too, for example: 'Be worthy of a reputation' (Confucius); and 'The world is preserved by three things: truth, justice, peace' (Jewish saying).

Hymn suggestion

Come and Praise Vol 2 'Make us worthy, Lord' No 94

Prayer

Dear God,

Teach us to be honest in our dealings with other people. Help us not to tell lies and give us strength to be honest about admitting our mistakes. Help us to be honest in saying we think someone is wrong even when doing this makes us unpopular. Amen.

44 More!

Introduction

Imagine that you are at a birthday party. The person who has cut the cake hasn't made a very good job of it and the slices are uneven. When yours arrives it looks absolutely lovely – but your neighbour's is bigger. How do you feel about this?

Story

Oscar had a good home and was well fed. But, like most dogs, he was always on the lookout for anything extra to eat. One day he was passing the local butcher's on one of his morning adventures.

'Hi, Oscar,' shouted the butcher, who knew him well. 'Got a treat for you here. Catch.'

So saying, he threw a nice juicy piece of meat in the dog's direction.

Oscar caught it in his mouth, and wagged his tail to show his thanks. 'Right, I'm going to take this back to my garden where I can enjoy it in peace,' he thought to himself.

Now, Oscar lived in a cottage just outside the village. To get to it he had to cross over a bridge. Beneath the bridge ran a very slow-moving stream. On this particular morning it was very calm and the water was hardly moving at all.

'Nearly home,' thought Oscar as he trotted up onto the bridge. Then, looking over the side of the bridge, he saw something underneath – another dog with a huge piece of meat in his mouth.

'His piece of meat is far bigger than mine,' thought Oscar. He stopped and looked down again. The dog looked straight back at him.

Oscar growled in the back of his throat. 'Why should he have a bigger piece than me? I'm going to do something about that!'

With a snarl, Oscar leaped off the bridge to attack the dog below him. He hit the water with a tremendous splash, and his piece of meat swirled away as the water shot up his nose and into his mouth.

For a few seconds he floundered about, puzzled and angry. Of course, if he'd been a human being he would have known that what he had seen was his reflection – but his greed for more had cost him what he had in the first place.

Information for the teacher

1   There are some interesting March connections on the theme of 'food'. The first packaged food was sold in the USA on 6th March 1930, and Kellogg's Corn Flakes first appeared on the 7th in 1897. Johnny Appleseed, the legendary apple tree planter of the USA, died on 11th March 1847. A useful link with dogs is that 10th March 1886 was the occasion of the first Cruft's Dog Show in London.

2   This story could be used as one of a small series which involve 'reflections'. There is a well-known Chinese folk tale in which a wife finds a mirror in her husband's belongings. On looking in it she sees 'another woman' and accuses him accordingly!

In Greek mythology Narcissus was so impressed with the beauty he saw in his reflection that he jumped into the water to touch it and was drowned – hence 'narcissism' to mean 'the love of oneself'.

The children will be aware of the significance of the mirror in the Snow White story.

Thus a strong moral link could be established between a thread of stories around the same theme.

Hymn suggestion

Come and Praise Vol 1 'Who put the colours in the rainbow?' No 12

Prayer

Let us pray this morning that we may see ourselves as we really are.

Let us recognise our faults and try to do something about them.
Let us not concern ourselves too much about the faults of others.
Amen.

45 Not quite perfect

Introduction

Imagine that you are going to get a present. It is the best computer that money can buy, with every possible gadget. You would expect it to be perfect, wouldn't you?

Story

The twins had never seen their mother so excited. Both Floella and Simon listened, fascinated, while Mrs Garbutt spoke to her husband.

'It's amazing, Clive,' she said. 'It's really amazing.'

'Well, you've always been kind to her . . . you deserve it!'

'But . . . being able to buy the best!'

For years Mrs Garbutt had looked after the old lady next door as well as she could. She'd done her shopping, made her regular meals, mowed the lawn . . .

'And then she said to me that she'd been left quite a lot of money and she wanted me to have a special present. I could choose something and have the very best.'

'Well, what have you decided to get?' asked Dad.

'You know, I've always wanted a real Persian carpet – just a small one to put in the middle of the room. That's what I'm going to choose. On Saturday we'll go into that special carpet shop on the outskirts of the town.'

When Saturday came Mr and Mrs Garbutt and the twins drove out to Suleiman Carpets. The shop was like nothing the children had ever seen before.

'It's like being in a strange country,' whispered Floella.

'Yeah,' agreed Simon. 'It even smells different, doesn't it?'

'And have you seen those funny little brass things everywhere?'

'You mean – like teapots?'

Meanwhile, Mum and Dad were talking to a salesman.

'We're looking for a small Persian carpet.'

'Of course – would you like a coffee while you're choosing – and a drink for the children, perhaps?'

The twins explored the mysterious shop thoroughly until, about half an hour later, Mum had decided which carpet she wanted.

'It's very expensive but it's just what I want,' she said to the salesman. 'It's absolutely perfect.'

'No, madam – it's not.'

'Sorry? I don't understand.'

'I said it's not perfect.'

'But if it's not perfect how can you be charging all this money for it?'

'Let me explain,' went on the salesman. 'Persian carpets are the finest in the world – there can be no doubt about that. But the people who weave the carpets believe that only God, or Allah as they say, can create a perfect thing. Therefore in every carpet they make, no matter what a work of art it is, they make a tiny deliberate mistake.'

'And this carpet has such a mistake?'

'Look,' said the salesman.

Then, with his finger, he traced round one of the beautiful intricate patterns on the carpet – and pointed out how one tiny, tiny bit of the pattern didn't quite fit.

'Well, we would never have spotted that!' gasped Mum.

'No madam, only an expert can find the mistake – but it is one of the ways in which we can tell if the carpet is absolutely genuine.'

'Well,' gasped Dad. 'We've certainly learned something today.'

Information for the teacher

1   Some quotations from the Qur'an and sayings from Muhammad encapsulate the feeling behind the main point of this morning's story, for example:

> 'Your God is the most generous ... who taught man what he knew not.'

> 'Worship Allah as if you see Him; if you do not see Him, know that he sees you.'

> 'Be careful of your duty to Allah.'

2   For those near enough, a visit to the Victoria and Albert Museum in London would be a useful follow-up. Among its comprehensive collection of items from the Muslim world are carpets.

Hymn suggestion

Come and Praise Vol 1 'Peace, perfect peace' No 53

Prayer

Dear God,

Although we can never be perfect, help us at all times to do our best.

Teach us not to be too easily satisfied with our efforts and help us always to try and seek improvement. Amen.

46 The healing of the blind man

Introduction

One of the most noticeable things about the stories of Jesus is that he was always trying to help people.

Story

Jesus and his disciples did a lot of travelling around. For a time they stayed with two sisters who were called Martha and Mary.

The house where Martha and Mary lived was in a village called Bethany. This village was near to the city of Jerusalem. One day Jesus and his friends decided to go for a walk. The disciples knew that something interesting almost always happened when they went out for walks.

As usual, it was hot and the road was very dry and dusty. As they walked along, they heard a man's voice calling out in the distance. When they got closer they saw that the man who was making all the noise was sitting by the side of the road. He had one hand stretched out in front of him.

'Can you help a blind man?' he called out, over and over again.

'Isn't it sad,' said Peter. 'Because he is blind all the poor man can do is beg.'

'Can you help a blind man?' the voice called out again.

Jesus stopped in front of him. He paused for a moment and then carefully spat on the ground. Then he bent down and made clay with the dust and water.

'Now, my friend,' said Jesus, 'keep still for a moment.'

Not knowing what was happening the blind man kept still and quiet.

Jesus bent down. 'This won't hurt,' he said. Then he spread the clay over the man's eyes.

'Who are you?' asked the blind man. 'Why are you doing this?'

'You are talking to Jesus,' said Peter. 'Listen carefully to what he tells you.'

'One of my friends will lead you over to a pool of water,' said Jesus. 'When you get there, carefully wash all the mud off your eyes.'

After the man had been taken to the pool, Jesus and his friends went on their way. Meanwhile the blind man slowly washed each tiny piece of mud away from his eyes. Then, holding his breath, he slowly opened one eye, and then the other.

Suddenly a great shout tore through the air.

'I can see!' shouted the man. 'I can see! I can see!'

People nearby looked round to see what all the fuss was about.

'Look – that's the blind beggar, isn't it?'

'What's he shouting about?'

'He doesn't seem blind any more.'

'How strange.'

The people went up to the man who had been blind. They formed a circle round him and jostled each other as they sought to look at him more closely.

'You're not blind any more.'

'That's amazing!'

'What happened?'

'Yes . . . come on, tell us. How come you can see now?'

The blind man looked around him. He blinked his eyes. 'It was a man called Jesus,' he said. 'He made this mud and put it on my eyes. Then he told me to go to the pool and wash it off. When I washed it off I could see. I can see – I can actually see. Isn't it wonderful?'

Information for the teacher

1   A useful address here might be Guide Dogs for the Blind Association, Hillfields, Burghfield Common, Reading RG7 3YG, www.gdba.org.uk

2   The original source for this Bible story is John 9, 1–41. There are other Biblical references to Jesus curing blind people: Mark 8, 24; Matthew 9, 27–31; Matthew 20, 30–34; Mark 10, 46–52. Blindness in Biblical times was common and blind beggars lined the most-used roadways. Apart from the blindness of old age, another cause was ophthalmia (inflammation of the eye, its membranes or its lids), which was not only infectious but was also worsened by the dust and glare caused by the prevailing climate.

3   The calendar link with this story is again the focusing of attention on Jesus and his ministry, leading up to the events of the first Easter.

Hymn suggestion

Come and Praise Vol 1 'From the darkness came light' No 29

Prayer

Let us bow our heads and listen to the words of a famous prayer:
   'God our Father, guide and strengthen us by your Spirit that we may give ourselves in love and service to one another and to you.' Amen.

47 The idols

Introduction

All children enjoy being told that, sometimes, adults can learn from children. This morning's story is about a very wise boy called Abraham.

Story

'It's wrong,' thought Abraham, 'I just know it's all wrong.'
   He was standing in his father's shop looking round. On every shelf, different sized clay statues were stacked in rows. Abraham's father made these statues and then sold them to people. The people took them to their homes and worshipped them as gods.
   'It's ridiculous,' thought Abraham, as he fingered one of the clay models. 'How can people worship these things that my father makes in his back room, when there is only one God who should be worshipped?'
   Continuing to walk round the shop, Abraham moved the statues from here to there, worrying all the time.
   'If only my father would use his skill to make clay pots and dishes – that would be far more sensible. No good can come of making these statues.'
   Finally Abraham stopped. He would have to be cruel to be kind. It was the only way to make his father see sense. With a sigh he went into the workshop and brought out a hammer. Slowly, and with tears in his eyes, for he knew how hard his father worked, he began to break each statue. Eventually there was only one statue

left. It was easily the biggest in the shop. Abraham lifted it down and stood it amidst the wreckage of the others. Then he leaned the hammer beside it.

Sometime later, Abraham's father, Terah, came home. When he saw the mess in the shop he was furious. Shouting for Abraham, he pointed at the pile of broken statues.

'What's happened here? Who is responsible for this? What do you know about it?'

'Ah,' said Abraham, 'well, when you were out a terrible quarrel broke out among the statues and the biggest statue got so angry about it that he got a hammer and broke all the others up.'

Terah gazed dumbfounded at his son.

'The biggest statue broke the others up? You expect me to believe rubbish like that? How could a statue do that – it has no power!'

'True,' said Abraham. 'Why then do you worship a statue and sell them to other people to worship? How can any man worship something which has no power?'

For a very long moment there was silence. Then Terah looked for a long time at Abraham.

'Son,' he said, 'sometimes we need to learn a lesson. You have taught me one today.'

Information for the teacher

1   A *midrash* is a traditional story which highlights characters and events to reinforce scriptural teachings. This morning's story is a *midrash*. Abraham is the Father of the Jewish Nation and there are several such stories about him. Other stories about Abraham can be found in the Torah and in the Old Testament. (Genesis 22 is the story of Abraham and Isaac his son.)
    The Torah is written in Hebrew. The Hebrew language has no vowels in it and is read from left to right.

2   This story could be told in either February or March, to coincide with the Jewish festival of Purim. This festival celebrates an event of over two thousand years ago when Haman, an official in the royal court of Persia, wanted to exterminate all the Jews in Persia. He arranged for lots to be cast to decide how this should be done. (The word for 'lots' is 'purim'.) However, Esther, the Jewish queen of the Persian King Ahasuerus, found out that the plot would start by the hanging of her uncle Mordecai. She warned the king in time and Haman was hanged. (Bible reference: Book of Esther)

Purim has been celebrated joyfully ever since and every time Haman's name is mentioned in the synagogue on this date it is greeted with rude noises. Many of the latter are made with a grogger, which is a noisy rattle.

3   A useful address for Jewish affairs is: Jewish Education Bureau, 8 Westcombe Avenue, Leeds LS8 2BS.

Hymn suggestion

Come and Praise Vol 2 'And ev'ryone beneath the vine' No 149

Prayer

Let us give thanks this morning that we are free to come to school, have teachers to help us learn, have the chance to celebrate things and can talk and sing and pray together.

48 The Ethel Langton story

Introduction

Sometimes, if we are caught in an unexpected situation, we have to act in a way which requires all our courage and determination. Listen to Ethel Langton's story.

Story

Ethel Langton was fifteen years old and she was the daughter of a lighthouse keeper. Mr Langton's lighthouse was near the Isle of Wight, a quarter of a mile out to sea. In March 1926 this lighthouse overlooked one of the busiest stretches of water in the world. Huge liners, tankers, tugs and merchant ships sailed daily by, to and from Southampton.

Without the St Helen's light shining at night, hundreds of seamen's lives would have been at risk. The light itself was an oil burner. Every day the wick had to be trimmed and the oil filled up. The light was situated on top of a twenty-foot tower and could only be reached by climbing an outside steel ladder. Doing this was very dangerous in bad weather.

'Right, my love,' said Mr Langton to his daughter on Saturday, 20th March 1926. 'Your mum and I are going ashore to do the week's shopping. We'll see you and Badge at dinner time.'

'OK, Dad,' replied Ethel, looking at the calm sea and scratching Badge's ear. Badge was the family dog.

Used to the routine, Ethel read for a while after her parents had gone. After a short time she was aware that the waves were being whipped up by an ever-increasing wind.

'Hope they get back before the storm starts, Badge,' she said to the dog. 'Otherwise they'll have a rough trip.'

Ethel's hopes were dashed when the storm worsened with sudden and savage ferocity. Now the waves were pounding the beach, spume filled the air and the wind howled terrifyingly. The hours of daylight slipped away frighteningly quickly and Ethel realised that her parents could never make it back in these conditions.

'There's nothing else for it, Badge,' she said. 'I'll have to climb up and see to the light. But first let's have something to eat.'

Then came another unpleasant surprise. The only food she could find was half a loaf of bread and a few spoonfuls of sugar. She shared this with Badge and then braced herself to deal with the light.

As she opened the door the savage wind almost blew her over. Determinedly, she got down and crawled over to the ladder attached to the light tower. Getting her foot onto the bottom rung, she began the terrifying climb. Halfway up her scarf was torn from her neck and disappeared into the dusk. When she was almost at the top, one of her feet was blown off a rung and for a few dizzying seconds she hung on only by her hands.

Finally she reached the light. Checking it out, she got it lit before darkness fell, and then began the perilous descent.

Through the night, Ethel made several journeys to see that the light was working properly. Hardly daring to sleep for more than a few minutes at a time, soaking wet and desperately hungry, she felt sure the storm would soon die down.

'When it does,' she said to Badge, 'Mum and Dad will be back in a flash – and won't I be glad!'

With the coming of dawn she fell into an exhausted sleep in an armchair. She was awakened by Badge nuzzling her.

'Oh, Badge,' she said, 'what's the weather like?'

The roar of the wind and the crashing of the waves soon told her. 'We could be in for another busy night,' thought Ethel. 'I'd better get up and prepare the light.'

This time, when she reached the light, Ethel had to trim the wick, fill it up with oil and wind the mechanism. This took her well over an hour – but the light was now ready to be lit when darkness fell.

Back indoors Ethel thought longingly of a hot meal and she and Badge lay tightly together to try and keep warm. The next day passed in another roaring frenzy, to be followed by several more terrifying climbs up the ladder during the night.

By the next morning Ethel was completely exhausted. She was so cold, tired and hungry that she could hardly stand. 'But I may have to do more than that,' she thought. 'Maybe I'll have to keep the light going for another night!'

As the day went on, however, the storm began to abate gradually and in late afternoon she saw a lifeboat put out from the shore. Her parents were on board and her ordeal was soon over.

That was not the end of the story, however. Ethel's courage was described in all the newspapers and, at fifteen, she became the youngest person ever to receive the Lloyd's Medal for Meritorious Service.

Information for the teacher

1 This storm in March 1926 was described at the time as being the 'worst in living memory' for those parts.

2 A useful comparison could be made between facilities available in 1926 and those available now. Significant items might be things like helicopters, frozen food in deep freezers, etc.

Hymn suggestion

Come and Praise Vol 1 'He who would valiant be' No 44

Prayer

Let us bow our heads and give thanks to those people who, all over the world and every day, show courage in helping their fellows. Let us all learn from their determination and unselfishness.

49 What is your opinion?

Introduction

Sometimes people's cruelty to animals is almost unbelievable – as this morning's story shows.

Story

'I've got to get help for these poor creatures – I just *must*.'

The man who thought these words to himself was a lorry driver.

On one of his latest jobs he had been asked to drive a truckload of forty Shetland ponies across the border of Northern Ireland, towards Dublin in the south. He had been absolutely appalled at the condition they were in. This is their story.

The ponies were sold at an auction in the Shetlands. Then they were taken by boat from the Shetlands to Northern Ireland. Later they were crammed into the lorry which took them on to southern Ireland. When they reached Dublin they were to be sold at Smithfield Market.

The ponies' journey from the Shetlands to Dublin took three weeks. During all this time they had hardly any food or water and no thought was given to their travelling conditions.

When the lorry driver had delivered them to the market in Dublin, he reported the ponies' terrible condition. A vet was rushed to the scene. He was horrified at what he found. Only nine of the ponies were left at the market and all of these were in a distressed state. They had pus running from their eyes and noses and all of them had a disease called ringworm. Some of them could hardly stand, they were so weak.

'Well, at least I know where these nine will be properly looked after and given a good home,' said the vet.

He contacted Redwings Horse Sanctuary, near Norwich, and made arrangements for the ponies to be taken there. The good news is that all nine ponies made a good recovery in the caring atmosphere of Redwings.

But what of the other ponies, who had been crammed in – forty to the truck? Nobody knows their fate but there have been reports of such ponies being sold cheaply and ridden until they drop dead of exhaustion or illness.

How can some human beings behave so cruelly?

(The information in this story comes from a Redwings newsletter.)

Information for the teacher

1   Redwings Horse Sanctuary (Hill Top Farm, Hall Lane, Frettenham, nr. Norwich, NR12 7RW, www.redwings.co.uk) organises school visits and anyone interested should contact the School Visits Department at the above address. The sanctuary looks after 1,200 horses and there are schemes like 'adopt a pony or donkey' which cost just £6 per year.

The sanctuary, via managers, vets and welfare staff, are anxious to help educate children in the 'battle to prevent unnecessary suffering'. There is also a newsletter available from the same address.

2   A useful calendar and literary link here is with *Black Beauty*. There are obvious connections between the two stories, and the author, Anna Sewell, was born on 30th March 1820.

Hymn suggestion

Come and Praise Vol 1 'All the animals' No 80

Prayer

Let us pray this morning for all animals everywhere who are suffering at the hands of human beings.

Let us remember that, though they have no words with which to complain, they still feel pain and distress.

Let us pray for the guidance of those people who cause animals to be hurt. Amen.

50 I need some help

Introduction

It is hard to imagine a more frightening situation than the one in which John found himself. When you listen to John's story, I'm sure you'll agree!

Story

The small plane droned peacefully through the sky above Wales. In the distance Les Rhoades, the pilot, and John Anderson, his passenger, could see the distant outline of Cardiff airport.

'Soon be there now,' said Les.

'Smashing little plane, this,' answered John, looking out along the wing of the Rally Minerva aircraft.

'Yes, it's . . .' Suddenly, Les gave a choking noise and slumped forward in his seat.

'Les? *Les!*'

John reached across and shook the pilot without success. Les was deeply unconscious, and the plane began to rock uncertainly.

'What shall I do?' gasped John aloud. 'I've never even *touched* the controls of a plane before.'

Gritting his teeth and forcing himself to stay calm, John radioed the Air Traffic Controller at Cardiff airport with an emergency Mayday call.

'I need some help,' he said as calmly as he could, and then explained the situation.

On the ground the controller reacted quickly to the emergency. 'How can we get him down?'

'What's the best thing to do?'

'What about contacting Robert? He's airborne at the moment.'

Robert was flying instructor Robert Legg who was flying nearby with a pupil in his Piper Warrior. He was quickly contacted by radio.

'OK,' replied Robert, 'I understand. I'll call him on my radio.'

So began a nerve-racking time. Robert called John on the radio and, bit by bit, told him what to do with his hands and feet to keep the plane flying.

'From what you tell me, you've got plenty of fuel,' said Robert. 'All we're going to do at the moment is give you a bit of practice.'

'OK,' answered John. 'I've never done anything like this before.'

So, in the skies above the airport, the two planes began circling as John tried to get used to the controls.

'You're doing absolutely great,' said Robert encouragingly. 'I think we're about ready to land now.'

'If you think so,' answered John.

Inch by inch the Rally Minerva dropped as Robert's calm voice told John exactly what to do. Slowly it was lined up with the runway and began to sink even lower.

Out of the corner of his eye John could see things flashing past as he listened to the voice in his ear and struggled to keep the plane on an even keel. Then, with a *clunck*, he felt the wheels touch the ground.

Still concentrating for all he was worth, he eased back the speed and the plane gradually rolled to a stop. He was back on the ground – and safe!

Information for the teacher

1   This incident took place on 31st March 1992. Les Rhoades, a businessman, was twenty-three-year-old John Anderson's father-in-law. Sadly, Mr Rhoades had suffered a heart attack and was dead on arrival at Llandough Hospital, Cardiff.
Speaking of the incident afterwards, Robert Legg said of John: 'He made a perfect landing. He did marvellously well.'

2   There are several Bible references which are appropriate to this story:

> 'One man wins success by his words; another gets his due reward by the work of his hands.' (Proverbs 12, 14)

> 'Prepare yourself for testing, Set a straight course, be resolute, Do not lose your head in time of disaster.' (Ecclesiasticus 2, 1–2)

> 'Woe to faint hearts and nerveless hands.' (Ecclesiasticus 2, 12)

Hymn suggestion

Come and Praise Vol 1 'He who would valiant be' No 44

Prayer

Dear God,
   We pray that we may be given the skill, courage and resourcefulness to deal with difficulties in our lives. We also give thanks for those many people who are always ready to help us. Amen.

April

51 Is that really what you want?

Introduction

You might know somebody who never seems to be content. 'I wish I had that ... I wish I could go there ... I wish I was ...' This morning's story is a particularly good one for discontented people to listen to.

Story

Many years ago two kings lived near each other on islands in the Pacific Ocean. King Tuwara was a crafty fellow who was always trying to get the best for himself and his subjects. King Wa-Kulikuli was foolish and envious and always thought other people had more and better things than himself.
   Now it so happened that Wa-Kulikuli came one day to visit the island which Tuwara ruled. He had never been there before and he was amazed to see a huge curtain hanging outside Tuwara's house.

'That's a beautiful curtain. I haven't got any like that. Can I have it?' blurted out Wa-Kulikuli.

Tuwara smiled and said, 'Oh no, I'm terribly sorry.'

The curtain was actually to keep mosquitoes from getting into Tuwara's house and biting everybody. Tuwara, however, was rather ashamed that his island had mosquitoes when he knew that there were none on Wa-Kulikuli's island. 'We keep that cloth up because it looks beautiful and it keeps out any cold winds which might blow,' went on Tuwara.

So the two kings went into the house and, as happens on the islands, darkness fell very quickly. As it did so the buzzing of mosquitoes began on the other side of the curtain.

Because there were no mosquitoes on his island Wa-Kulikuli didn't know what they were so he said to Tuwara, 'What's that noise?'

'Ah,' said Tuwara. 'Those are my friends. They come to sing me to sleep when it gets dark.'

'How marvellous,' gasped Wa-Kulikuli. 'I've got nothing like that. Can I see them?'

'No, no, nobody can see them,' said Tuwara. 'They're terribly shy and wouldn't ever want to be seen. That's why we keep the curtain up.'

Not only did Wa-Kulikuli believe this but he got desperately greedy in his foolish way. 'Look, my friend,' he said, 'I'd like those creatures to come and sing me to sleep. Let me buy them from you.'

Tuwara could hardly believe his ears. This silly man actually wanted to buy the mosquitoes which were such a pest to him and all his people! But Tuwara was very crafty – and Wa-Kulikuli had something he wanted.

'Not a chance, old friend,' he said. 'I just couldn't sell them.'

'Now look,' went on Wa-Kulikuli, mopping his brow. 'I really do want those creatures to sing me to sleep. I'll give you anything you like for them.'

Tuwara paused and stroked his chin.

'They are my loyal subjects, you know ... but ... perhaps I could arrange to let you have them in exchange for those shellfish you have on your island.'

Everybody around knew that the shellfish on Wa-Kulikuli's island were the best around. But the foolish king had lost all sense of reason – more than anything else he wanted those mosquitoes!

'It's a bargain,' he cried. 'Bring those singing subjects of yours to my island and I'll give you the shellfish.'

Next morning Tuwara captured the mosquitoes in the cave where they lived. He collected them all up in a basket which was so carefully lined that none could escape. Soon the two men were on a boat heading for Wa-Kulikuli's island. When they arrived Tuwara put the basket down on the beach and stood beside it.

'Come on, come on,' cried Wa-Kulikuli impatiently, 'let them out.'

'I couldn't do that,' sighed Tuwara. 'Remember they have been loyal subjects. If they see me here they won't want to leave me.'

So Wa-Kulikuli agreed to collect up all the beautiful-tasting shellfish on his island and put them in Tuwara's boat. When this was done Tuwara said solemnly, 'Let us get completely out of sight before you open the basket, my friend. I certainly wouldn't want any of the mosquitoes to follow me now!'

Well, Wa-Kulikuli could hardly wait to get rid of Tuwara. How he wanted to see these loyal subjects who would come to sing to him every night! The second Tuwara's boat disappeared from sight the foolish king threw the lid of the basket open while all his people looked on.

At once there was an angry buzzing and the mosquitoes swarmed out, biting everyone in sight. From that time onwards nobody could rid the island of them and the people once more sighed and complained at the foolishness of their king.

Meanwhile Tuwara was very happy. He had got rid of his troublesome mosquitoes and obtained some fine food for his people. 'Foolish is the man who wants everything,' he said to his wife.

Information for the teacher

1   This story is adapted from *Tales from the South Pacific Islands* by A Gittins.

2   There are so many folk tales in which greedy, selfish, discontented people get their comeuppance that it is worth making a collection of them. As with this one, they are often ideal for drama. Indeed, for the teacher who wishes it, and has a little more time for preparation, this morning's story could be presented in dramatic form.

3   In dealing with the often self-destructive emotions mentioned above there is an appropriate – and reassuring – Bible reference: 'Each man should examine his own conduct for himself; that he can measure his achievement by comparing himself with himself and not with anyone else.' (Galatians 6, 4)

Hymn suggestion

Come and Praise Vol 1 'The Family of Man' No 69

Prayer

Let us bow our heads and think this morning about how foolish it is to waste time and effort being envious of what other people have.

Let us pray that we can be contented people; let us give thanks for the good things in our lives; let us remember all those who are less fortunate than we are. Amen.

52 This month

Introduction

Many people think April is the most exciting month of all. To be outside is to see signs of spring all over, on land, on water and in the air. Perhaps one of the best ways to describe April is to say that it is the month of promise.

This month

April is the month when we think particularly about two birds. The first is the swallow and these birds can be seen arriving in April. Long ago when people didn't know so much about hibernation and migration they thought swallows spent the winter months hiding in mud at the bottom of ponds!

Here is a poem about swallows:

> The swallow, for a moment seen,
> Skim'd this morn the village green;
> Again at eve, when thrushes sing,
> I saw her glide on rapid wing
> O'er yonder pond's smooth surface, when
> I welcom'd her back again.
>
> (Anon.)

The cuckoo also comes in April and his song is heard most often during this month and May. Many people think that cuckoos are scarcer these days but in fact it is just that they find it harder to get a home. Where hedges have been cleared, perhaps for building, the nests of birds like hedge sparrows and meadow pipits have been swept away with the hedge. Where once the uninvited cuckoo used to use nests like these for rearing, now he has to look further afield.

There are many old traditions associated with cuckoos. For instance, you should take careful note of what you are doing when you first hear the cuckoo call. An old tale says that what you are doing then will be what you will do for the rest of the year!

April is associated with showers and one of the worst ever floods occurred on 17th April 1421 when nearly a hundred Dutch villages were flooded and one hundred thousand people were drowned, lost or injured. On a more cheerful note, we can remember another saying: 'April showers bring May flowers.'

April, of course, has its own flowers too. Cow parsley, primroses, cowslips and dog violets start to appear and attract bees and wasps. Trees start to 'burst out' at this time of year and a close look at them will often show squirrels busily racing about building their nests, known as 'dreys'.

Near their sets young badgers come out to play at dusk and newts are safely wrapping their eggs in the leaves of water plants.

Probably no month has had as many poems written about it as April. Here are just two, which cheerfully tell that spring is here:

> For lo, the winter is past,
> The rain is over and gone;
> The flowers appear on the earth;
> The time of the singing of birds is come.
>> (Song of Solomon 11, 11–12)

> But a little while ago
> All the ground was white with snow;
> Trees and shrubs were dry and bare,
> Not a sign of life was there;
> Now the buds and leaves are seen
> Now the fields are fresh and green,
> Pretty birds are on the wing
> With a merry song they sing!
> There's new life in everything!
> How I love the pleasant Spring!
>> (Anon.)

Information for the teacher

1   Both the swallow and the cuckoo had days designated to them in times past. Old calendars noted 15th April as Swallow Day in Britain – presumably because this date was significant for increased sightings of the returning bird.

20th April was the cuckoo's day and there are several other 'traditions' associated with hearing this bird's first song, as well as the one mentioned in the text. For girls, the number of times they heard a cuckoo call was the number of years they would have to wait before marriage. On a gloomier note for older people, the number of bursts of song indicated the number of years they had left to live!

2   Grass snakes can be seen near water at this time of the year and April is the month when adders perform their dance of court-ship.

Hymn suggestion

Come and Praise Vol 1 'Think of a world without any flowers' No 17

Prayer

Dear God,

Thank you for another month which gives us so much to see and listen to and learn about. Help us to use our senses so that we can enjoy the natural things around us. Amen.

53 Ruswarp the faithful

Introduction

Sometimes humans can learn a lot from the behaviour of animals – as this morning's story shows.

Story

The early April weather was ideal for walking. The air was fresh and the sun shone brightly out of a clear blue sky.

'This is the place to be when the weather is like this,' said the walker to himself as he climbed slowly up the mountain path of a lonely but beautiful part of Wales. 'Nobody about, peace, fresh air and ...'

The walker's thoughts were interrupted by a sudden faint whine.

'Why, that sounds like a dog,' he thought. 'But how would a dog get out here?'

With the stones and pebbles of the path slipping beneath his boots, the walker climbed higher – and nearer to the faint noises of the dog. Finally, on turning a bend in the path, he was shocked to see the creature which was making the noise.

There, lying just alongside the path, was a brown and white collie. Piteous whimpers came from the dog's mouth and he was obviously too weak to stand. His body was so thin that his bones were almost sticking through the skin and his nose had the dryness of a very weak or sick dog.

'But what are you doing here, old chap?' asked the walker, getting down to stroke the poor dog's head. 'It's a bit of a mystery, isn't it?'

Sometime later the mystery was solved.

Not far from the starving dog the dead body of a man was found. Experts later decided that the man had been dead for three months, and this solved more of the mystery.

In January a man called Graham Nuttall, who was a keen hill walker, travelled from his house in Lancashire to walk in Wales. He told a friend that he would be back later that day and when he didn't arrive the police and rescue teams were alerted. Despite a search of the area, neither the man nor his dog, Ruswarp, could be found.

What had happened was that the man had fallen, become unconscious and finally died. Ruswarp, his fourteen-year-old collie, decided that the best thing to do was wait by his master until help arrived. He waited, guarding Mr Nuttall's body, for three months, drinking water from a nearby stream, but – as far as anybody could tell – going without food.

Despite his sadness at losing his master, the faithful Ruswarp's story had a happy ending. He was so weak that he had to be carried down the mountainside, but once safe he began to make a good recovery.

'We don't quite know how this wonderfully loyal dog managed to stay alive,' said a member of the RSPCA. 'We would expect a dog of his age to be able to stay alive in the wild for about five or six weeks with water and without food. But for three months ...! He's a remarkable dog, this Ruswarp!'

Information for the teacher

1 Mr Nuttall came from Burnley and had taken the train to Llandrindod Wells on 20th January. His body was found in a stream near to where the dog was lying.

2 This story could provoke thoughts on the treatment of animals by humans. A useful quotation here might be: 'God places animals in our care – to reject them or treat them cruelly is to do wrong in the eyes of God.' (Muhammad)

3   A useful address here is:

RSPCA, The Causeway, Horsham, West Sussex RH12 1HG, www.rspca.org.uk

4   Readers may notice a great similarity to the famous story of the Scottish dog, Greyfriars Bobby. He displayed similar loyalty to his master in Scotland in the nineteenth century.

Hymn suggestion

Come and Praise Vol 1 'All the creatures of our God and King' No 7

Prayer

Dear God,
   Thank you for all the love, faithfulness and loyalty of our pets. Give us the grace to treat them as they deserve. Amen.

54 Don't count your chickens before they're hatched

Introduction

The title of this morning's story is a warning, as you will find out when you listen to the story of Hannah.

Story

Hannah lived many years ago in the country. She milked cows, raised chickens and hens – and dreamed.
   'Ah, if only ... Wait until ... That'll be the day.'
   Such thoughts were often going through her head when she went about her jobs. One of these jobs was taking a can of milk to the local market to sell. She always carried the can balanced on her head. This particular day the can was very big and very full.
   'Aha,' thought Hannah, as she walked along. 'I'll get quite a bit of money for this milk. When I've got it I'll go straight away and buy some more eggs.'
   Pausing in her thoughts, she carefully climbed over a fence, holding the milk can carefully on her head. Once she was on the other side, she set off quickly, avoiding the big stones on the path. Her mind slipped off into its daydreams once again.

'Yes. I'll get some eggs and then, along with the ones I've already got, they should give me about two or three hundred chickens. I'll wait until the market prices are at their highest for chickens and then I'll bring them all to market. Now, let's see – two hundred and fifty chickens at a good price will give me ...'

At that moment a farmer's dog came bounding up to Hannah, barking excitedly. She held on to the milk can firmly with one hand, and shooed the dog away. Seeing that she wasn't interested in playing, the dog soon trotted off, leaving Hannah to get on her way – and continue her thinking.

'Now, where was I? Oh yes, I've just sold two hundred and fifty chickens at the market for a good price. It will be more than enough for me to buy a lovely new dress.'

By now Hannah had fallen in step with quite a few other people who were walking to the market. She smiled at them but made no attempt to talk – she was far too busy with her thoughts!

'That lovely new dress. Right. It'll be blue to match my eyes. It'll have a long, full skirt and puffy sleeves and by the time I get it the great fair won't be too long off. I'll wear it to the fair and when there's dancing all the young men will come and ask me for a dance. But I'll be waiting for someone special so I'll just shake my head ...'

So wrapped up in her thoughts was Hannah that she *did* shake her head – and the milk can crashed to the ground, emptying its contents all over the stony path.

Information for the teacher

1   This story is adapted from one of Aesop's fables. A useful story from the Bible to parallel this is the tale of the man who built bigger and better barns, filled them with produce so that he could retire and enjoy the 'good life' and died the night of his retirement. (Luke 12, 16–20)

A useful Biblical reference in connection with both stories might be:

Be most careful how you conduct yourselves:
Like sensible men, not like simpletons.

(Ephesians 5, 15)

Hymn suggestion

Come and Praise Vol 1 'The wise may bring their learning' No 64

Prayer

Let us think this morning about taking care of the small things in our lives. Let our dreams not get in the way of what we should be doing now.

Let us pray that we might be reliable, sensible people who never let our friends and relatives down.

To help remind us about these things let us listen to the words of a poem:

> For want of a nail a shoe was lost
> For want of a shoe a horse was lost
> For want of a horse a rider was lost
> For want of a rider a battle was lost
> For want of a battle a kingdom was lost
> And all for the want of a horseshoe nail.
> > (This poem is by Benjamin Franklin and
> > relates to the death of Richard III.)

55 The mystery

Introduction

Have you ever noticed that when somebody does something bad, it often brings the best out of somebody else? This morning's story is about a mystery which was never solved – and it is also about courage, skill and determination.

Story

'You can now unfasten your seatbelts, and I wish you a smooth and comfortable flight.'

The voice of Captain Ian Harvey filled the cabin of the airliner as it reached its cruising height and settled on course. It flew through the night, which was lit by occasional flashes of lightning, and the passengers settled down to enjoy a meal.

For stewardess Sue Cramsie this was a busy time.

'I expect they're all as hungry as ever,' she thought as she handed round the trays of food. 'Funny though – there seems to be a peculiar smell around.'

As she sniffed again, Sue felt a chill of fear run up her back. The smell was of something burning! She hurried to the back of the plane to investigate, but she never got there. Just as she turned there was a blinding explosion, the cabin filled with smoke and Sue was hurled unconscious to the floor.

'We're going to crash!' yelled one of the passengers.

'Keep calm,' shouted another.

'The stewardess . . .' gasped a third, as the smoke cleared and revealed a terrifying sight. On each side of the aircraft's cabin there was a huge hole, and lying dangerously near to both of them was the unconscious stewardess.

'Let's get her to safety,' said one of the passengers quietly, and two men dragged Sue to a safer position.

Meanwhile, up in the cockpit, Captain Harvey and his co-pilot, First Officer Dusty Miller, were struggling to keep the aircraft from falling out of the sky. The explosion had taken them completely by surprise and had seriously damaged the controls.

'Dusty,' gasped Captain Harvey, 'get back there and see what the problems are. I'll try and hold her.'

Sweat poured down Captain Harvey's face as he held the bucking, almost unbearably heavy control column. Without a word, First Officer Miller got up and went to investigate. He was back, grim faced within a couple of minutes.

'It's not good,' he said. 'Half the control rods have gone, there's two whacking great holes in the fuselage and the tail's hanging on by a whisker. Sue's hurt and unconscious but there's no panic. The passengers are looking after her.'

'Right,' said Ian Harvey. 'We're going back to London. Radio now – say we're badly damaged, stewardess seriously injured, have emergency services standing by.'

With desperate care, Captain Harvey turned the plane back towards London. Lurching and groaning through the sky, it wallowed in the night until the runway lights came into view. Strapped in and tense, the passengers watched the lights get nearer and nearer – and then with a sudden screaming of engines the plane lifted into the sky again.

'She nearly stalled that time,' shouted Captain Harvey. 'We'll try again.'

This time, despite all the problems, the damaged plane touched down smoothly on the runway. Sue was rushed to hospital in an ambulance, and the calm and brave passengers were shepherded to safety.

Then Captain Harvey, First Officer Miller and some ground staff experts carefully inspected the damaged plane. It was a miracle that it had ever got back to the airport and only a brilliant pilot could have helped it to do so.

At first it was thought that the plane had been struck by lightning, but a later inspection showed that the explosion had been caused by a bomb somebody had put on board.

Who had done so, and why, has remained a mystery. What is not a mystery is that on that terrifying night, everybody aboard aircraft G-AIVL had behaved in the best possible way. Sue Cramsie made a complete recovery and was soon back at work.

Information for the teacher

1   This incident occurred on 13th April 1950. The aircraft was a BEA Viking, and the flight was from London to Paris. Captain Harvey had previously been a distinguished bomber pilot in the Second World War, and his skill and courage on this occasion received great publicity. The explosive device had been planted in the towel compartment in the toilet.

2   A few appropriate books from the school's reference library could make a useful hall display to enhance this assembly.

Hymn suggestion

Come and Praise Vol 2 'You've got to move' No 197

Prayer

Let us pray this morning for all those people who drive buses, steer ships, pilot aeroplanes, drive trains.

Let us pray for all those people who work in transport and let us give thanks for their skill and experience which keeps passengers safe.

Amen.

56 A day out

Introduction

I expect most of you know how much your grandparents like a day out. For some people one of the most enjoyable ways of spending a day like this is to go on a coach outing . . .

Story

'It's great – just look at that view of the sea.'

'In ten minutes we're going to stop down there for a cup of tea.'

'Did you bring a picnic, Betty?'

Colin Henry smiled. He was driving a big, fifty-seater coach.

Behind him he could hear people chatting – saying the same sort of things they always said on outings like this.

'As long as they enjoy it,' he thought, 'that's what it's all about.'

He thought about the busy streets of Liverpool, where most of his passengers came from, and the lovely seaside views of Devon they were looking at now. He had made this journey so often that he didn't really need to think about it.

Suddenly, a feeling of terror crept up the back of Colin's neck and made his skin prickle with fear.

'No, I must be wrong,' he thought, and eased his right foot down once again on the brake pedal. But again he had that sickening feeling that there was nothing there – his brakes really had failed!

'I've got to try and hide it as long as I can,' thought Colin as the coach began to pick up speed on its descent into the seaside town of Paignton.

Faster and faster and faster it went. Now the driver could no longer pretend. It took all his skill and strength to hang onto the steering wheel as the runaway vehicle swayed and screeched round the downhill corners. All conversation had stopped and the white-faced passengers gripped the seats in front of them as they were flung from side to side.

Sweat poured down Colin's forehead as he sought to control the coach, and at the same time find some way to stop. Then, among the houses which flashed by, he saw one ahead that was obviously empty – it was now or never.

'Hang on!' shouted Colin and aimed his coach at the empty house. A telegraph pole which stood in the way was smashed to pieces and the vehicle ploughed into the front wall.

There was a momentary pause, and then ... whoosh! – flames and smoke began to leap out of the engine compartment.

Next door to the empty house lived Maurice Ildster. Shocked and frightened by the terrific noise, he dashed out of his house and saw the wrecked coach and the spreading flames. Instantly he returned inside and came back with a fire extinguisher.

'It's OK, I'm coming,' he yelled. Racing up to the coach, he began to fight the spreading flames. Within seconds his prompt action had put the fire out. Throwing down the extinguisher, Maurice then began to help the shocked and shaken passengers out of the coach. Miraculously, not one of them was seriously hurt.

The emergency services had now been alerted and next on the scene was a fire engine. Poor Colin the driver was trapped in his cabin and had to be cut out. Soon he was on his way to hospital with back injuries.

'It was a miracle,' said one of the passengers, Mrs Betty McCarron, a little while later. 'But for the courage and skills of our wonderful driver, and the quick thinking of the young man with the fire extinguisher, I'm sure most of us would have been killed.'

Information for the teacher

1   This incident took place on 17th April 1992 in Paignton. The driver of the coach was Colin Henry, aged forty-two, and his elderly passengers were all from the Maghull area of Liverpool and at the start of a day trip. The hero with the fire extinguisher was Maurice Ildster, a thirty-five-year-old soldier.

2   The sense of 'movement and fire' could be enhanced by some appropriate recorded music for this assembly. Two suggestions are *Ritual Fire Dance* by Falla, and Stravinsky's *Firebird Suite*.

3   For background information on roads, traffic and transport, a useful web site address is

www.detr.gov.uk (Dept of the Environment, Transport and the Regions)

For more details on accident prevention, a useful address is:

ROSPA, Edgbaston Park, 353 Bristol Road, Edgbaston, Birmingham B5 7ST, www.rospa.org.uk

Hymn suggestion

Come and Praise Vol 1 'Travel On' No 42

Prayer

Let us pray for all those who are making journeys today on land, sea or in the air. May they reach their destinations safely. Amen.

57 How did they do it?

Introduction

How do they do it? Why did it happen? There are sometimes questions which nobody can answer, because there are still a lot of mysteries in the world. Today's story is the sort of mystery we all like – one which has a very happy ending.

Story

'Isn't it fantastic?' said Peter

'It certainly is,' replied Elizabeth. 'I wonder what England will be like?'

'Well, we'll soon find out.'

The two children, son and daughter of Professor Hunter, were leaving their home in Canada and going on a visit to England with their parents.

'There's only one snag, though,' said Elizabeth.

'What's that?'

'Well, I don't like leaving our pets all that time.'

As if they could understand, the pets looked up from the carpet where they were all lying comfortably. 'They' were Luath, a beautiful golden Labrador retriever; Badger, a bull terrier who was now old and partly blind, and Tao, a sleek and comfort-loving Siamese cat.

'Oh, don't worry,' went on Peter. 'Dad's going to take them all to Uncle John's, so they'll be well looked after while we're away.'

So the arrangements went ahead. Professor Hunter took the three pets to the home of John Longbridge in his car. This was a day's journey because the two homes were three hundred miles apart, through some of Northern Canada's most wild and bitter countryside. On his return, the family left for England.

What happened next will always remain something of a mystery. Although the animals were being well looked after by Mr Longbridge, they must have become homesick for their own house and family. One morning, when he got up, they had all disappeared.

So began a fantastic journey. Through some of the loneliest, most difficult countryside in the world, the two dogs and the cat began a three-hundred-mile trek to retrace an unknown route.

We know that Tao was once nearly drowned and separated from her companions for three days, yet she caught up with them again. All survived dense wooded wilderness and raging rivers and streams. Finally, thin, exhausted and desperately hungry, they arrived home just hours after the Hunter family had got back from England.

Information for the teacher

1   The details of this story, such as they are, were researched and written about by Sheila Burnford in her book *The Incredible Journey*.

2　A calendar link could be made with another unusual journey which took place in April: on 12th April 1961 Yuri Gagarin made his 30,000 km/h (18,000 mph), 89-minute trip round the globe in his spacecraft *Vostok 1*. Other April links: Richard Trevithick, who died on 22nd April 1833, drove his first steam carriage in London in 1802 – this was one of the forerunners of the locomotive and heralded a great development in transport; John Metcalf, a blind man who died on 26th April 1810, earned his living at one time as a stage-coach driver!

3　If the aspect of the story concerning the loyalty and faithfulness of animals is to be developed further, an impressive link is with the story of Greyfriars Bobby. For fourteen years, Bobby, a Skye terrier, guarded the grave of his master Mr Gray, who died in Edinburgh. So famous became the little dog that, on his death, his collar and dinner bowl became exhibits in the Huntly Museum, Edinburgh.

Hymn suggestion

Come and Praise Vol 2 'All the animals' No 80

Prayer

Let us think this morning about the qualities, the courage, and the loyalty of so many animals.

Let us learn from them, appreciate them, and make sure that if animals are ever in our care we treat them with respect, care, kindness and consideration.

58 Milkman extraordinary

Introduction

Every day we see people we know and take for granted – until they do something special.

Story

Michael Buckley was happy. It was a brisk April day and he had just completed his milk round. As he drove his empty milk float through the streets of Tylerstown in Mid Glamorgan in Wales, he had nothing more serious on his mind than a nice cup of tea.

'Soon be home now,' he thought to himself as he turned the float into a long street.

'But ... what's that? It can't be ...' Michael gasped as he happened to glance up at one of the houses he was passing. A second glance, however, confirmed his worst fears. Standing on a bedroom windowsill was a tiny child.

Trying not to frighten her, Michael stopped his milk float as quietly as he could.

'Don't worry, pet, you'll be all right,' he called, as he tried to walk as casually and unconcernedly as he could to the front door of the child's house. Once there, he gave a short rap on the door – all the while keeping his eye on the child, who was now obviously frightened and teetering backwards and forwards on the ledge.

'Come on, come on, hurry up,' muttered Michael as he hammered again on the door. Still nobody answered and as he looked up the milkman suddenly saw the little girl lose her balance completely.

Things then happened with a rush. With a cry of fear, the little girl began to fall towards the concrete path beneath her. Leaping away from the front door, Michael dashed in the falling child's direction and flung himself in a full-length dive. He caught her inches above the concrete.

The story had a completely happy ending. Despite Michael's efforts, fourteen-month-old Cerys Shirley did hit her head on the concrete and had to be taken to hospital. However, she was only bruised, and William Shirley, her father, had some nice things to say about her rescuer.

'We can't thank Mike enough,' said Mr Shirley. 'His quick thinking certainly saved Cerys's life. She had climbed over some toys and somehow got out onto the windowsill.'

'Anybody would have done the same as I did,' said the modest milkman.

Information for the teacher

1   This story happened in April 1990 and Michael Buckley attributed his life-saving dive to the fact that he had played a lot of rugby in his younger days. He was forty when this incident happened.

2   It is a useful exercise to ask the children, after an assembly like this, to find items in newspapers about the heroic actions of 'ordinary' people. Local newspapers are very valuable in this context. In this way a very useful file of assembly stories can be built up.

Come and Praise Vol 1 'Cross over the road' No 70

Prayer

Let us give thanks this morning for those 'ordinary' people whose courage, quick thinking and speed of action is so often 'extra-ordinary'.

May

59 James Merryweather

Introduction

Every town these days has its library, post office, police station – and its fire station. Although fire stations and fire brigades are very important, it took the efforts of one man, more than anybody else, to make others realise this. His name was James Merryweather.

Story

The warm May sunshine shone down on a miserable scene. A group of people in black clothes moved slowly and tearfully through a London cemetery in a long funeral procession.

Watching them, with his hat in his hand, stood a burly, determined-looking man.

'It need never have happened,' he said to the friend who stood beside him. 'In fact, it *should* never have happened. More people dead because their house burnt down when the fire could have been put out.'

'I know, James, but what can you do?' asked the friend.

'I'm going to form my own fire brigade, that's what I'm going to do,' replied James Merryweather.

It was 1862 and James, a skilled engineer, had been trying for years to get the London Fire Establishment to take an interest in his steam fire engine. Despite many fires, and many deaths, they still preferred to use the old method of pumping water by hand. James argued that this was slower and nothing like so effective.

Now, tired of having to help the authorities, he organised his own fire brigade.

'I want brave men,' he said to anybody who joined him, 'but they will have the best fire engines possible. They'll be able to get to fires quicker than anybody else and they'll be able to put them out much more rapidly.'

There was no shortage of volunteers and soon James's fire engines were a familiar sight as they raced round London dealing with various fire alarms. His reputation grew.

'Have you heard about James Merryweather's fire brigade?'

'Yes, he really gets things done.'

'Far better than anybody else.'

'Well, he's always thinking about new ideas and working them out, isn't he?'

Finally, in 1866, the authorities decided they must do something better. The London Metropolitan Fire Brigade was formed and James's steam pumps were accepted everywhere and put into use.

'Great,' said James. 'Now we'll be able to put out fires more efficiently. But what we've also got to do is to try and make sure that they never start.'

So James became one of the first people to think seriously about fire precautions. He wanted experts to look over buildings before people moved in to live there, to make sure they were as safe as possible from fire risks. In 1897 he said that no theatre should ever be allowed to open until officers of the Fire Brigade had made sure it was safe.

While James was doing this, he was still building bigger and better fire engines, and writing the first book on proper fire-fighting methods.

'I don't know where you find the time to do it all,' said one of his friends.

'I must,' replied James. 'Don't you see how important it all is? If what I do can save only one life, it's worth it. Remember, it might be your life – or your son's or daughter's or mother's.'

So James carried on his ceaseless work and by the time he died he had invented more than two hundred and fifty improvements to fire-fighting equipment.

Information for the teacher

1 This is ideal material to fit into the theme of 'Those who help us', which often features in a series of assemblies.

2 There are some interesting May calendar associations to link with this story. For instance, it was as far back as 13th May 1680 that the first Fire Insurance Company began selling insurance.

Disastrous fires occurred on these dates: in New Jersey, USA, on 6th May 1937, when the airship *Hindenberg* caught fire after crossing the Atlantic: and on 11th May 1941, when London suffered its worst air raid, during which fourteen hundred people died and Westminster Abbey, St Paul's Cathedral and the British Museum were all damaged by fire.

The worst-ever number of casualties caused by a fire was in Japan in 1923 when sixty thousand died in a fire caused by an earthquake.

3 The first fire brigades were organised by the Romans. These were known as the corps of *Vigiles* (watchmen) and were created following a great fire in Rome in the year AD 6.

4 In another context, 'fire' is often a theme linked with RE, particularly at this time of the year with the symbolic link between Whitsun and fire. Flowers appearing over the heads of Apostles in Christian art symbolised the presence of the Holy Ghost.

St Anthony of Padua is the patron saint of protection against fire.

5 A useful web site address in this context is: www.fire.org.uk

Hymn suggestion

Come and Praise Vol 1 'Water of life' No 2

Prayer

Let us give thanks this morning for those people whose skill, inventiveness, courage and determination do so much to help others. We pray that their advice and suggestions may be listened to for the good of us all. Amen.

60 Leading the way

Introduction

Imagine a whole lot of strange children suddenly appeared in the playground of your school when your class was out there. What do you think might happen? This morning's story is one to make us think about a situation like this.

Story

Muhammad (pbuh) was on his travels again. He had reached a town after a long journey through the desert, and he liked what he saw.

'This is a pleasant place,' he said to himself. 'There are plenty of cool trees and comfortable buildings, and everybody seems to be well enough. What a very nice place to live.'

Muhammad rested in the town for a few days. As usual, he talked to a lot of people and even in such a short time he became well known.

One morning, just before he was preparing to leave, there was a great commotion in the town.

'There's a whole lot of them!'

'They're coming in through the gates now.'

'Never seen anything like it.'

'Goodness knows what happened to them.'

Muhammad was swept along with the crowd of people who pushed through the town's narrow streets towards the entry gate. When they reached it they split into two groups, one on either side of the road. There they watched, silently, as a long crocodile of people wound its way out of the desert through the town's gate.

The line moved slowly because the people in it looked near to collapse. Bleached by the sun, what few clothes they wore hung in rags and tatters from their starved looking bodies. Many were bandaged, some helped weaker friends to stagger along and all had a dazed and beaten look.

Muhammad became more and more restless as the pitiful group staggered to a stop and stood with downcast eyes.

'I've heard about them,' said a man next to Muhammad. 'Their town was ransacked and they've been wandering in the desert for weeks.'

'That's what I heard, too,' said another man, staring at the group.

Muhammad could stand it no longer. He stepped in front of the townspeople.

'How much longer are you going to stand and stare?' he asked. 'When is somebody going to do something?'

Sheepishly most looked away, but not one man.

'Wait!' he cried, and hurried to his house nearby. Within seconds he was back with a pile of clothes over his arm and food and drink in both hands.

He hurried to the group of worn-out people and began to give these things to them. When his friends saw what he had done they moved hurriedly away – and returned equally quickly with more clothes, more food and drinks and even sums of money.

Muhammad watched all this quietly.

'It is as I thought,' he said to one of his friends. 'If one person sets a good example there will be plenty who will follow him.'

Information for the teacher

1 A useful calendar link for this story is 7th May. It was on this date in 1945 that the Second World War ended in Europe – and there is a modern counterpart of this tale which is very evocative. At a parade in Moscow, German prisoners of war were paraded through the streets. Many of them were in a pitiful condition. The watching crowds had themselves suffered innumerable hardships and privations, but as the line of men went by an old woman broke through the line of Soviet troops guarding the prisoners and gave a hunk of black bread to a wounded German soldier. Within seconds others in the crowd were pressing what little they had onto the desperate prisoners.

2 A Muslim is required to give two-and-a-half per cent of his income to the needy or poor. A concern for others is a fundamental tenet of the religion and is reflected in many of the sayings of Muhammad.

Hymn suggestion

Come and Praise Vol 2 'God in his love' No 76

Prayer

This morning let us listen to the words of a Muslim proverb and then spend half a minute thinking quietly about them. The words are: 'He is best loved who does most good to others.'

61 Determination

Introduction

Somebody once said that it is not important what you have in life – it's what you do with what you have that counts. This morning's story begins on the M6 motorway.

Story

The thirty-eight-ton lorry was approaching a traffic queue on the motorway.

'Better start slowing down,' thought driver Stuart Braye, easing his foot onto the brake. To his horror, the lorry didn't slow down fast enough – his brakes had failed! Even though the lorry had slowed to only thirty miles an hour, the crash was a bad one. For thirty minutes Stuart was trapped in his cab, and then he was rushed to hospital for an emergency operation.

'You're lucky to be alive,' said the doctor when Stuart recovered consciousness. 'Very lucky – but I'm afraid we've had to remove one of your legs.'

Although he was shocked, Stuart felt so thankful to be alive that he made a quick recovery. Learning to walk again, however, was very difficult. It was six months before he could be fitted with an artificial leg, and then he had to have another operation.

Stuart used this time to study on a business course so that he could prepare himself for a more suitable job when he was better, but all the time he worried about how he would be able to run again.

'I've always liked running and been a bit of an athlete,' thought Stuart to himself, 'and I'm not going to give up now.'

So he started to learn to run again. It was very painful and so that no one could see how much he had to struggle he ran round the streets near his house in the darkness when everybody else was in bed. Agonisingly slowly, Stuart began to get better and better at running. He got an extension for his artificial leg, called a 'Flexifoot', from America, and this helped him enormously. He joined an athletic club and began to train seven days a week.

Gradually Stuart's determination began to pay off in several ways. He began to set up fast times in races and became a well-known member of the British Amputees Sports Association. His courage, determination and success also led to his being invited to give talks to doctors and to patients who had recently lost one or both of their legs.

Stuart Braye is the sort of man who doesn't know the meaning of 'giving up'.

'Don't call me disabled,' he says, 'just say I'm physically challenged!'

Information for the teacher

1 This story could be linked to several medical anniversaries in May. Florence Nightingale was born on 12th May 1820; Edward Jenner made the first successful smallpox vaccination on the 14th in 1796; the Royal Flying Doctor Service began in Australia on the 15th in 1928.

2 Useful addresses could include:

Royal Association for Disability and Rehabilitation (RADAR),
12 City Forum, 250 City Road, London EC1V 8AF.
www.radar.org.uk

REACH (The Association for Children with Hand or Arm Deficiency) contact Mrs Sue Stokes, 12 Wilson Way, Earls Barton, Northants NN6 0NZ. www.reach.org.uk

Hymn suggestion

Come and Praise Vol 1 'A man for all the people' No 27

Prayer

Let us think this morning about the example people like Stuart Braye set us. Let us pray that their courage and determination helps others who are in difficulty and distress. Amen.

62 Getting what you deserve

Introduction

People sometimes try to get things for themselves by being sly and deceitful. This morning's story is a warning about the results of such behaviour.

Story

Up on the hillside the wolf looked down on the flock of sheep. As the evening wind ruffled his coarse coat, he thought to himself, 'I'm so hungry, and there's nothing I'd like more for supper than one of those sheep down there.'

As he thought this, his eyes flicked to the burly figure of the shepherd who was guarding the sheep. He looked alert and fast-moving enough to see and deal with any approaching wolf. But the wolf had an idea. Lying nearby was an old sheepskin.

'If I were to disguise myself in this sheepskin and then mingle with the flock,' he thought, 'I could bide my time and then kill the fattest sheep for my supper. The shepherd would never even know I was there.'

Slipping into the sheepskin, the wolf found that it covered him perfectly. He approached the flock stealthily, and in no time at all he was among them. Not only did the shepherd not see him arrive, but the other sheep paid no attention to him either. Pretending to munch grass like the sheep, the wolf smiled to himself.

'So far so good. Now it's just a case of being patient and choosing a good supper.'

Now it so happened, that exactly the same thoughts were going through the shepherd's mind.

'I need a good supper tonight,' thought the shepherd, poking his fire and sharpening his knife. 'One of these sheep will do very well.'

Dusk was already beginning to blur the outlines of the flock and the shepherd knew he must make his choice quickly before darkness fell. Moving among them he spotted a sheep which looked particularly rounded and meaty. Quickly, he killed it and was about to drag the carcass to his fire when he saw what he had killed – a wolf in sheep's clothing!

Information for the teacher

1 There are various useful calendar references for this story. The 13th of the month is St Servatius's Day. This saint features in an old proverb to do with sheep shearing: 'Who shears his sheep before St Servatius's Day loves more his wool than his sheep.' (Servatius died in 384.)

Alternatively, the story could be linked with an anniversary of a renowned storyteller, of which there are several in May: Baron Münchhausen was born on the 11th in 1720; Charles Perrault (author of 'Mother Goose') died on the 16th in 1703; Paul Dukas (composer of 'The Sorcerer's Apprentice') died on the 17th in 1935; Arthur Conan Doyle (of the 'Sherlock Holmes' stories) was born on the 22nd in 1859.

2 A most useful story to link with this one is that of the wolf of Gubbio. This creature had done a great deal of damage and killing and was being hunted by the people of Gubbio. One day St Francis was walking when he encountered this sly and ruthless wolf. He immediately treated it with respect, called it 'Brother Wolf', protected it and set about teaching a creature who knew no better how to behave to others.

Hymn suggestion

Come and Praise Vol 2 'All the animals' No 80

Prayer

Let us pray this morning that we may be given the strength to avoid sly and deceitful behaviour. Let us always be truthful, honest and straightforward. Let us remember that even if no one else knows we have done something dishonest, we do.

63 Thank you, doctor

Introduction

There are many reasons why we are lucky to be alive today rather than hundreds of years ago. One of them is that many people in the world now have excellent doctors, nurses, hospitals and medical care to see that they stay healthy and are treated quickly if they become ill. It was not always the case . . .

Story

It was a beautiful day in May 1347. The sun shone down on the sparkling waters of the Mediterranean Sea and the people of the Sicilian port of Messina went happily about their business. It was then that the eleven ships were seen at the harbour mouth.

'Look, those galleys must be from Genoa.'

'Yes, no doubt about that.'

'But . . . why aren't they steering properly?'

'They're all over the place.'

'They're crashing into each other!'

'They're not going to stop in time by the harbour wall . . .'

'No, they're ramming it!'

As if jerked about by unseen puppet strings, the eleven ships careered into each other, steered wildly erratic courses, and finally crashed brutally into the harbour wall.

The citizens of Messina put out in small boats to help, and boarded the galleys. There they found the reason for the strange behaviour of the ships.

Practically every member of the crew in each ship was dead, and those sailors still alive were desperately ill and not able to do their job properly.

'What is it?' 'What disease have you got?' 'How can we help?' These were the questions the survivors were asked.

But soon the people of Messina were no longer asking questions – they were too ill. A sudden and painful illness of three days was followed by death on the fourth day. Soon the mysterious illness was sweeping through Italy to Germany, France, England and the whole of the rest of Europe.

Towns and villages were wiped out and millions of people died. There were no well-trained doctors and proper medicines such as we have today and people believed all sorts of strange things would save them. Some kept goats in the house with them all the time, believing that the smell would keep out illness. Others believed spiders sucked away all poisons from their house.

Eventually the mystery illness passed, but not before it had killed forty-two million people in Europe.

Information for the teacher

1   The Black Death swept through Europe in the middle of the fourteenth century. It struck Britain in 1348. Agricultural labourers died in their thousands, crops withered, robbers roamed everywhere and 'normal' living was a thing of the past. It is thought that this bubonic plague started in China and was spread through Europe by ships which carried aboard locusts, fleas, rats and other vermin.

2   All religions concern themselves with the wellbeing of others and the healing of the sick. Biblical references related to such a theme could include Luke 17, 11–19 and Mark 7, 31–5.

3   Two saints could be examined in more detail in connection with this story: Saints Cosmas and Damian. Christians of Arabic birth, these third-century twins devoted their lives to medicine and to surgery, such as it was in their day. They were killed for their Christian beliefs, but remain the patron saints of medicine. St Luke too was a doctor, but is remembered more for his gospel writing.

4   For notes and leaflets on the National Health Service, the appropriate address is: Department of Health, Richmond House, 79 Whitehall, London SW1A 2NL. Inquiries should be directed to the Public Enquiry Office. www.doh.gov.uk

5   Useful May 'medical' anniversaries to link with this story are: the birth of Florence Nightingale on the 12th in 1820; the inauguration of Australia's Flying Doctor Service on the 15th in 1928; the birth of Edward Jenner, discoverer of vaccination against smallpox, on the 17th in 1749.

Hymn suggestion

Come and Praise Vol 1 'From the darkness came light' No 29

Prayer

Dear God,

Let us be thankful for good health, and let us pray for all those who don't have it. May they have the strength and will to recover.

Let us also give thanks for the skills and knowledge of doctors and nurses, and those who find medicines to cure illnesses. Amen.

64 The sisters

Introduction

This morning's story is one of unselfishness. It is about two sisters and their mother.

Story

Lily and Janet were twin sisters. They lived with their mother, many years ago. Their father was dead and the family did not have much money.

When they went to school both girls had a chance to sing – and they were a sensation.

'Have you heard Lily sing? She's wonderful!'

'She is, but I think Janet is even better.'

'No, you can't separate the two, they are both marvellous.'

So it went on. The girls sang together, and by themselves, and their fame spread from their school throughout the village, and even to the nearby town. They sang in concerts and their mother was very proud of them.

One day they sang at a concert in another village. By now they were in their teens and quite used to performing. That evening, unknown to them, a famous singing teacher from Vienna was in the audience. After the concert he came to see them.

'That was delightful, girls. May I introduce myself? My name is Hans Gonert and I train opera singers. I think you could both become famous singers, but you need training. I'd like to take you both to my school in Vienna and teach you. I know you'll want to talk about this so I'll come and see you in the morning to discuss details.'

Lily and Janet could hardly contain their excitement. But as they walked home each had thoughts which were exactly alike, but which they didn't mention to the other.

Where was the money going to come from, to live in Vienna? Who was going to look after their mother, who was now getting old and frail, while they were away? Finally Lily spoke.

'It's a marvellous opportunity, Janet, but I think you're better than me and I'm not sure I want to go anyway. You go and I'll stay home.'

'Nonsense. You go and I'll stay,' replied Janet.

Being twins, and knowing what the other was thinking, the two girls suddenly stopped and threw their arms round each other. Both wanted desperately to go, but . . .

'I know the answer,' said Lily. 'We'll both go, but this is how we'll do it. First of all you go. I'll get a job here to help you out with the money and I'll stay and look after Mum. Then, when you've trained, you come back and I'll go and train.'

When the girls put this to Herr Gonert the next day, he accepted, and Janet went off to Vienna.

Meanwhile, back at home, the job which raised the most money to help pay for Janet's training was working on a market stall. Every day, in all weathers, Lily stood outside shouting her wares and working from almost dawn till dusk. Then she went home and looked after her mother. Each week she sent money off to Janet and each week she received a long letter back telling her about how wonderful the training was and what marvellous progress Janet was making.

Finally, after several years, Janet's training was over. The next day she caught the train for the long journey home so that Lily could take her place. Lily met her at the station and the two girls hugged each other silently for a minute.

'You'll love it, Lily,' said Janet. 'There'll be some great jobs when you've trained and Vienna is a lovely city.'

'I'm sure it is,' said Lily.

Janet looked at her sharply.

'Your voice, Lily! What's the matter with your voice?'

'Oh, it's nothing,' croaked Lily in her rough voice, 'but, you see, shouting in a market all day . . . well . . .'

'You mean, you can't . . . you can't . . .'

'No, Janet. It's gone, I'm afraid. I'll never be able to sing like you now, no matter how much I train.'

Janet looked at the tired but smiling face of her sister and felt the tears run down her face.

'Oh Lily . . . Lily.'

So it was. Janet went back to Vienna and became a famous opera singer and Lily stayed at home, worked in the market and looked after her mother. When Janet gave concerts she always dedicated one song on the programme to her sister Lily, and whenever Lily heard and read of her sister's fame she felt so proud.

Information for the teacher

1   The perfect location for this story is 20th May. This was the date on which the painter Albrecht Dürer was born in 1471. The story of Janet and Lily is loosely based on that of Albrecht and his brother, Franz.

Albrecht and Franz were both painters. Franz, the elder brother, took a heavy labouring job to pay for Albrecht's studies on the understanding that the roles would be reversed when Albrecht's studies were finished. Sadly, when this was the case Franz's hands were ruined by his work and he could no longer paint. As a testimony to his brother's sacrifice Albrecht painted a picture of his brother's hands clasped together in prayer. This magnificent and beautiful picture has remained world-famous ever since. It appears on many cards and would be a most useful acquisition as a teacher's resource.

2   Lily's hoarsened voice and Franz's ruined hands were, in a sense, beautiful because of what they achieved. Some quotations about beauty may be apt here:

'Beauty is a combination of qualities . . .' (dictionary reference).

'Beauty is truth, truth beauty' (John Keats, 1795–1821).

'Judge not according to appearance' (St John, 7, 24).

Hymn suggestion

Come and Praise Vol 1 'For all the beauty of the earth' No 11

Prayer

Dear God,

Let us give thanks for those people who make sacrifices so that others can benefit. Let us give thanks for our parents and friends who want only the best for us and who try to help us and guide us.

Teach us to value unselfishness and give us the strength to practise it. Amen.

65 Fair shares

Introduction

As you know, most old stories have good and bad characters in them. It is possible, though, to have a story which is interesting even though there are only good characters in it. Perhaps you will agree after listening to this morning's story.

Story

Omar and Anwar were very sad. They were the sons of a farmer who had just died. Although their father had been old and tired, they missed him very much.

'He always gave us such good advice,' said Omar.

'Yes,' agreed his brother. 'Nothing was ever too much trouble for him. He was the kindest of men.'

So the two brothers opened the letter their father had left them.

My dear sons [it said] thank you for all the happy times you helped me to enjoy over the years. I wish you both every happiness. If you go to the barn you will see that what I have left is divided equally between you.

So the two sons went to their father's big barn. He had asked one of his servants to stack his precious bags of corn against the walls. There was exactly the same number of bags in each pile. In front of one of them there was a little notice saying 'Omar'. In front of the other a notice saying 'Anwar'.

'Just like him,' said Omar, 'fair and thoughtful to the last.'

'Yes, you're right,' replied Anwar.

Now, although both had been very good sons, they lived very different lives. Omar wasn't married and only had himself to think about. On the other hand, Anwar had a wife and three children.

That night, after they had got into their separate beds, the brothers lay thinking.

'I wonder if my father has been quite fair?' thought Omar to himself. 'He's left the same number of sacks to both of us – but I have only myself to worry about and I have all I need. Now, Anwar, he needs all he can get to care for those children of his. I think I'll go and rearrange our inheritance.'

So, slipping out into the bright moonlit night, Omar made his ways to the barn. Leaving the door open to let the moonlight in, he dragged ten sacks from his pile and put them on Anwar's pile.

133

'Now, I feel better about that,' he said to himself. Then he went back to his bed and fell into a sound sleep.

Meanwhile, Anwar was tossing and turning in his bed.

'What's the matter?' asked his wife.

'It's my father's arrangements for Omar and me. They just don't seem right.'

'What do you mean?' asked his wife.

'Well, I'm such a lucky man,' went on Anwar. 'I've got you and we've got our three lovely children. What more could we possibly want? Omar, he's just got himself. I think he deserves a bigger share than me.'

'I agree,' said Anwar's wife. 'But what can you do about it?'

'I'm going to creep over to the barn now and move some sacks from my pile to his. Nobody will ever know about it.'

So, as the moon continued to shine down, Anwar crept stealthily to the barn. Working quickly and quietly, he transferred ten sacks from his pile to Omar's.

Next morning, both brothers were up bright and early – for each had separately decided to go to the barn to check that they hadn't left any trace of their night-time visit.

When they reached the barn they met each other and were astonished to see that each pile had exactly the same number of sacks in it as on the day before.

(Adapted from a story in *The Caravan of Dreams* by Idris Shah.)

Information for the teacher

1   This story is ideal for this morning's calendar link, which is with the week of storytelling that the Federation of Children's Book Groups annually promotes in May. This event should be watched out for, particularly as one of the expressed aims of such a week was 'to reflect harmony among peoples and a wealth of cultural heritages.'

The address for the Federation of Children's Book Groups is:

The Federation of Children's Book Groups, 2 Bridge Wood View, Horsforth, Leeds, West Yorkshire LS18 5PE.
www.fcbg.mcmail.com

Hymn suggestion

Come and Praise Vol 1 'I listen and I listen' No 60

Prayer

Let us think this morning about the many stories we hear in our lives. Let us learn from the wisdom which is so often contained in these stories. Amen.

June

66 The cheat

Introduction

Every year in June a famous horse race takes place at Epsom in England. This is the Derby. This morning's story is about this race, a horse that ran in it, and two men.

Story

A huge crowd was packed on Epsom Downs racecourse. A hot June sun shone down, people selling drinks and food shouted their wares and there was the sound of good-natured voices everywhere.

'Roll up for the greatest race in the world.'

'Which horse is going to win?'

'Running Rein – it's a certainty.'

'Not a chance! Orlando – that's the one for me.'

The date was 1844 and a tall man in a top hat stood watching the surge of the crowds around him. This was Sir George Bentinck and his job was to see that cheating, in any type or form, did not take place anywhere on the racecourse.

Another man in a top hat was looking around too. This was the owner of the horse Running Rein. Mr Goodman – that was his name – was very anxious for the race to start, and equally anxious for it to finish. If his horse won he would be fifty thousand pounds richer. This was an enormous sum of money in 1844.

The horses left the saddling enclosure and moved to the starting line. The crowd got more and more excited.

'They all look good.'

'What a race this is going to be!'

'Get ready . . .'

'They're off!'

Kicking clods of turf behind them as they ran, the horses leapt from the starting tape and pounded towards Tattenham Corner –

the bend before they entered the straight run up to the finishing line. The brightly coloured silks of the jockeys flashed in the sunlight as each rider crouched low over his horse's neck, urging it to even greater speed. The roar of the crowd got louder and louder as two horses began to widen the gap between themselves and the other runners.

'Come on, Running Rein!'

'Come on, Orlando!'

Neck and neck, the two racing animals galloped flat out towards the winning post – and then, suddenly, with a last desperate burst of speed, Running Rein edged ahead, and the race was won.

Sir George Bentinck watched with interest the speed with which Mr Goodman got his horse away from the winner's stand and out of sight. He was even more interested, and suspicious, when he noticed the brown stains where Running Rein had been standing.

'There's only one thing *that* could be,' said Sir George to himself as he swept his fingers through the stained grass. 'That's dye. But why would anyone want to put dye on a horse?'

So Sir George began an investigation which was to last a year. During this time he found out that Mr Goodman had bought some brown dye from a hairdresser in Regent Street in London. He also found out that Mr Goodman had used this to dye a horse's legs brown. The horse was a four-year-old called Maccabeus who had won many races. Once his legs had been dyed brown he became known as 'Running Rein' and because the Derby is for three-year-olds only he had a big advantage over all the other runners.

'Now I've got all this information, I can show everybody what a cheat Mr Goodman is,' said Sir George to his friends.

So the case came to court and the courtroom was packed with jockeys, owners, trainers and members of the public. Even in places as far away as Australia and America people had heard what was happening and were taking an interest. Sure enough, Sir George proved that Mr Goodman was a cheat and a liar, and that his horse was a fake. The result of the race was changed, Running Rein was disqualified and Orlando was placed first.

The man who had tried to win the world's greatest horse race by cheating now stood in disgrace.

Information for the teacher

1   This story could be linked to the Wednesday in early June when the Derby takes place every year.

2 The phrase 'honesty is the best policy' might be discussed in connection with this story. This could be extended to consider 'conscience' – whereby if we have done something dishonest and nobody else knows about it, nevertheless we do.

Hymn suggestion

Come and Praise Vol 2 'Make us worthy, Lord' No 94

Prayer

Dear God,
  Help us at all times to resist the temptation to cheat in any way. Help us to be honest and truthful at all times. Amen.

67 *The cooking pot*

Introduction

If you play a mean, nasty trick on somebody it often seems to come back eventually and hurt *you*. This morning's story shows this.

Story

'Oh dear, oh dear, oh dear,' thought Sunil to himself.
  'No matter how hard I work I never seem to be able to get enough money to feed my family properly. Well, it's no good moaning. I'll just have to try and work harder.'
  Now Sunil was a good man. He did work and what's more he helped as many people as he possibly could. Nothing was too much trouble for him. As a result, when the great goddess Durga heard his thoughts she decided to help him.
  The next day he was working a long way from home. Late in the morning he sat down for a rest and dozed in the sun. The goddess Durga spoke to him.
  'Sunil, take this pot – it will keep your family well fed for ever.'
  'What . . . what . . .?' Startled, Sunil awoke suddenly – and found a cooking pot beside him.
  'That was the goddess Durga speaking to me,' he thought, 'but what did she mean about the pot?'
  He picked up the pot, looked at it, turned it round, and then tipped it upside down. At once rice poured from it. Every time he turned it upside down limitless rice poured out.

'This is fantastic,' muttered Sunil, 'My family will never go hungry again. Thank you, great goddess, thank you.'

After work, Sunil made his way home. It was tremendously hot still and he was tired and dirty. When he came to an inn with a water trough he thought he would go in for a wash before he got home.

'Can I wash as usual?' he asked the innkeeper.

'Yes, go ahead.'

'Oh – and while I'm washing, will you look after this pot, please? It is very, very precious.'

While Sunil was away getting washed the innkeeper looked at the pot.

'Hmm,' he muttered. 'He's never had anything precious in his life! What can be so special about this?'

Then he turned the pot upside down and found out!

'Fantastic,' thought the innkeeper. 'Fantastic – I could feed my family for life if I had this pot. Now, how to get it . . .?'

The innkeeper scurried off to the cellar and found a pot which looked exactly like the one Sunil had asked him to look after. He swapped the two over.

'Got my pot?' said Sunil when he'd finished washing.

'Right here,' answered the landlord.

Sunil hurried home with the great news. Imagine his feelings when he turned the pot over and out came . . . nothing!

'The only time this pot has left my side was when I stopped at the inn,' he thought. 'That innkeeper must have changed pots.'

Now, Durga the goddess had seen all this happen. She was furious – first of all with Sunil for his carelessness, and even more so with the mean and deceitful innkeeper. She spoke to Sunil. 'Another pot awaits you.'

Sure enough, there was another pot, just like the first. Joyfully, Sunil turned it over – and out leapt a group of evil spirits who gave him a beating. Desperately, Sunil righted the pot and they disappeared back into it.

'That was awful,' he gasped. 'But I'm sure Durga is guiding me to show me how I can get the first pot back.'

So saying, he set off for the inn again. Going innocently up to the innkeeper, he spoke as before.

'I'd like to wash, please. Would you look after my pot in the meantime? Please be careful with it – it's even more precious than the first one.'

The innkeeper could hardly wait until Sunil was out of the way. Greedily he turned the pot over – and out shot the evil spirits. Not content with giving him a good beating, they were about to tear his inn to pieces when Sunil, who had been hiding and watching, rushed back to get rid of them by turning the pot over.

'Thank you, thank you,' gasped the innkeeper. 'I'm sorry – you must know what I did to your first pot to do this to me. Please – let me give it back to you at once.'

The innkeeper hurried off and came back with the first pot. This time Sunil checked it – and sure enough, out came the rice again.

Because he was such a kind man, Sunil gave the innkeeper a large supply of rice before he made his way home again. From that day onwards he and his family never went hungry again.

Information for the teacher

1 Durga, the Hindu goddess, is the wife of the great god Shiva, and is also known as Sati, Kali, Ambika and Devi. She is the 'all-comprehending one' whose hands hold 'delight and pain'. This story seems a very appropriate example of her twin characteristics of benevolence and fierceness.

2 Perhaps the calendar links for this story could be reflections of 'unfairness' in the modern world, and the continuing need for peace, consideration for others and equal opportunities. June contains some tragic anniversaries of people who did not receive these things: on the 11th, in 1982, forty-two British soldiers were killed at Fitzroy during the Falklands War; on the 15th, in 1952, Anne Frank's diary was published – she had kept it from 1942 to 1944, when she was sent to a concentration camp; on the 29th, in 1925, a law was passed in South Africa banning all black people from holding skilled jobs.

Hymn suggestion

Come and Praise Vol 2 'I come like a beggar' No 90

Prayer

Let us think this morning about fairness for all. Let us never begrudge or be envious of the good fortune of others and let us always be prepared to share our own good fortune. Amen.

68 Sarah Gooder's story

Introduction

For most children living in Britain today it would be hard to imagine what life was like for someone the same age one hundred and fifty years ago. Sarah Gooder's story gives us some idea.

Story

The men in the room were all silent. Then one of them spoke.

'Well sir, that's how it is. We need somebody to help us. Will you do it?'

The man who spoke had a tired, careworn face and his clothes were poor and well worn. His friends, who gathered round him, looked very much the same, but all had a look of absolute determination on their thin faces.

'If what you say is true, I promise that I will find out all I can about the situation – and do my utmost to put it right.'

The second speaker looked very different from all the other men. He was tall and elegantly dressed and his voice was calm and educated – but he too looked worried by what he had heard.

The tall, well-dressed man was the Earl of Shaftesbury and on this day in 1832 he had met a group of working men to hear what conditions were like in mines and factories all over the country. What he had heard had made him almost ill with its dreadfulness.

'There's women and children working in coalmines for sixteen hours a day. They never see the light of day and they're treated like slaves. It's the same in factories, where some children are so tired after sixteen hours working at a machine that they just fall to the floor and sleep. How old are these children? you ask. Well, some of them are only four.'

This is what one of the men had told Lord Shaftesbury. As soon as the group had gone, he began to think of how he could deal with this problem. He realised that he would have to find out exactly what was happening, prove it, and then get Parliament to pass laws to protect these desperate children.

So began a life's work for Lord Shaftesbury. First of all he visited coalmines and investigated conditions for the workers there. It was while he was preparing his first report on Children's Employment Conditions that he met Sarah Gooder. This is what she told him.

'The worst thing about my job is that I'm scared of the dark and it's dark all the time. I'm so scared I daren't even sing to cheer myself up.'

Lord Shaftesbury asked, 'How long do you work each day, Sarah?'

Sarah replied, 'I'm not really sure. I know that I get to the coalmine at half past three in the morning of each day and I work there until half past five in the afternoon.'

'Have you got a hard job to do?' asked Lord Shaftesbury.

'I've got to open and close ventilators in the mine all day,' said Sarah. 'That's not such a bad job – some of the other children have worse jobs. Jenny and Violet have to drag trucks of coal. They've got to do this crawling on their hands and knees because the roof is too low for them to stand up. It's too low for ponies to drag the trucks, so they have to do it.'

Lord Shaftesbury asked Sarah what she did when she was not at work.

Sarah replied, 'I just sleep. I'm too tired even to eat. I fall asleep over my food. I'm always tired. I never ever play – and I've got nothing to play with, anyway.'

'How old are you, Sarah?' asked Lord Shaftesbury, and she told him, 'I'm eight.'

Lord Shaftesbury wrote his report about Sarah and the other children, and people were absolutely horrified when they read it. There was a great uproar and people demanded that the Government should do something to stop these terrible things. Eventually Parliament ruled that no women or girls should ever work in mines again, and boys had to be ten before they could do so.

Information for the teacher

1   Legislation to prevent children working in mines was difficult to achieve because many of those who sat in the House of Lords were wealthy mine owners. In Lord Shaftesbury's diary there are entries like this one: 'The object of years within my grasp . . . a notice to investigate the condition of all the wretched and helpless children in collieries . . . I must have public knowledge and public opinion working within it.'

2   Children may be aware of the famous statue of Eros at London's Piccadilly Circus. They are less likely to know that this stands over a memorial to Lord Shaftesbury, symbolising Christian charity.

3   There are several calendar links which can be made with this story. On 6th June 1844 the Factory Act of England established an Office of Factory Inspectors whose job was to ensure the health and wellbeing of those employed in factories. Charles Dickens died on 9th June 1870.

Dickens was poor in his youth, and in his many novels he highlighted the desperate plight of poor children.

4   All religions advocate care and concern for children. Perhaps the most famous Biblical reference to children is in St Mark, 10, 14: 'Suffer the little children to come unto me, and forbid them not: for of such is the Kingdom of Heaven.'

Hymn suggestion

Come and Praise Vol 1 'From the darkness came light' No 29

Prayer

Let us give thanks this morning for people like Lord Shaftesbury who, by their hard work, determination and concern, have made the world a better place for others.

69 Keep on trying

Introduction

Sometimes, when things seem very difficult, we are tempted to say, 'I give up.' This morning's story is about some people who wouldn't give up.

Story

It was a bright June day and the air high up in the Lake District was fresh and inviting. It was perfect for walking and Charles and Muriel Leeming were enjoying the exercise as they strode out on the high ground.

'What a day!' said Charles.

'You're right – and what a view,' answered Muriel, pointing to the countryside six hundred feet below them.

Torver, their eight-year-old Yorkshire terrier, let out an excited bark. He was certainly enjoying himself too.

The two people and their dog continued on their way.

'That's Clough Head Peak up there,' said Charles.

'Yes, one of the best spots on Helvellyn,' replied Muriel.

'Look at Torver, he's going to beat us to it!'

'He would . . . but that path's very narrow. Torver, be careful, be caref—'

Charles's voice petered out as, up ahead, the little dog suddenly lost his footing on the narrow path. With a scattering of small stones and a desperate yelp, he scrambled to pull himself up – and then suddenly he was gone. Charles and Muriel leaned helplessly over and watched their pet roll side over side down the slope of jagged scree. Twice he bounced off clumps of bushes and then, under the flying dust and stones, he disappeared.

'Oh Charles,' murmured Muriel tearfully, 'the poor, poor little chap.'

For the rest of the day the Leemings searched for their pet. Unfortunately they heard nothing from him, nor could they find him anywhere.

'I'm afraid he must have died in the fall,' said Charles, 'and perhaps his body is trapped in a crevice somewhere.'

Miserably, the two walkers returned to their home in Lancashire. Next day they described the incident to their local vet, Mr David Higginson.

'How awful for you,' said Mr Higginson. 'But you know, these Yorkshire terriers are tough little fellows. He might have survived the fall, but, being dazed, just wandered off somewhere.'

'But what can we do?' asked Muriel. 'Where do we begin to look for him?'

'Well look, leave it to me,' Mr Higginson went on. 'I have an idea. It may come to nothing but it's worth a try.'

So Mr Higginson got in touch with a vet he knew in Keswick, which was near where the Leemings had been walking. When he explained what had happened, the Keswick vet said he knew of an animal charity nearby which might be able to help.

When they heard the story they moved into action straightaway. Posters were given out containing the details of Torver and his story was told in local newspapers and broadcast on the radio. Hundreds of people were on the lookout for the missing terrier.

Then, five days later, all the effort and determination put into the search for the little dog paid off. Four miles from Keswick a man spotted a particularly battered and bedraggled Yorkshire terrier lying under a caravan. When he was encouraged to come out he walked with a limp but didn't seem badly hurt. Yes – it was Torver.

Information for the teacher

1 Torver was returned safe and sound to the Leemings. His story received considerable publicity, and a photograph was published of the dog looking fit and well and reunited with his owners.

2 This theme of determination, not giving up, and pressing on regardless of discouragement is one which could be followed up by compiling a selection of stories which reflect these qualities in varying ways. National and local newspapers are useful here and many folk tales reflect the same virtues.
Biblical stories which might be used here could include Noah and the Flood (Genesis 6–8); Daniel in the Lion's Den (Daniel 6); Moses in the basket of reeds (Exodus 2); David and Goliath (I Samuel 17); and Paul's journeys (Acts 13–28).

3 A useful address is:

Countryside Commission, John Dower House, Crescent Place, Cheltenham GL50 3RA. www.countryside.gov.uk

For those near enough, the National Park Centre at Brockhole in the Lake District is open to school parties and would provide first-hand local 'colour' relating to the story.

Hymn suggestion

Come and Praise Vol 2 'Let the world rejoice together' No 148

Prayer

Dear God,
We ask this morning that you may help us to be determined and caring, able to cope with disappointments, and to be reliable people at all times.
We give thanks for the many lives that are saved because of these qualities. Amen.

70 A life to treasure

Introduction

We all get a great deal of pleasure from people who entertain us. They might be footballers, musicians, actors, artists or magicians. This morning's story is about a man who wrote wonderful music – but whose life was strangely bound up with the sea.

Story

The Russian warship *Prokhor* was wallowing in very rough seas. These were the days when ships were driven by sails and the captain gazed anxiously upwards.

'There's only one way to get out of this trouble,' he called. 'Send someone aloft to get more sail unfurled.'

An officer sprang to obey his orders. 'You – you – and you,' he shouted to three seamen. 'Get aloft on the mainsail.'

Slowly the three men climbed high up into the masts of the ship. One was a young cadet named Nikolay. The wind howled and shrieked round them as if trying to tear the clothes from their bodies. From one side to the other the ship yawed wildly and all three struggled desperately to hold on as their hands grew numb with cold.

'Get along and unfurl that sail,' shouted the senior sailor to Nikolay.

Inch by inch the young cadet edged his way through the swaying rigging.

'Nearly there,' he thought to himself. Suddenly the ship lunged violently to one side. One second Nikolay was reaching to unwind the ropes binding a sail – the next he was plunging downwards through the storm-lashed darkness.

Before he had time to think, he crashed into the pounding waves and sank rapidly. The freezing water filled his mouth and ears as he fought to swim back to the surface. No sooner had he done so than tough hands hauled him back on board.

'You were lucky there, son,' said one old seaman. 'Most people who fall off the rigging like that hit the deck – and that's the end of them.'

After his miraculous escape, Nikolay continued his career at sea. A new interest was taking up more and more of his time, however. He had bought a harmonium and every spare minute he was off duty he composed music. Tune after tune flowed out from his small instrument and finally he realised that he wanted to spend the rest of his life making music.

'As soon as I get back to St Petersburg I'm going to give up the sea and see if I can compose more,' he thought to himself. And so he did. Within a year he had written a great symphony which was soon performed. Then followed a second symphony and an opera.

Success followed success. Nikolay got married and was appointed Director of a School of Music. It seemed as if he just couldn't stop writing great music – and then one morning he got up with a strange feeling.

'I can't think of anything,' he thought to himself. 'There are no musical thoughts coming into my head.'

The next day was the same – and the next – and the next.

'I'm finished,' thought Nikolay. 'I've got no ideas left. I might as well give up. I've got nothing left.'

So he gave up his home in the great city and went to live in Odessa, a town by the sea. There he began to take long, lonely walks by the sea on which he had once earned his living.

One day, as he was walking along the beach, the tide was ebbing out slowly. As he watched the swirling water and heard it hissing on the sand he suddenly felt a tune forming in his mind again. Rushing home, he set about composing it properly. It was as if the sound of the waves had set his mind off again and never again had he any difficulty in writing great pieces of music.

The rest of Nikolay's name was Rimsky-Korsakov and you will almost certainly have heard some of his music. Now is your chance to listen to some more, knowing a bit about the man who wrote it.

Information for the teacher

1 The last sentence of the story provides an opportunity (if appropriate) to listen to some of Rimsky-Korsakov's work. There is plenty to choose from and among selections which seem most appropriate for primary school children are 'The Flight of the Bumble Bee', *Sheherazade*, and *Sadko*.

2 The reason for linking Rimsky-Korsakov with this month is that he died on 21st June 1908.

3 There is a very telling quotation about music in Shakespeare's *Merchant of Venice*. It is obviously for adult consumption but a little tactful adaptation by the teacher could certainly get its message across to children:

> The man that hath not music in himself,
> Nor is moved with concord of sweet sounds,
> Is fit for stratagems and spoils;
> The motions of his spirit are dull as night,
> And his affections dark as Erebus:
> Let no such man be trusted.

Hymn suggestion

Come and Praise Vol 1 'A living song' No 72

Prayer

Let us give thanks this morning for those composers whose music has given so many people so much pleasure.

Let us give thanks, too, for musicians everywhere whose skill and talents help us to enjoy music. Amen.

71 This month

Introduction

June is usually one of the loveliest months of the whole year, and one in which there is a great deal to see and do out of doors.

This month

June is a month which writers and poets like to describe. One poem goes like this:

> Full early in the morning
> Awakes the summer sun,
> The month of June arriving,
> The cold and night are done;
> The cuckoo is a fine bird,
> She whistles as she flies,
> And as she whistles 'cuckoo',
> The bluer grow the skies.
>
> (Anon.)

If you take a walk in fields or woods on a June day you would expect to see lots of flowers. There are pink and white dog roses, and wild hyacinths. Yellow and white daisies are scattered throughout fields and in damp spots there are large, blueish-purple flowers called meadow cranesbill. You might also see flowers which look like large buttercups and these are called marsh marigolds. As well as looking, it is a good idea to take deep breaths and then you might get the lovely smell of honeysuckle, which is a plant which twines round other plants and hedges.

If you go anywhere near a pond, watch out for tadpoles, which by June have longer legs and shorter tails. Sticklebacks are around and there is certainly lots of activity above the surface of the pond. Watch out for dragonflies, butterflies and moths in the air.

Perhaps the fruit we all think of most, in connection with June, is the strawberry. The Romans called strawberries *fragaria* but our name for them comes from the fact that this is a fruit which spreads long runners over the ground: we say that it 'strews' these, and so they were first called 'streoberries' and eventually 'strawberries'. There's a special way to pick strawberries so that you don't damage them. Each berry should be snapped off with the first finger and thumb, about a quarter of an inch from the berry along its stem. You should always be careful to touch the actual berry as little as possible because this causes it to 'smear', or bruise.

Some birds like berries, of course, and there are plenty of them to see and hear during June. Although the poem we heard earlier mentions the cuckoo, this bird will be heard less than in May. This is because he leaves earlier than others for warmer conditions. So don't expect to hear many cuckoos after about the third week of June. Other birds to watch out for and listen to are hedge-sparrows, blackbirds, goldcrests, chaffinches and linnets.

Finally, if you live in southern England, then listen out at dusk on a calm, quiet June night. You could well hear the whirring noise of stag beetles flying about. If you see one, you can tell if it's male because it will have things that look like antlers, but which are really long jaws.

Information for the teacher

1   James Lowell said, 'What is rare as a day in June?' Practically all the points mentioned in the assembly text can be extended further. For instance, there are more interesting stories relating to strawberries. In earlier times, and for several obvious reasons, they were considered a much greater delicacy than they are today. In consequence highwaymen were very active in way-laying strawberry consignments – not surprising when their rarity brought as much as £10 for 1lb of strawberries in London.

2   There are an unusual number of poems and pieces of prose which could be used with children during June. 'A hot day' by A S J Tessimond is particularly good, with many telling lines ('A tree, June lazy ...'). Other good choices of poems are 'An Indian Summer on the Prairie' by Vachel Lindsay, 'On a Midsummer's Eve' by Thomas Hardy, and 'Summer' by Christina Rosetti.
    For prose, a dip into Laurie Lee's *Cider with Rosie* is rewarding.

Hymn suggestion

Come and Praise Vol 1 'For the beauty of the earth' No 11

Prayer

Dear God,

Please help us to use our senses to appreciate summer's beauty. Help us not only to enjoy the sights, smells and sounds of the countryside, but to be aware of how important it is to look after it in every way we can. We thank you for the pleasure we get in sharing lovely summer days. Amen.

72 John

Introduction

You all know that if you are going to have a party there has to be a lot of preparation beforehand. It's the same for things like sports days or swimming galas or school trips. This morning's story is about a man who had to prepare people for a great event.

Story

Zacharias was a priest in the temple at Jerusalem in the time before Jesus was born. He and his wife Elisabeth were very excited.

'I wonder if it will be a boy,' muttered Elisabeth to herself as she went about her daily jobs. She and Zacharias had no children so they were looking forward to the birth of their first child.

When the great day arrived, a boy was born and he was called John. Many people thought that when he grew up he would be a priest like his father, but John had other ideas. He was very fit and strong and did a lot of thinking by himself. One day he spoke seriously to his father.

'I must leave home,' he said. 'I feel that the job I have to do in life can't be done here.'

'But where will you go?' asked Zacharias.

'I am going to live in the desert,' replied John. 'There I will get the chance to talk to people who pass by. I feel that I have a lot to say to them.'

So John left Jerusalem and went to live in the desert. He lived alone and life was very hard. Then he began to make regular journeys to the great river which was nearby. This was the River Jordan and many people passed along it every day.

'Listen to me, I have something to tell you,' said John to these people. 'You must try and live better lives than you are doing now.'

'What do you mean?' asked a tax collector who was passing by.

'Well – you, for instance. You collect taxes. Do you ever cheat and take more tax than you should, keeping the extra for yourself?'

The tax collector looked shiftily away.

'Well, if you do, you must stop and live a better, fairer life – being generous to others rather than trying to cheat them.'

'And you, soldier – it is easy for you with your power to treat people badly. But you shouldn't. Remember, someone as strong as you can help people rather than frighten them.'

So John went on talking to the travellers by the River Jordan. Soon he became so well known that people went especially to hear him speak. They asked him questions.

'What can we do to live better lives? Can you help us?'

As well as advising them, John then baptised many people in the waters of the river. He also kept on telling them that a man, much more important than he was, was soon coming to show them how they must live. John's listeners did not know it but the man he was preparing for was Jesus.

Information for the teacher

1 The Bible references for this story are as follows: Luke 1 and Mark 1. Moving on further, the story of Jesus's baptism is in Matthew 3, 16–17; and that of John's death in Mark 6, 27–9.

2 John was supposedly born at a village four miles west of Jerusalem and showed an early predilection for the austere life. Honey was one of his main foods in the desert and he wore a cloak of camel's hair tied with a belt. It was John's regular baptising of people in the Jordan that gave him the name 'John the Baptist'.

   As well as having many listeners, John also attracted some close followers and friends (Matthew 9, 14; Luke 7, 18).

3 The Roman authorities were always apprehensive about potential 'troublemakers' who gathered followers. Herod Antipas considered that John fell into this category and had him arrested. He was subsequently beheaded at the request of Salome.

4 John the Baptist's Day is 24th June. One of his symbols is camel's hair ('And John was clothed with camel's hair, and with a girdle

of a skin about his loins', Mark 1, 6). St John the Baptist is the patron saint of Florence.

Hymn suggestion

Come and Praise Vol 1 'The journey of life' No 45

Prayer

Let us pray this morning for those who prepare. Let us give thanks for their work and care, and pray that their preparation is appreciated and rewarded. Amen.

73 Six wise men?

Introduction

'I know I'm right!' I'm sure you have heard people say that. Sometimes, though, it is better to listen to another point of view first before being certain that we are right – as this morning's story shows.

Story

The king was fabulously rich.

'I want to use some of my riches to find really wise men,' he said to his courtiers. 'Go and find me six of the so-called wisest men in the kingdom and tell them I want to reward them for their wisdom.'

So six wise men were brought before the king.

'Now,' said the king, 'the wisest among you will be rewarded with a large sum of money – or, if you prove equally wise, the money will be shared between you.'

'Ah,' thought each of the men, 'I'm sure I am wiser than these others. It will just be a question of proving it when the king sets his test.'

'Right,' said the king, clapping his hands and bringing his servants scurrying towards him. 'Get six very large blindfolds and tie them tightly round each of these wise men's heads.'

This was done and then, with a servant leading each of them, the six men were taken outside into the palace gardens. Silently tethered in the garden and, of course unseen by the men, was an elephant.

'This is what we are going to do,' said the king. 'Each of you will be led out to feel something. When you have all felt it you are free to discuss what you think it is – and decide together – or you can make your own choice without discussing it with the others.'

The first wise man was led by his servant up to the elephant. His hands were placed firmly on the elephant's tusk and he was told not to move them.

'This is a great thick spear,' he thought to himself. 'I don't need to talk to anybody about that. I'm sure I'm right. So I'll get all the money.'

The second man was led up to the elephant and when his hands were placed on the elephant's leg he was positive he was holding a tree. His thoughts about winning everything for himself were exactly the same as the first man's.

The third man was sure he had hold of a rope as he held the elephant's tail; the fourth believed the elephant's chest was a wall and the fifth thought he had hold of a carpet when the servant put his hands on the creature's ear!

The sixth man was just the same as the rest. When he was lifted to sit briefly on the elephant's back he thought he was on a large covered rock.

When all had had their turns, the king ordered the elephant to be taken away. When this was done the blindfolds were removed and the wise men were asked to tell the king what they had touched.

'A spear, Your Majesty.'

'A tree, Your Majesty.'

As each man said what he thought he had touched, the others could hardly contain their laughter for thinking how stupid their fellow competitors were. When they had all finished the king ordered the elephant to be brought back. As it lumbered into view, the faces of all six men dropped in astonishment. How could they have been so wrong?

'You have all proved your lack of wisdom,' said the king. 'Each of you was so greedy to get all the money for himself that he was sure he was right and didn't want to share his opinion with the others. But if you had discussed what each of you felt you would have realised it was an elephant. Then each of you would have got something – instead, all of you get nothing.'

Information for the teacher

1   This is an adaptation of an old Hindu story. In at least one other version the wise men are competing for the hand of the king's daughter.

2   A useful calendar link for this story could be 27th June. On this date in 1880 Helen Keller was born. She was to lose her sight and hearing completely before she was two, but overcame her difficulties and became well known and admired for her championing of the handicapped.

3   The idea of wisdom being a sharing of knowledge is captured in a quotation from Tolstoy: 'The highest wisdom has but one science – the science of the whole'.

4   A good source for stories of this type is *Faith Stories for Today* by Angela Wood (BBC Consumer Publishing).

Hymn suggestion

Come and Praise Vol 1 'Join with us' No 30

Prayer

Dear God,
   Teach us the value of sharing – our talents, our good fortune, our worries, our disappointments. Help us to learn that by sharing these, and other things, in our lives we become much wiser people. Amen.

July

74 Be prepared

Introduction

This morning's story has a very simple message: Be prepared!

Story

It was a glorious summer's day in July. The sun shone down brightly and a few wispy clouds drifted lazily by in a deep blue haze. The countryside was peaceful and still – well, almost still.
   'Gosh, this is warm work, but it will certainly be worth it eventually.'
   This was an ant speaking. He didn't really have too much time for speaking because he was working too hard. Backwards and forwards he scurried, collecting grains of wheat and then stacking

them away in a hole. All round him, his friends were busy on the same job.

Now it happened that a grasshopper had been watching the ant who had spoken.

'Hey, you!' called out the grasshopper.

'Are you speaking to me?' asked the ant, as he hurried on another journey.

'Look at me for a minute,' said the grasshopper.

The ant shot him a quick look. 'Well?'

'You see what I'm doing, don't you,' went on the grasshopper. 'I'm doing nothing. I'm sitting here enjoying the sun – doing absolutely nothing – and it's great.'

'Good for you,' replied the ant. 'But if I did nothing now I'd pay for it later.'

'What do you mean?' asked the grasshopper.

'If you don't know that, then you're sillier than I thought,' said the ant. 'Now, if you'll excuse me, I've got work to do. Then I can sit and do nothing.'

So the day went by, the grasshopper basking in the sun, the ant working hard. The next day was very similar, and the next . . . but as the weeks went by the weather began to change. The sky clouded over, a cold wind began to cut through the trees, rain fell, and then flurries of snow came down. Winter had arrived.

Warm and contented in his home the ant ate the food he had collected in the summer and waited patiently for the weather to change again. One day he had a visitor.

'I've called to see you,' said the grasshopper.

The ant looked at his visitor. Gone was the confident creature who had poked fun at him back in July for working. Now the grasshopper was shaking with cold and looked and sounded very miserable.

'It's nice of you to visit me,' said the ant, 'but what is it you want?'

'Food!' cried the grasshopper. 'All that food you stacked away in the summer. I can't get any and I'm starving. Please let me have some of your food.'

'I'm sorry,' said the ant, 'but I've just been checking my supplies and I've got just enough to see me through the winter. You should have thought about this in the summer when all you wanted to do was enjoy yourself.'

Information for the teacher

1 This is one of those old tales which can be adapted to feature different creatures or people. It can also be very easily dramatised and used in this form in an assembly preparation.

2 The most popular Biblical story in the 'Be prepared' theme is that which tells of the girls at a wedding. Five of the ten girls took spare oil so that their lamps would be certain to stay lit when the bridegroom arrived. Five didn't bother, and consequently their lamps went out and they couldn't borrow any more oil.

Hymn suggestion

Come and Praise Vol 1 'Give me oil in my lamp' No 43

Prayer

Dear God,

Please help us to help ourselves. Give us the wisdom to take care and make preparations, and not to rely on other people to get out of difficulties which have come about through our own carelessness.

Amen.

75 One of Scotland's brave

Introduction

This morning's story is about a man whose bravery and determination saved the lives of every single person who was on a ship with him. This is Jim Maxwell's story.

Story

'Isn't it beautiful?'

'Look at that scenery.'

'Oh, I *am* looking forward to this trip.'

The passengers strolled round the deck of the ship pointing out the sights to each other. It was a beautiful July evening in 1827 and the ship, the *Clydesdale* had just left Scotland on its journey to Ireland.

As darkness fell, the passengers went below to their cabins to enjoy a good night's rest. Captain Turner paced the bridge, and the pilot, Jim Maxwell, stood at the wheel, guiding the ship through the night.

It was when the ship was about halfway on its journey that both captain and pilot became aware of a familiar and terrifying smell.

'Something's burning,' said Captain Turner.

'You're right, Skipper,' replied Maxwell.

'Keep her on course for Ireland,' ordered the captain, and went in search of the smell.

He didn't have to look very far. When he reached the top of the engine room ladder, he not only felt a blast of hot air but he also saw the first flames begin to burn the starboard side of the ship.

'Emergency!' bellowed the captain at the top of his voice. Within seconds, every member of the crew was at work fighting the flames with buckets of water. The passengers were alerted and rushed on deck to the fore part of the ship, where the flames were least likely to reach them.

'We're in desperate trouble,' thought Captain Turner. 'Our only hope is speed. If we can reach land before the boilers blow up or we're burnt to death, we have a chance.'

Now, unknown to Captain Turner, Jim Maxwell had disobeyed orders. Thinking that they would have a better chance of beaching on the familiar coasts of Scotland, he had steered the ship round on a course for home.

So began a nightmare journey. More and more of the ship was on fire despite the crew's non-stop efforts to beat back the flames. The engines became white hot with the strain the terrific speed imposed upon them, and the passengers grew more and more terrified.

The calmest man on board was Jim Maxwell. The soles of his feet began to blister with the heat coming from below decks, black smoke billowed around him, almost choking him, and his clothes began to singe as the flames licked upwards.

'Leave the wheel, man! Lash it on the course we want and get up on deck.'

Captain Turner shouted this not once but three times to the brave pilot.

'No, we need a man at the wheel to guide us in,' replied Jim.

Finally, the ship began to blaze around him and the wheel in his hands started to char and singe.

'Get some water on him,' shouted the captain.

So a chain of sailors began to pass buckets of water, and the last one threw each bucket of freezing water over the pilot's smouldering clothes. Still he held on, burnt hands gripping the wheel as bucket after bucket of water crashed over him, keeping the roaring flames back for a few seconds each time.

'Land!' cried one of the passengers suddenly. 'Land! Land!'

Sure enough, the familiar outline of the Scottish coast came clearly into view as the doomed ship raced ahead. A huge crowd on the shore gasped in horror as the floating inferno surged towards them.

'They'll never make it.'

'She'll blow up any second.'

'I wonder how many have died already?'

With his eyes fixed firmly on the coast ahead Jim steered the ship towards a shallow beach. Then, with a screaming of timber on the stony shore, the bows of the *Clydesdale* ground to a sudden stop. At once the people on the shore rushed to help the terrified passengers and exhausted crew. Jim Maxwell was found slumped unconscious over his burning wheel, and tender hands rushed him ashore and to hospital.

After some weeks there, he made a full recovery and returned to his work on ships. Thanks to his courage and determination not a single life had been lost on the *Clydesdale*, and he had become one of the most famous men in Scotland.

'Just doing my job,' was all this modest, brave man would say about the night he steered the blazing ship to safety.

Information for the teacher

1 The *Clydesdale* was bound for the west coast of Ireland, having just left the Clyde, when this incident occurred. When Jim Maxwell's story became known a public subscription was opened for him.

2 Useful addresses are: Royal National Lifeboat Institution, West Quay Road, Poole, Dorset D15 1HZ, www.rnli.org.uk and the FireNet web site www.fire.org.uk

Hymn suggestion

Come and Praise Vol 1 'A man for all people' No 27

Prayer

Let us think this morning about the courage of people like Jim Maxwell. Let us remember, too, the support people need in difficult situations. Give us the strength to be always someone who will 'lend a hand'.

76 What can I do to help?

Introduction

Have you ever noticed how often we make excuses about things? 'I'm too busy to do that ... What good could I do? ... I'm not clever enough to do that ...' and so on. This morning's story is about a man who used his time, energy and talents to help others.

Story

It was a summer's evening and the man was watching a programme on television. He was comfortable and well fed, but the children he saw on the television screen were starving and crying. They were living in a country called Ethiopia, where the weather was so dry that families couldn't grow enough crops to keep themselves alive.

'These people need help,' thought the man to himself, 'and there must be thousands of others like them who also need help. Now what can I do that would be useful?'

This man was a musician so, with some friends, he wrote a song. Then he got some more friends to help him make a record of the song. By the time all this had happened it was getting near to Christmas.

This was just what the man wanted because the song was called 'Do they know it's Christmas?' and he hoped lots of people would buy the record. He was right. The song told of the suffering of people in Africa and it sold millions of copies all over the world.

'Now I must use the money to help those starving children,' thought the man. So he started a fund called Band Aid and he went to Africa himself to see how the money was being used to help.

'Well, it's certainly helping,' thought the man, 'but they need so much! I must organise something else to get more money to help.'

This time he had a brilliant idea. What if he held a huge pop concert, got lots of stars to sing and play at it – and then used all the profits to help those desperate people in Africa? Better still – what if he held *two* pop concerts ...

So the man started to work really hard again. He hired Wembley Stadium in London, and the John F Kennedy Stadium in Philadelphia, USA. Between them these two stadiums could hold a hundred and sixty thousand people! Next he started to organise the groups and stars to sing at the concerts, and finally he booked the date – 13th July.

'I must think of a special name for these concerts,' thought the man. 'I think a good name could be ... Live Aid.'

So the two huge concerts were held. Each stadium was packed and the events were broadcast throughout the world. As well as the singing, the huge screens showed scenes from Africa when there was a pause in the music. The whole thing was a tremendous success and the staggering sum of forty million pounds was raised.

With this money the man got ships to take food to Africa and lorries to carry it further, right to where it was needed most. Thanks to him, thousands and thousands of lives were saved. The man's name was Bob Geldof.

Information for the teacher

1   Bob Geldof started this work in 1984. The Live Aid concerts were held on 13th July 1985. His further work included a cookery book (the *Food Aid Cookery Book*) and Sport Aid (May 1986) which included many sponsored running events.

2   One common link between major religious figures is the help they gave to others.

3   Several useful quotations can be used in advocating help for others and making sure that we are not 'insensible to other men's needs' (Job).

   'Don't refuse to help the poor ... deny the hungry ... be mean to those who need money.' (Adapted from Ecclesiasticus 4)

   'He is best loved who does most good to other creatures.' (Islamic proverb)

   'Give a man a fish and you feed him for a day. Teach a man to fish and you feed him for life.' (Confucius)

   'Let us learn to give and not to count the cost.' (St Ignatius)

4   In view of the titles of the organisations inspired by Bob Geldof a definition of 'Aid' may be useful: 'to render assistance to; promote the success of; assist; help; succour'. (Funk and Wagnall)

5   A useful parallel to this story could be the work of Mother Teresa. Born in Yugoslavia in 1910, she went to India in 1948 to be a teacher. She was so shocked by conditions there that she spent the rest of her life seeking to improve them. Her 'Prayer for Peace' has been translated into over four hundred languages, and in 1979 she was awarded the Nobel Peace prize.

Hymn suggestion

Come and Praise Vol 2 'Bread for the world' No 75

Prayer

Let us give thanks this morning for the energy and determination of people like Bob Geldof who, when they see a need, do something about it.

77 Rumours

Introduction

Sometimes, particularly when people get excited, they say things which they are not certain are true. They say them as if they were, though – and that's how 'rumours' start.

Story

The hare was a very nervous creature, always fearing the worst.

'I wonder what dreadful thing is going to happen today?' he said to himself one morning. 'What a worry life is! What's that?'

Just beyond the bushes where he was crouching there was a heavy, soft thud.

'It's the ... it's the earth falling in! The end of the world! The earth is falling in!'

Racing off as fast as he could, the hare fled. He hadn't gone very far before he bumped into a deer – another nervous creature.

'What is it?' asked the deer anxiously.

'Run!' said the hare. 'There's danger everywhere ... it's the earth ...'

At once the deer started running in panic. When he reached a pack of buffalo he called out. 'Hurry, run for your lives!'

Hearing the panic in the deer's voice, the buffaloes thought it would be better to be safe than sorry. They started to pick up speed in a dusty gallop.

Everywhere the rumour spread: danger – run for your life. Boars, tigers, even elephants moved uneasily and quickly in the hare's path.

Eventually the rumour reached the lion. When he heard that everything had started with the hare he set out to find him.

'Now look here,' said the lion when he had stopped the running animals, 'tell me exactly what happened.'

'The earth,' gasped the hare, 'is breaking up. I heard it. We must get away!'

'What did you hear?' went on the lion.

'A terrible thud – terrible – just like the earth breaking.'

Well, the lion continued to question the hare until he decided that he had heard enough.

'Right,' he said, 'now get on my back and take me to exactly where this happened. You other animals – I want you to wait here until we get back.'

The huge crowd of animals shifted about nervously while the lion ran back to the clump of bushes where it had all started. The hare, clinging to his back, was terrified. Eventually they reached the bushes – and there, lying on the ground, was a huge, heavy fruit. It had fallen behind the bushes where the hare had been sitting.

'There,' said the lion, 'that's what you heard – that heavy fruit falling to the ground.'

The hare looked down shamefacedly. 'I'm ... I'm sorry for all the trouble I caused,' he said.

'Well, I think you've learned a lesson,' went on the lion. 'Now you've got to go back and tell the other animals exactly what happened.'

Information for the teacher

1   In this old story the lion is meant to represent the Buddha who had been reborn in this new guise to give the sort of advice to the animal world which he had already given to humans.

2   The idea of rumours and the confusion they can generate is one which can be readily followed up with children as they have an almost innate grasp of this subject! This can lead on to a more serious consideration of telling the truth, particularly in the context of human relationships, and although this is a story with a Buddhist background an African proverb is a useful reminder here:

> A word is like water.
> Once spilled it cannot be gathered again.

Hymn suggestion

Come and Praise Vol 2 'A still small voice' No 96

Prayer

Dear God,

Help us to remember how much harm we can do by using the wrong words. Teach us to speak with truth, kindness and consideration so that what we say never causes any trouble or hurt to anyone else.

Amen.

78 Enough for everybody

Introduction

The end of the summer term in school is an exciting time. There are sports days and class outings and everybody looks forward to these. This morning's story is about a class trip.

Story

'It's going to be great.'

'All those trees that we can climb after the picnic.' 'And there's a boating lake too . . .'

'. . . and Miss Jennings says we can get boats out if we like.'

Class 5 was full of excitement. It was the morning of the class trip. The register had been called, the coach was waiting at the end of the lane and Mrs Waters and Mr Brown, the helpers, had taken all the picnic stuff along already.

'All right, get in twos and calm down.'

Miss Jennings looked completely different in her jeans and with her hair tied back in a ponytail – but Class 5 still knew when it was time to stop messing about.

Half an hour later, the coach was cruising along the motorway heading for Marefield Forest. The sun glinted through the windows, nobody felt sick and in ten minutes they would be there!

Sure enough the coach pulled into the carpark right on time. There was only one other coach there.

'Right,' said Miss Jennings. 'Now, every group has got two hours to do their activity. Those who are going boating will be with Mrs Waters; the Nature Trail people are with Mr Brown.'

Miss Jennings went on briskly to tell everybody where they would be and who they would be with.

'At exactly twelve o'clock,' she said finally, 'everybody will come back to the little clearing which is marked on your maps. There is never anybody there so we'll have the place to ourselves for our splendid picnic.'

There was a great cheer when she said this.

Well, it was a fantastic morning. Geoff Wall tore a hole in his trousers climbing a tree, Emma Bywaters lost a shoe in the lake and Sertan Uhal found a box of ten horseshoes buried near a tree.

At twelve o'clock everybody was hungry and the leaders headed their groups back to the marked clearing. Then there was an unpleasant surprise.

'Somebody else is there.'

'It's those kids from that other school.'

'Miss Jennings said nobody else ever came here.'

'They've pinched our spot.'

'It's not fair.'

Class 5 were unhappy. They stood on the edge of the clearing watching the other schoolchildren taking all the best spots and unpacking their picnic boxes. It just wasn't fair!

Miss Jennings had just arrived and was about to speak to them when suddenly the coach driver came up and pushed his way through to her. He looked very worried.

'Is there something wrong?' asked Mrs Jennings.

'Well . . . not exactly wrong,' said the coach driver, 'But you know the helpers brought that big hamper with all the picnic stuff along the lane for me to put on the coach . . .'

'Yes,' said Miss Jennings, in an apprehensive voice.

'Well . . . I didn't.'

'You mean . . .'

'We've got no food – it's still standing on the pavement back near the school.'

It was at that moment that a teacher from the other school came up to Miss Jennings.

'I'm sorry to butt in,' he said, 'but I couldn't help overhearing and . . . we'd be very pleased to share what we have with you. Wouldn't we, kids?' he suddenly shouted to all the other children who were just about to start eating.

'YES!' came a great shout back.

Well, within five minutes Miss Jennings and this teacher had got things organised. Class 5 was split into groups and each group joined some of the children from the other school. You know what it's like in school outings – and parties: there's always too much food, so there was plenty to go round.

What's more, everybody made new friends. Miss Jennings and the teacher from the other school seemed to get on very well together, and it was great.

'Best school trip I've ever been on,' said Sertan later in the afternoon.

'You bet,' replied Geoff, 'and to think when we first saw those other kids we didn't like them.'

Information for the teacher

1   There are obvious twin themes here – one of sharing, and the other of judging people before we know them. This story could be presented in assembly by having one child read it, while the others in the class act it out.

2   All religions advocate generosity to those less fortunate. Some useful quotations are:

'Be forebearing with one another and charitable.' (Ephesians 4,2)

'A kind word counts for more than a rich present; With a generous man you will find both.' (Ecclesiasticus 18, 16–17)

3   Obviously July is an ideal month to present this assembly and its presentation could be linked to some class outing.

Hymn suggestion

Come and Praise Vol 2 'Bread for the world' No 75

Prayer

Let us think this morning about some words spoken by a famous saint. These words are: 'Let us learn to give and not to count the cost.'

Amen.

(From a prayer of St Ignatius)

79 The traveller's friend

Introduction

Often we need determination to complete a task which seems very difficult. But 'sticking at something' often brings its own reward, as this morning's story reminds us . . .

Story

The river was deep and fast-flowing and the man who sat on a stone on its banks was tall, strong and broad shouldered.

'That Christopher,' people used to say about him, 'I reckon he could carry an elephant across that river!'

They were exaggerating, of course, but they were talking about Christopher's job. This was to carry people from one side of the river to the other. There was no bridge so Christopher sat there and waited for travellers who needed to cross. Then, taking them on his back he strode out into the water and delivered them, mostly dry, to the other side.

Well, one day Christopher was sitting on his usual stone when he heard a voice behind him.

'Would you take me across, please, sir?'

Christopher looked round and saw a small boy standing there. 'Certainly young man,' he said. 'Come on, hop onto my back.'

'This is an easy one,' thought Christopher to himself, 'this lad is as light as a feather – I wish they were all like this.'

So saying, the ferryman stepped into the fast-moving water and, feeling his feet crunch on the familiar stones, set off for the other side. It must have been when he was nearly halfway across that he felt the weight on his back suddenly begin to get heavier ... and heavier.

'I can't ... I can't understand it,' he gasped.

The weight was now almost unbearable. Christopher felt as if his legs were being forced down into the river bed. Sweat poured down his face and he gritted his teeth with the enormous effort he was making.

Finally, with the last drain of his strength, Christopher reached the other side of the river and collapsed exhausted onto the bank. Unable to understand what had happened, he heard the child's voice speaking to him.

'You have done well, my friend. My name is Jesus, and, you see, you were not only carrying me but the weight of all things people do wrong in the world as well. You don't need telling what a terrible weight that is.'

Information for the teacher

1   St Christopher's Day is 25th July and he died on this day some-time in the third century. He was supposedly a man of immense strength – 'twelve cubits in length' – and after this episode left

the river to be baptised and become a Christian. He was martyred for his faith during the reign of the Emperor Decius.

2   St Christopher is the patron saint of travellers. A famous wood-cutting depicting the incident of the story, and dating from 1423, has inscribed on it that whoever views the picture will be safe for the day.

Hymn suggestion

Come and Praise Vol 1 'Travel on' No 42

Prayer

Dear God,

Let us pray this morning for all those who are about to set off on journeys. May they be protected from all dangers and arrive safely at their destinations. Amen.

80 The pattern

Introduction

All our lives have a pattern to them, but it is what we do which often helps to decide what the pattern is. In July many eleven-year-old children leave their junior schools for the last time, ready to go to secondary schools in the autumn. This is part of life's pattern.

Story

Wayne was fed up.

'I don't want to leave Brookfield,' he said. 'I like it here and I don't want to go to that big secondary school in Charters Lane. It's a dump.'

None of the others in Mr Haine's class bothered much when Wayne said this. Although they all liked him, he wasn't very good at much. They were all looking forward to making new friends, learning French and having a zippy new uniform.

'It'll be great, Wayne.'

'We can't play rugby at this school.'

'I hear the drama club is really good there,' said Debbie Clark who happened to hear what they were talking about.

'Hmm,' muttered Wayne.

Now, although Wayne wasn't good at much at school, he did try hard and he knew what he wanted to be.

'Just like Dad – that's what,' he would say to himself.

Mr Dawkins, Wayne's Dad, was a motor mechanic and Wayne used to watch for hours as his Dad changed starter motors, adjusted points and cleaned oil filters.

'Hello Wayne,' said Mrs Dawkins when her son got home that afternoon.

'Hello, Mum. Where's Dad?'

'Need you ask?'

Wayne grinned. Dad was rebuilding an old Morris Minor in the garage at the bottom of the garden. Every spare minute he was down there.

When Wayne got to the garage his dad was bent over the re-built engine of the car. The bonnet was up and he was making some fine adjustment.

'Hello, son.'

'Dad, I don't want to go to the secondary school. It's a dump and they reckon there are bullies there and . . .'

Mr Dawkins straightened up and wiped his hands with an oily rag.

'Come here, son,' he said. 'Now look at this engine – there are the new plugs I've put in, the fan belt is tightened perfectly, the carburettor is cleaned out, there's petrol in the tank – but as it is at the moment the whole thing is no good to anybody. Now watch.'

Mr Dawkins squeezed past Wayne and got into the driver's seat. With a twist of the ignition key, he started the engine, and then came back and stood beside his son. They looked at the engine which had now come to life. It throbbed and the parts moved efficiently.

'See what I mean?' said Dad, but Wayne looked puzzled. 'An engine's a bit like a life – all the parts are there, but until they're working smoothly together it's no good. Going to secondary school is a bit like that. It's a part we have to do – and do as well as we can – and then it goes towards making our lives run like this engine is doing.'

Wayne had never thought about it like that. Suddenly he felt completely different. Of course he wanted to go to secondary school – how could he ever be a motor mechanic if he didn't?

Information for the teacher

1   This story is obviously end-of-term material with a bias towards those children who will be leaving the school at this time.

2   Two useful quotations might be:

'Idle hands make a man poor; busy hands grow rich.' (Proverbs 10, 4)

'One man wins success by his words; another gets his due reward by the work of his hands.' (Proverbs 12, 14)

Hymn suggestion

Come and Praise Vol 1 'The journey of life' No 45

Prayer

Let us pray this morning for all those who will be going to new schools in September. Let us hope that they find friendship and opportunity there and enjoy and benefit from both. Amen.

Anniversaries, facts, fancies, anecdotes and religious notes

Many assemblies can be developed from the fertile ground suggested by the above title. This section aims to provide a selection of such starting material.

Introduction

Much of the information here will serve as source material for locally-developed assemblies. Where a particular event can be linked to an assembly (or assemblies) already detailed in this book, then there is an appropriate reference to aid teacher planning.

A note about the various calendars which govern the festivals of different faiths is important. *The Gregorian calendar*, which is solar-based and used in most western countries, enables most festivals related to this to be fixed. An exception is Easter, which is a movable feast. *The Jewish calendar* is lunar-based and to adjust it to the solar year an extra (embolismic) month is added seven times in each nineteen-year period. *The Islamic calendar* is lunar-based without adjustment, which means that Muslim festivals advance by some eleven to twelve days each year. More than one calendar has been in use in India.

The impact for teachers of these calendar fluctuations is that an annual plan of great religious festivals can only be accurately made by reference to the relevant current calendars. Otherwise it is a question of moving source material about as appropriate.

September

1st   Feast Day of St Giles, patron saint of handicapped people. A day remembered in Ireland for the death of Patrick O'Bryen (1806). At 8 feet 5 inches in height, he was one of the tallest men who ever lived.

       Edgar Rice Burroughs, creator of Tarzan, was born in 1875.

2nd   On this date in 1752 Britain adopted the Gregorian calendar. The Great Fire of London began in the bakery belonging to a man called Farryner, who lived in Pudding Lane.

3rd   Because the Gregorian calendar was adopted, eleven days were 'removed' from the calendar. This caused riots because people thought eleven days were being taken from their lives.

Louis Sullivan, the architect who designed skyscrapers, was born in 1856.

Sinking of the 'Delaware' in 1863. (Link – Assembly 10)

4th   In 1567 Queen Elizabeth I allowed two Flemish merchants to work in England, and teach Englishmen their skill of glass-making.

In 1909 the first Boy Scout Rally was held in London.

5th   Count Barowloski died near Durham in 1837. He was ninety-six years old and had never grown to three feet high.

St Laurence Justinian, the patron saint of Venice, died in 1455.

6th   The 'Mayflower' sailed from Plymouth in 1620. Seventy-four men and twenty-eight women were on board. (Link – Assembly 1)

7th   In 1533 Henry VIII's wife Anne Boleyn gave birth to a daughter – Elizabeth.

8th   In 695 a monk supposedly heard angels singing and when he asked why they were celebrating he was told that this was the anniversary of the birth of Mary, mother of Jesus.

9th   In 1835 the 'sport' of bear baiting was banned by parliament.

In 1754 William Bligh, Captain of the 'Bounty', was born.

10th   William the Conqueror died in 1087.

Scape Goat Day: a traditional Jewish custom was that a goat was let loose in the desert on this day. This was the 'scape goat' and it carried with it all the sins of the people. (Link – Assembly 3)

11th   Death of Roger Crab in 1680. (Link – Assembly 1)

A famous quotation was supposedly written by Benjamin Franklin on this day in 1773: 'There was never a good war or a bad peace.'

12th   John Alden, the last of the 'Mayflower' Pilgrim Fathers, died in 1687.

13th   The Catholic Annual of this date in 1830 carried a health warning about eating only ripe, and moderate quantities of autumnal fruit at this time of the year. (Link – Assembly 4)

14th   Holy Rood Day. Rood is another word for cross and traditionally on this day children were freed from school and work so that they could gather nuts.

The actual cross on which Jesus was crucified was supposedly found by St Helena. To commemorate this, her son, Constantine, built a great church in Jerusalem and it was opened on this date in 335 with the ceremony of the Exaltation of the Holy Cross. The annual custom has endured.

Robert Raikes, founder of Sunday Schools, was born in 1735.

15th   The Liverpool–Manchester railway was opened in 1830.

This was the date in ancient Rome when the Circensian Games were held annually. An imitation of the Greek Olympic Games, the main event was the pentathlon – leaping, wrestling, throwing, boxing and racing on foot and by chariot.

Battle of Britain Day, commemorating the RAF's victory in 1940. (Link – Assembly 6)

16th   The German inventor of the thermometer, Gabriel Fahrenheit, died in 1736.

17th   The first person ever to be killed in an aeroplane accident died in 1908. This happened in America and his name was Thomas Selfridge. (Link – Assembly 24)

Sir Francis Chichester, solo round-the-world sailor, was born in 1901.

18th   Peter Sellers, one of Britain's funniest actors, was born in 1925.

The Emperor Domitian was a ruler of such cruelty that he had polished stones planted on all his walks. These acted like mirrors so that he could see if his many enemies were about to attack him. He was killed by his 'friends' on this date. (Link – Assemblies 21, 22)

Dr Johnson was born in 1709.

19th   Dr Barnardo died in 1905.

Mickey Mouse featured in his first cartoon in 1928.

An old Derbyshire belief is that a storm on this date means that the winter will be mild.

George Cadbury, chocolate maker and philanthropist, was born in 1839.

20th Eton School was founded by Henry VI in 1440.

Muhammad (pbuh) changed the name of the city of Yathrib to Medina.

Rahere, court jester and founder of St Bartholomew's hospital in London, died in 1144.

Jacob Grimm, fairytale writer, died in 1863.

21st This is St Matthew's Day. An ex-tax collector and disciple of Jesus, he died in the first century. By the time of his death his writings had become more prolific than any other gospel chronicle. It was said he used an angel's feather to write the first gospel, and his name is linked to many old sayings, for example, 'St Matthew's Day sends sap into the tree.'

22nd This is the date on which, in 286, the Emperor Maximian ordered the death of one of his generals and an entire section of his army because they refused to give up their Christian beliefs. So died St Maurice and six thousand, six hundred soldiers.

Michael Faraday, the scientist who invented the first dynamo to make electricity, was born in 1791.

23rd Today is St Thecla's Day. For refusing to give up her Christian belief, she was sentenced to be killed by wild beasts. They became calm in her presence, however, and wouldn't do her any injury. She died peacefully during the first century.

24th Traditionally this was the day on which harvesting began in medieval England:

> Harvest home, harvest home,
> We have ploughed, we have sowed,
> We have reaped, we have mowed,
> We have brought home every load,
> Hip, hip, hip, harvest home, hurrah!
> (*Link – Assembly 4*)

25th Samuel Pepys wrote in his diary in 1660 that this was the date on which he drank his first ever cup of tea.

26th In 1580 Sir Francis Drake and his fleet returned to England after taking great treasure from Spain.

The 'Queen Mary', then the world's greatest ship, was launched at Clydebank in 1934. A crowd of 200,000 watched King George V and Queen Mary perform the launching ceremony.

27th A woman was arrested for smoking a cigarette in a car in New York in 1905.

The world's first passenger railway (from Stockton to Darlington) opened in 1825.

28th Louis Pasteur died in 1885. He was the French scientist who introduced 'pasteurisation'.

This date is Michaelmas Eve, a time of nut-cracking amongst medieval church congregations, and one of those rare occasions when master and men were considered equal.

29th St Michael's Day, or Michaelmas Day. The Archangel Michael killed Lucifer the traitor angel and his feast day was very significant in the England of former years.

On this day rents were due and for those who couldn't pay, geese were often sent to landlords as presents in the hope that longer credit could be obtained.

There are many old sayings associated with the day, for example:

'The Michaelmas Daisy among dead weeds
Blooms for St Michael's valorous deeds.'

30th This was the date agricultural labourers (after 1351 and the Statute of Labourers) sought new jobs for the following year at market town fairs. (*Link – Assembly 7*)

The foundation stone of Nelson's Column was laid in 1840.

In 1846 the first tooth extraction under anaesthetic was performed.

Religious notes

Harvest Festival is usually celebrated in schools at the end of September and work in this book is aimed at this time.

September is also the month when the Hindu festival of Janam Ashtami could be considered. This festival celebrates the birth of Lord Krishna. The day before is one of fasting and prayer and a time when special sweets are put in images of Lord Krishna as a baby in a cradle.

Because of the many sides to Krishna's character – hero, people's champion, enjoyer of life – he is a very popular Hindu figure. As well as prayers, there are songs and plays about the great adventures of his life. The latter are told in the epic story, the *Mahabharata*.

The teachings of Lord Krishna are recorded in the *Bhagavad Gita*, which means 'Song of the Blessed Lord'. An example is:

'He who offers to me with devotion only a loaf, or a flower, or a fruit, or even a little water, this I accept from that yearning soul, because with a pure heart it was offered with love.' (9:26)

Jews observe Succoth, the Feast of the Tabernacles, at this time of the year. Similar to the Christian Harvest Festival, it is a time of family celebration in specially-created temporary buildings, usually set in gardens.

The Old Testament sets the guidelines for this festival:

'Thou shalt observe the Feast of the Tabernacles seven days after thou hast gathered in thy corn and wine – and thou shalt rejoice in thy feast, thou, and thy son, and thy daughter, and thy manservant, and thy maidservant, and the stranger.'

October

1st Traditionally this was the date on which the English pudding season started. These were filled with steak, leeks, mushrooms, spices and some were cooked for as long as sixteen hours.

Paul Dukas ('The Sorcerer's Apprentice') was born in 1865.

Lord Shaftesbury, social reformer, died in 1885.

2nd Mahatma Gandhi, Indian leader, was born in 1869.

Aristotle died in 322 BC.

A curious custom takes place at Braughing in Hertfordshire on this date. Church bells are rung initially in a solemn manner, and then joyfully.

This is to commemorate Matthew Wall, a sixteenth-century farmer who was on the way to his funeral when the coffin was dropped. Wall, who had been mistaken for dead, recovered consciousness in the fall, and was released from the coffin.

3rd In 1754, a French nobleman won a wager that he could ride from Fontainebleau to Paris in less than two hours. He completed the forty-two mile journey in just over one-and-a-half hours, but the horses he used died from overexertion. (*Link – Assembly 9*)

4th St Francis of Assisi died in 1226. Up to the age of twenty-five Francis was a wastrel. A serious illness changed this. He became a Christian and, much to the annoyance of his rich father, gave away large sums of money to the needy. (*Link – Assembly 11*) He wore only the poorest of clothes and lived frugally. Impressed by his devotion, many people became followers. Known as Franciscans, they too practised self-denial.

5th In 1930 the great British airship R101 crashed into a hillside at Beauvais, in France.

6th Thor Heyerdahl, explorer and leader of the Kon-Tiki expedition, was born in 1914.

W K Kellogg, inventor of corn flakes, died in 1951.

7th This was the date on which the famous diarist John Evelyn recorded a significant visit in 1644. This was to a galley in the harbour at Marseilles. Here he saw galley slaves double-chained about their waist and legs, in couples, and made fast to their seats '. . . commanded by cruel and imperious seamen'.

8th In 622 the prophet Muhammad entered Medina on a camel.

A strange duel took place in Paris on this date in 1361. A man called Macaire was suspected of having murdered another man called de Montidier. Unfortunately the only witness was de Montidier's dog. The king decided that a duel should be fought between dog and suspected murderer. During the course of this, so determined was the dog to seek retribution for its master's death, that Macaire confessed to the murder.

9th The famous district of Montmartre in Paris is particularly significant today. In 272 St Denis, patron saint of France and first Bishop of Paris, was beheaded for his beliefs. He is said to have carried his own head after the execution. The place where this occurred was called the 'mountain of the martyrs', or Montmartre.

Camille Saint-Saëns (composer of 'Carnival of the Animals') was born in 1835.

10th Lord Nuffield, car manufacturer and philanthropist, was born in 1877. (*Link – Assembly 8*)

11th Sir George William, founder of the YMCA, was born in 1821.

This is the day after which it is supposedly unlucky to gather blackberries. Thrown out of heaven by St Michael, Satan fell in a blackberry bush on 11th October and put a curse on the bush.

12th Elizabeth Fry, reformer of English prisons, died in 1845.

This is Christopher Columbus day in South America. In the USA it is celebrated on the second Monday in October.

13th Margaret Thatcher, former Prime Minister, was born in 1925.

The Roman festival of Fontinalia – water worshipping – took place annually on this date.

14th King Harold was killed at the Battle of Hastings in 1066.

The *Literary Digest* of 14th October 1899, carried some comment on the 'horseless carriage' saying that ... 'it will never, of course, come into as common use as the bicycle.' (*Link – Assemblies 8, 9*)

Martin Luther King was awarded the Nobel Peace Prize in 1964.

15th P G Wodehouse, author and creator of Jeeves and Wooster, was born in 1881.

Florence Nightingale was appointed to organise the military hospital at Scutari in the Crimea in 1854.

16th This was the date of John Brown's stand against slavery in the Battle of Harper's Ferry in 1859. Seizing the army base there, he thought that nearby slaves would rush to help. They didn't and he was executed. Slavery was only abolished in the USA after the Civil War.

'John Brown's body lies a-mouldering in the grave,
But his soul goes marching on.'

17th This is St Audrey's Day. The daughter of an East Anglian king, Audrey was famous for her good works in the seventh century.

18th St Luke's Day. As one of the most talented of Jesus' followers, Luke was a practising doctor and artist as well as the writer of a gospel. He was crucified in the year 63 in Syria. (*Link – Assembly 12*)

19th   Jonathan Swift, author of *Gulliver's Travels*, died in 1745.

20th   Grace Darling, lifeboat heroine, died in 1842. In 1838, along with her father, she saved the lives of nine people from the disintegrating ship 'Forfarshire' off the coast of Northumberland. She was awarded several medals but was only twenty-seven when she died of consumption. (*Link – Assemblies 2, 5*)

Christopher Wren, architect, was born in 1622.

In 1822 the first issue of *The Sunday Times* appeared.

21st   Nelson was killed at the Battle of Trafalgar on this date in 1805. The battle lasted four hours and the admiral was killed by a musket bullet.

Thomas Edison invented the light bulb in 1879.

22nd   The first successful parachute jump was made from a balloon on this date in 1797. The event took place in Paris and the parachutist was Andres Jacques.

23rd   This is the birthday of Pele (1940), the only footballer ever to score a thousand goals in first class matches.

24th   Cranberries were brought to England by voyagers returning from America in 1667. King Charles II was said to have liked them very much.

United Nations Day since 1946.

25th   The Battle of Agincourt took place in 1415. Henry V's army of thirty thousand defeated one hundred thousand Frenchmen. In Shakespeare's *Henry V* the reference to this victory on St Crispin's Day is significant.
   St Crispin was martyred by the Emperor Maximilian in 287. He preached his beliefs during the day and earned his living by making shoes at night. Thus, apart from the literary references, he is also the patron saint of cobblers, and perhaps long-distance walkers because . . .

Dear Saint, the saint of those who make good shoes,
Thee for my patron saint I also choose;
Where'er I walk in highway, trail or street,
Bring thou unblistered home my grateful feet.

In 1854 the Charge of the Light Brigade took place in the Crimean War.

26th Igor Sikorsky, inventor of the helicopter, died in 1972.

The Football Association was founded in 1863.

27th Captain James Cook, the explorer, was born in 1728.

28th Alfred the Great died in 901.

The Statue of Liberty was unveiled in New York in 1886.

29th Sir Walter Raleigh, explorer and seaman, died in 1618.

30th A minor planet, Hermes, just missed a collision with the earth, which would have destroyed both, in 1937.

Jean Henri Dunant, founder of the Red Cross, died in 1910.

31st The heathen festival of Hallowe'en was taken over by Christians for a threefold commemoration of Christian dead on All Hallows' Eve (31st) followed by All Hallows' Day and All Souls' Day.

Religious notes

The Jewish Festival of Rosh Hashanah takes place in the Jewish month of Tishri, which occurs in autumn.

This festival celebrates God's creation of the world; Abraham's sacrifice of a ram instead of his son; God as judge as well as creator; the need for atonement before God. Jewish years are calculated from Rosh Hashanah – thus it is also a new year celebration.

The Torah says: 'In the seventh month, on the first day of the month, shall be a solemn rest unto you, a memorial gathered with a blast of horns . . .'

The festival is started by the blowing of the sofar (ram's horn), which is a reminder of Abraham's sacrifice. Apples and bread are dipped in honey and eaten in the hope that this will bring a 'sweet' new year. New Year cards are sent to friends and relatives. These contain good wishes – *L'Shanah Torah Tikatevu*.

Despite the seriousness of the festival, it is not a time of gloom because it emphasises God's forgiveness and love. The festival builds up to Yom Kippur (The Day of Atonement), which is the holiest day of the Jewish year, and continuous prayers are said in the synagogue during this day.

Dashara is a Hindu festival which in some parts of India commemorates Rama's victory over Ravanna, whilst in others it is mainly concerned with the worship of the goddess Durga. The main day of the latter festival is Durga Puja. During the celebrations, clay statues of the goddess are made and treated with great respect and honour. After Durga Puja, the last day of the festival, they are symbolically thrown into the river – recognising the fact that the goddess will now have left these temporary homes.

November

1st   All Saints' Day. Saints are people of all ages and backgrounds who have achieved sainthood by being exceptional Christians. Two requirements were laid down for sainthood by Pope Innocent III in 1199: first, that the person concerned should have lived a life of inspiring virtue and second, performed miracles after his or her death.

An interesting aside to All Saints' Day is that it was customary amongst better-off families in the sixteenth century to present an apostle's spoon to a child at his baptism. This spoon had the figure of the child's patron saint carved on its handle.

2nd   This is the day when the Christian church remembers all its members who have died. A possible link is with Chinese Buddhists who also set aside a day for remembering – and helping – the dead. Of particular concern are homeless spirits without descendants, for whom large paper boats are burned to help them across the 'seas of hunger and thirst'.

This was the date in 1936 when the BBC's first television service began. (*Link – Assembly 18*)

3rd   This being the month associated with saints, this date is the one on which St Winefride is remembered. Killed for her beliefs in the fifth century, a well of pure water is supposed to have sprung up on the spot where she died.

4th   Felix Mendelssohn died in 1847.

5th   'Now boys with squibs and crackers play,
        And bonfires' blaze turns night to day.'
                                        (*Poor Robin's Almanack*)

The plot to kill King James I in 1605 was hatched because of his supposedly unfair treatment of Catholics. Robert Catesby was the mastermind and Guy Fawkes the plotter designated to light the fuse to the gunpowder which would have blown up the Houses of Parliament.

A traitor betrayed the plot and the conspirators were all executed by 1606.

An interesting piece of trivia is that at St Peter's School in York, bonfires are lit there but never is a 'guy' burned. Guy Fawkes was an old boy of the school.

6th   In 1893 Peter Tchaikovsky, composer, died.

7th   Marie Curie was born in 1867.

The River Thames flood barrier was completed in 1982. It took eight years to complete at a cost of four hundred and fifty million pounds.

8th   In 1922 Dr Barnard, the heart transplant surgeon, was born. (*Link – Assembly 19*)

9th   The first motor bike was ridden in 1885.

10th   Thirteen-year-old Fritz Kreisler (born in Vienna) made his American debut as a concert violinist on this date in 1888.

11th   St Martin's Day. Martin, Bishop of Tours, died in 397. Perhaps best known for the story of the torn cloak, the fragment of the cloak given to the beggar was preserved as one of France's most holy relics.

This was also the date on which the Armistice was signed to end the First World War in 1918. Millions of men lost their lives in this conflict and as a permanent memorial to them the Menin Gate in Ypres, Belgium, was engraved with the names of fifty thousand men who have no known graves.

Traffic through this gate is halted every evening whilst the 'Last Post' is played on a bugle.

12th   King Canute died in 1035. The story of the limit of his powers (being unable to control the incoming tide) is still an effective one with children. (*Link – Assembly 17*)

13th   Robert Louis Stevenson was born in 1850.

14th   Prince Charles was born in 1948.

Medzhid Agayer died in the USSR. He was one hundred and forty-three.

15th St Albert's Day. He died in Germany in 1280 and was considered one of the greatest scholars who had ever lived.

16th The Suez Canal, one hundred miles long, was opened in 1869, after ten years of work.

Jack Sheppard, the infamous highwayman, was hanged in 1724.

17th One of Britain's most famous generals, Monty, or Field Marshall Viscount Montgomery of Alamein, was born in 1887.

18th This was the date, in 1963, on which the Dartford Road Tunnel was opened. This allows traffic to drive under the River Thames between Essex and Kent. (*Link – Assembly 8*)

The UK premier of the record breaking film *Titanic* on this date in 1997. It grossed over one billion dollars world-wide.

19th In 1703 a prisoner died in the Bastille prison in France. He had been imprisoned for over twenty years, wore a velvet mask at all times and was mostly in solitary confinement. Later the subject of a famous book (*The Man in the Iron Mask* by Alexandre Dumas), the identity of the prisoner was shrouded in mystery. One supposition was that he was a criminal who looked so much like the king of France that he had to be masked.

20th Princess Elizabeth (now Queen Elizabeth II) was married in 1947.

21st The balloon designed by the Montgolfier brothers first flew in 1783. It attained a height of three thousand feet.

'Schinderhannes' died in 1803. He was the German Robin Hood.

22nd St Cecilia's Day. The patron saint of music, Cecilia was martyred in 230.

The SOS call sign was adopted internationally: 'Mayday' comes from *m'aidez* (French for 'Help me'). (*Link – Assembly 17*)

23rd St Clement's Day. Clement was an early Pope who was put to death by being thrown into the sea tied to an anchor. Because anchors were made by blacksmiths, he became their patron saint.

24th   In 1815 Grace Darling, heroine of the famous sea rescue, was born.

25th   St Catherine's Day. Catherine was a fourth-century martyr.

In 1823 the first pier was opened – Brighton.

8am, 25/11/1872 was the last entry in the log book of the 'Marie Celeste', a ship found sailing in the Atlantic with no one on board.

26th   The first Thanksgiving Day was held in the USA on this date in 1789. The original cause for Thanksgiving was the harvesting of the first crops by the Pilgrim Fathers in 1621.

27th   The first policewomen (Misses Allen and Harburn) started their duties in Grantham in 1914.

28th   Enid Blyton died in 1968. Her books for children have sold over fifty million copies and have been translated into one hundred and sixty-five languages.

Margaret Thatcher resigned as Prime Minister on this date in 1990. After eleven years at No. 10 Downing Street she was the longest serving Prime Minister since the 1820s.

29th   Concorde first flew in 1969. The agreement for its English–French joint development was signed on this date in 1962.

30th   St Andrew's Day. The brother of Peter, Andrew was a missionary in the Middle East until his crucifixion on this date in 70 AD.

There is an interesting 'weather saying' associated with this date: 'As November, so is the following March.'

Religious notes

One of the movable feasts which occurs in this month is Guru Nanak's birthday.

Chanukah, the Jewish Festival of Light, and a celebration often linked with Diwali and Christmas in primary school RE themes, also occurs at this time of the year.

From a Christian viewpoint, the significance of All Saints' Day has already been mentioned and, at the end of the month, thoughts of Christmas are stirred by the arrival of Advent. This begins on the nearest Sunday to 30th November.

Advent Sunday is the beginning of the Christian church's year, except in the Greek church where it begins on 11th November, St Martin's Day.

December

1st   St Eligius, a French Bishop, died in 659. He is memorable because he is the patron saint of so many groups of people ... goldsmiths, blacksmiths, miners, locksmiths, clock makers, carriage makers, tool makers, cab drivers, farmers and jockeys!

2nd   The rebuilt St Paul's Cathedral was dedicated in 1697.

3rd   1962 was one of the worst winters ever recorded in England. On this date fog paralysed London for four days and one hundred and six people died as a consequence. (*Link – Assembly 20*)

4th   In 1957 severe fog also contributed to a railway accident at Lewisham, in south London, in which ninety people were killed. (*Link – Assembly 19*)

5th   Mozart died on this date in 1791 at the age of thirty-six. Ironically his last composition was a Requiem Mass.

6th   This is the Feast Day of St Nicholas, Bishop of Myra, patron saint of Russia and sailors, who died in 342. Renowned for his wisdom and generosity, Nicholas has become a figure closely associated with Santa Claus and Father Christmas.

       The reason for his connection with sailors is that in 1807 some Italian seamen from Bari brought his remains back from Myra and lodged them in a church in Bari.

7th   On the Sunday morning of this date in 1941, Japanese aircraft from six aircraft carriers attacked the United States naval fleet at Pearl Harbour. Nineteen ships were sunk or badly damaged and over two thousand men were killed.

8th   Horace, the Roman poet, was born on this day in 65 BC. Greatly admired during his lifetime, many of his sayings are ideal assembly starters.

       'No lot is in all respects happy.'

       'Once a word has been allowed to escape it cannot be recalled.'

'When your neighbour's wall is on fire it becomes your business.'

'Seize today, and put as little trust as you can in tomorrow.'

9th The first Christmas card was created on this date in England in 1842. (*Link – Assemblies 25, 26*)

Arthur Pearson died in 1921. He founded St Dunstan's Home for the Blind.

10th In 1959 the Crowther Report recommended the raising of the school leaving age to 16 in England.

Alfred Nobel, the Swedish engineer who founded the Nobel prizes, died in 1896.
The Nobel prizes are awarded annually for achievements in physics, chemistry, medicine, literature, and service to the cause of peace.

This date is Human Rights Day.

11th Hector Berlioz, the French composer, was born in 1803.

12th This was the date of Marconi's first transatlantic radio message in 1901.

Robert Browning, author of 'The Pied Piper', a valuable assembly resource, died in 1889.

13th St Lucy's Day. A native of Syracuse, St Lucy was martyred in 304. She is particularly remembered in Sweden every year in a Festival of Lights, symbolic of her aid to early Christians.

14th In 1918 women voted for the first time in a British general election.

15th Alexandre Eiffel, designer of the Eiffel Tower, was born in 1832. The tower in Paris is three hundred metres high.

16th Ludwig van Beethoven was born in 1770.

Wilhelm Grimm (one of the Grimm brothers) died in 1859. (*Link – Assembly 16*)

Camille Saint-Saëns, French composer of 'Carnival of the Animals', died in 1921.

17th In 1903 Orville Wright made the first aeroplane flight, near Kittyhawk in North Carolina, USA. He was aloft for twelve seconds and covered a distance of about forty metres. (*Link – Assembly 24*)

18th In 1865 slavery in the USA was abolished.

19th This was the date in 1981 when the tragedy of the lifeboat from Mousehole in Cornwall occurred. Trying to rescue survivors from the freighter 'Union Star', the lifeboat was fighting conditions of eighty-knot winds and twenty-metre-high waves when it sank.

20th A fish caught off Madagascar in 1952 was recognised as being of a prehistoric species, a coelacanth.

21st St Thomas's Day. Thomas spread the gospel in the Middle East and India before dying in the first century. He is the patron saint of builders.

22nd Beatrix Potter (creator of *Peter Rabbit*) died in 1943.

George Eliot died in 1880. The plot of her novel *Silas Marner* contains some parts very well suited for assembly material. 'George Eliot' was in fact Mary Ann Evans.

This was also the date when 70mph speed limits were introduced on British roads in 1965. (*Link – Assembly 8*)

23rd Christmas Island was discovered by Captain Cook in 1777.

24th In 1933 the British Museum acquired the *Codex Sinaiticus*, an ancient manuscript of the Bible, written in the fourth century.

There is an ancient legend that on Christmas Eve the cock crows all night, thus keeping all evil at bay.

25th The Queen's Christmas Broadcast was televised for the first time in 1957.

A useful quotation for Christmas Day comes from *Sketches by Boz* by Charles Dickens: 'There seems a magic in the very name of Christmas. Petty jealousies and discords are forgotten . . . would that Christmas lasted the whole year through.'

26th Boxing Day derives its name from the time when church poor boxes were opened on this date so that their contents could be distributed to the needy.

This is also St Stephen's Day. Stephen was the Christian church's first martyr, being stoned to death in 33 AD.

27th   St John's Day. John was the last of the original disciples to die – in Ephesus in about 100 AD.

28th   This was the night of the Tay Bridge disaster in 1879. The bridge collapsed in a storm as a train was passing over it. Seventy-five people died. (*Link – Assembly 23*).

29th   The man who invented the raincoat was born on this date in 1776. His name was William Macintosh.

30th   In the severe winter of 1962 this was the day on which the worst snowstorm since 1881 hit England. (*Link – Assembly 20*)

Rudyard Kipling was born in 1865. He won the Nobel Prize for Literature in 1907.

31st   The chimes of Big Ben bringing in the New Year were first broadcast in 1923.

Apart from being Hogmanay in Scotland, it is also a Hindu festival and the Shinto festival of Joya No Kane. Bells are rung at this time to give thanks for the good things of the past year and to prepare for the coming year.

Religious notes

Bodhi Day (Mahayana) is a movable feast in December when Buddhists celebrate the Buddha's enlightenment, as he reflected sitting under a Bodhi tree. 'Buddha' means 'the enlightened one' and the experience took place over two thousand five hundred years ago.

Chanukah, the Jewish Festival of Lights, is also a November–December movable feast.

Christmas Day on the 25th of the month was not established until the time when Julius I was Bishop of Rome (337–352). Julius fixed this as the date, after various Christian communities had celebrated the birth on dates as diverse as 6th January and 29th March, with others in between.

January

'Then came old January, wrapped well
In many weeds to keep the cold away.'
(*Edmund Spenser, 1552–99*)

The ancient Jewish year, which began on 25th March, held its legal position in Christian countries up until the eighteenth century. It was not until 1752 that 1st January became the legal, as well as the 'popular' start to the English new year.

1st   This is the time for 'New Year Resolutions'. Charles Lamb said: 'The man who does not propose to himself to be better this year than he was last, must be either very good or very bad indeed.'

Many countries around the world held huge celebrations to welcome 1st January 2000 as the dawn of the third millennium. Due to time zone differences the Pacific islands of Kiribati were the first to see the dawn of the new millennium and Western Samoa the last.

The BBC began broadcasting its first programmes in 1927.

Traffic policemen were introduced in Great Britain in 1931.

In 1954 flashing indicator lights became legal requirements on all motor vehicles in Great Britain. (*Possible assembly starter for a 'signs' theme*)

2nd   The Roman poet Ovid died on this day in the year 18. He is remembered for many thought-provoking 'sayings': 'To be loved, be lovable' and 'While fortune smiles you will have a host of friends, but they'll desert you when the storm descends.'

General 'Tom Thumb' (real name Charles Stratton), probably the most famous dwarf, died in 1883. He was 31 inches (84cm) tall.

In 1914, at Hendon, a woman pilot looped the loop for the first time. Her name was Trehawke Davies. (*Link – Assembly 50*)

In 1984 a report said that acid rain was contaminating Britain's lakes and rivers.

3rd   In 1847 the Californian town of Yerba Buena had its name changed – to San Francisco.

On this date in 1661 Samuel Pepys noted in his diary that he had been to the theatre and that it was 'the first time that I saw women come upon the stage'. Prior to this, boys and young men had taken women's parts.

4th   During the Middle Ages monks compiled a catalogue of flowers for each day of the year, linking each flower with a saint. Today's flower is the common hazel and it is linked to St Titus.

Jacob Grimm (of the Grimm brothers' fairy tales) was born in 1785.

Louis Braille was born in 1809. He was three years old when an accident caused him to lose his sight. According to *The Young Louis Braille* by C H Abrahall, it was feeling the indentations on dominoes which was one inspiration for his devising the system known as Braille. (*Link – Assembly 46*)

This was the date in 1944, during the Second World War, when Hitler ordered the mobilisation of all children over ten.

5th St Simeon Stylites died in 459. He lived for 36 years on a pillar 60 feet from the ground, wearing an iron collar and animal skins. Twice a day he preached to people who came to hear him. He was greatly admired for his patience, humility and wisdom. He was 69 when he died. (*Link – Assembly 31*)

In 1927 in New York the first demonstration of Movietone took place. This was a synchronisation of moving pictures and sound.

6th This is the feast of Epiphany, which marks the time when three Wise Men first saw Jesus. 'Epiphany' comes from the Greek word which means 'appearance'. The Twelve Days of Christmas end with the Feast of Epiphany. In mediaeval England all twelve days were celebrated, with great festivities on the last night before serious work on the land began the next day. It is traditionally unlucky to have decorations up after Twelfth Night.

In 1928 the Thames burst its banks. Fourteen people were drowned, there was serious flooding and valuable paintings were damaged in the Tate Gallery.

In 1931, during excavations in Iraq, a royal palace dating from 550 BC was discovered.

In 1941 the world-famous pilot Amy Johnson was missing, believed drowned, after her plane disappeared while flying over the Thames Estuary. (Her body was never found.)

7th In some parts of Japan this is a festival date on which rice cooked with herbs is eaten to prevent both bad luck and bad health.

8th   St Nathalan's Day. His generosity to others gained him saint-hood but he is probably best remembered for losing his temper, then chaining his ankles in repentance. Throwing the key to his chains into the sea, he later bought a fish in Rome and, on cutting it open to cook, found the key inside. (*Link – Assembly 31*)

Galileo, the astronomer, died in 1642.

Elvis Presley was born in 1935.

9th   Davy's safety lamp was first used down a coal mine in 1816.

In 1920 the Government announced plans to build 100,000 new houses during the year.

In 1948 four hundred Jamaicans arrived in London on the ship *Empire Windrush* to look for work in the rebuilding of post-war Britain.

10th The Penny Post was introduced by Sir Rowland Hill in 1840.

'Buffalo Bill' (William F Cody) died in 1917.

'Tintin', the famous cartoon character, first appeared in Belgium in 1929.

After a twelve-day ordeal in which he tried to save his ship (the *Flying Enterprise*), Captain Henrick Carlsen had to abandon it forty minutes before it sank. This was in 1952 and was an early 'disaster' covered by TV. (*Link – Assembly 48*)

11th Tradition has it that if today is mild moles start their tunnelling operations and throw up the first mole hills.

In 1905 the price of liner tickets to cross the Atlantic went up. To get from London to New York now cost £6.

12th Charles Perrault was born in 1628. He wrote. 'Cinderella' and 'Sleeping Beauty'.

In 1807 a ship full of gunpowder exploded at its moorings in the Dutch city of Leyden. One hundred and fifty-one people were killed and 2,000 injured, and 200 buildings were levelled. The blast was heard 50 miles away and the anchor of the ship was later found in a field outside the town.

Britain's first supermarket was opened in Manor Park in 1948.

13th St Veronica died in 1497. She was a poor peasant girl who lived such an exemplary life that she became prioress of a nunnery. How the name Veronica came into being is significant. When Christ was carrying his cross a girl wiped his face with a cloth. After she had done so the cloth miraculously bore an imprint of his features – a *Vera Iconica* ('true portrait'). The cloth still remains in St Peter's in Rome.

During the 'flu epidemic of 1922, 804 people died during the week ending on this day.

14th This is the feast day of St Kentigern, a Scottish saint whose Day is celebrated in Glasgow and elsewhere in Scotland.

On this date in 1205 one of the coldest ever spells hit Europe. A hard frost gripped England until 22nd March. From then on, 14th January was thought of as the coldest day of the year – something borne out in 1734 when Siberia registered temperatures of −120°F and birds fell frozen from the sky.

Albert Schweitzer was born in 1875.

Lewis Carroll (author of *Alice in Wonderland*) died in 1898.

15th This is the day on which St Paul, the first hermit, died in 342.

This is Martin Luther King Day in the USA. The civil rights leader was born in Atlanta, Georgia, in 1929. He was assassinated in Memphis, Tennessee, in April 1968.

16th Promises! An advertiser said that on this day in 1749, at London's Haymarket Theatre, he would play sounds from every musical instrument on a walking stick, and would then squeeze himself into a quart bottle. A huge crowd bought tickets and turned up – but the 'magician' didn't. There was a riot and the theatre was wrecked.

17th This is the feast day of St Anthony, the patron saint of domestic animals, who died in 356. (*Link – Assembly 49*)

On this date in 1939 the Nazi Government in Germany banned Jews from being dentists or vets and they were not allowed to drive cars, or go to cinemas and theatres.

18th Every year on this date the festival of St Peter's Chair is held in Rome. This is held in St Peter's Church, where the chair on which the saint is said to have meditated is enshrined. The ceremony commemorates the founding of the papacy.

This is the date on which the annual week of prayer for Christian Unity begins.

Rudyard Kipling died in 1936.

In 1923, because of inflation, there were 112,000 Deutsch-marks to £1. (*Link – Assembly 29*)

19th   James Watt, the inventor (steam engine), was born in 1736.

In 1903 a new bicycle race was announced in Paris – the Tour de France.

20th   This is St Sebastian's Day. Born in Narbonne, he was an early Christian who was killed by the Romans and buried under the Appian Way. During his life he managed to persuade one Roman governor to release many Christian prisoners. He lived during the third century.

John Howard, the prison reformer, died in 1790.

In 1961 John F Kennedy became the USA's youngest president. In his inaugural speech he said: '. . . ask not what your country can do for you; ask what you can do for your country.'

21st   This is the feast day of St Agnes (died 304). She is the patroness of purity.

In 1930 the BBC made the first world broadcast.

In 1935 Snowdonia, the first British National Park, was established. (*Link – Assembly 40*)

22nd   Sir Francis Bacon, the great philosopher, was born in 1561. Despite his great mental powers, he was guilty of taking bribes when he was a judge. Hence the poet Alexander Pope described him as: 'The wisest, greatest, meanest of mankind'.

In 1901 Queen Victoria died at Osborne House on the Isle of Wight. She had reigned for 63 years.

In 1959 on this date it was announced that TV was growing rapidly in popularity and that two thirds of the British population now had a set.

23rd   St Eusebius died in 400. He ate only once every four days.

'Bodyline' bowling by the English cricket team in Australia caused great controversy in 1933.

The first jumbo jet landed at London's Heathrow Airport in 1970.

24th This is the feast day of St Timothy, bishop and martyr who was killed in 97 AD while trying to quell rioters in his temple.

The Boy Scouts were founded by Baden Powell in 1908. (*Link – Assembly 40*)

Winston Churchill died in 1965. He was ninety.

25th This is the feast of St Paul and celebrates his conversion to Christianity. (Bible reference: Acts 9, 1–31) Tradition maintains that weather for the year can be foretold by how it is on St Paul's Day:

> 'If St Paul's Day be fair and clear,
> It does betide a happy year.'

Robert Burns, the Scottish poet, was born in 1759. At Burns Night celebrations the haggis is eaten. The recipe for a haggis is minced heart and liver of sheep, suet, oatmeal, and seasoning – sewn into the sheep's stomach and boiled for three hours.

On this date in 1915 Alexander Graham Bell established a new long-distance record for a telephone call – 4,750 miles from New York to San Francisco.

26th Australia Day – commemorating the landing of Captain Arthur Phillips in 1788. On the same day in 1865 the sending of convicts from England to Australia ceased.

27th St John Chrysostum's Day. Born in 347 AD in Antioch, John was a brilliant orator ('Chrysostum' means 'golden mouth') whose Christian message made him enemies who succeeded in getting him banished. He died, ill and exhausted, while travelling in 407. Thus he was not a martyr but his sainthood came from his devotion and sincerity.

Mozart was born in 1756.

Lewis Carroll (*Alice in Wonderland*) was born in 1832.

In 1906 the River Thames caught fire as oil on the surface ignited.

In 1926 the first TV pictures were demonstrated in London by John Logie Baird.

28th Henry VII died in 1547.

Francis Drake died in 1596 on his ship off the coast of Panama.

In 1807 London's Pall Mall became the first street in the world to be lit by gaslight.

In 1986 the American space shuttle *Challenger* exploded on lift-off, killing its crew of seven.

29th St Francis's Day. He is the patron saint of writers and journalists. He died in 1662 and is known fully as St Francis de Sales.

The Victoria Cross was first awarded on this day in 1856. The medals were made from guns captured in the Crimea.

In 1947 one of the coldest ever spells of winter weather in Britain saw temperatures at −16°F. (*Link – Assembly 32*)

30th King Charles I was beheaded in 1649.

Edward Lear, poet, died in 1888.

Mahatma Gandhi was assassinated in New Delhi, India, in 1948. 'Mahatma' means 'Great Soul'.

In 1958 a bill was passed in the House of Lords marking lifetime peerages for men and women. For the first time in over six centuries women were admitted to the House of Lords.

31st Guy Fawkes was executed in 1606.

While on the subject of 'bonfires', on this night in 1804, with the country apprehensive about a French invasion, a warning bonfire was accidentally set alight near Berwick. This triggered off the lighting of many others and by morning all the southern Scottish counties were armed and ready to fight.

In one year, up to this date in 1922, the cost of living in Germany had risen by 73.7%.

Car front-seatbelts became compulsory in the UK in 1983.

Religious notes

Epiphany is the Christian feast which occurs twelve days after Christmas. It was originally associated with the baptism of Christ. An interesting link with the traditional story of the three wise men and their gifts is that these same gifts are presented at the altar in St James Palace, Chapel Royal, by members of the British royal family at this time of year.

January 25th has already been mentioned in the foregoing notes as St Paul's Day. It has another significance in that the week of prayer for Christian Unity is timed to end on this day.

The Hindu festival of Vasanta Panchami takes place in the month of Magha (January/February) and is a celebration of Sarasvati who is the goddess of learning and wisdom.

February

February (along with January) was one of the two months by which Numa Pompilius extended the Roman year from ten to twelve periods. The name came from the word 'februare', meaning 'to purify'.

1st   This is St Bride's Day. She is the patroness of Ireland.

In 1811 the beacon on Bell Rock lighthouse was first lit. In earlier times the Abbot of Aberbrothock had put a bell on this rock, off the Firth of Tay, to warn mariners of its presence. A pirate called Ralph the Rover cut this bell adrift and sent it into the sea. Later his ship was wrecked on the same rock and he was drowned. (Junior children find this a very telling story!) (*Link – Assembly 48*)

In 1915 passport photographs were first introduced in Great Britain.

In the same year, Sir Stanley Matthews, possibly England's most famous ever footballer, was born. He played until he was fifty.

2nd   Candlemas. On this date many churches have candlelit processions to celebrate the presentation of Jesus in the temple. In former times candles were thought of as 'representations' of the all-important sun, and were considered a talisman against such dreads as famine and plague. One other reason for the Church's emphasis on candles was to counteract these pagan celebrations. Candles and light symbolise good, truth, knowledge, hope and an early reference to Jesus the child said that he was 'a light to lighten the Gentiles' (Luke 2, 32). Candlemas Day is another of those which has traditional weather lore attached to it:

'If Candlemas Day be fair and bright,
Winter will have another flight;
But if it be dark with clouds and rain,
Winter is gone and will not come again.'

Tradition also names the snowdrop as the flower for 2nd February. It is said to have been created from a snowflake by an angel to give Adam and Eve hope when they had been expelled from the Garden of Eden. (*Link – Assembly 37*)

3rd   In Japan this is seen as the last day of winter and, to celebrate, people throw beans at each other.

Felix Mendelssohn was born in 1809.

This is the feast day of St Blaise, a saint with the power to cure throat problems.

On this day in 1953 hurricanes and high tides brought disaster to Britain's east coast. Two hundred and fifty people were drowned and thousands were made homeless. (*Link – Assemblies 32 and 48*)

4th   Charles Lindbergh, the first man to fly solo over the Atlantic, was born in 1902. (*Link – Assembly 50*)

In 1929 the first Green Belt area round London was approved. This was a five-mile tract near Hendon.

On this date in 1953 sweet rationing ended in Great Britain.

5th   St Agatha's Day. Agatha was being tortured for being a Christian when an earthquake erupted. It stopped when her torture stopped. She died peacefully in 251 AD.

Robert Peel, founder of the British police force, was born in 1788.

The *Reader's Digest* was first published in 1922.

In 1983 an unknown Mozart symphony was found among a pile of old papers in Odense, Denmark. It was calculated that the composer had written it when he was nine years old.

6th   On this day in 1918 the Representation of the People Act came into force, allowing women to vote in General Elections. They had to be over thirty, and householders. (Equal voting rights for all adults were won in 1928.)

In 1927 a ten-year-old boy in short trousers made a sensational debut playing the violin at a concert in Paris. His name was Yehudi Menuhin.

In 1958 the Manchester United football team's aeroplane crashed in Munich following a European cup tie. Seven of the players died immediately.

In 1964 Britain and France agreed to build a Channel Tunnel.

7th   Charles Dickens was born in 1812.

This was the day, in 1845, when William Lloyd went into the British Museum and deliberately broke the priceless 300-year-old Portland Vase, which had been discovered in Rome. He was fined for the vandalism. The vase, shattered into 2,000 pieces, was laboriously repaired by a man called Doubleday.

On this date in 1960 Israeli archaeologists discovered some parchment scrolls containing Biblical texts. The scrolls were estimated as having been written 1,700 years ago.

8th   Jules Verne, the author of *Around the World in Eighty Days*, was born in 1823.

9th   St Apollonia's Day. During her torture for being a Christian, in Alexandria, Apollonia's teeth were removed to make her renounce her faith, which she would not do. She died in 249 AD and is the patron saint of dentists.

This was the date in 1855 when, after a fall of snow in south-west England, mysterious footprints appeared next morning. These ran for nearly one hundred miles – over roofs and haystacks. They were cloven hooves – the mystery was never solved.

After eighteen days of continuous rain, London suburbs started to flood on this date in 1926.

In 1939 the British Government announced that London families on an income of less than £250 a year would be given free air-raid shelters.

10th St Scholastica's Day. Scholastica died in 543. She was the sister of the better-known St Benedict who founded the Benedictine monastery at Monte Cassino in Italy.

Samuel Plimsoll was born in 1824.

This was the date, in 1913, when rescuers found the dead bodies of Captain Scott and his two companions in their snow-covered tent near the South Pole. Scott's diary was found with them.

On this date in 1942 the first Golden Disc for a successful recording was presented. It was to Glenn Miller and his band for their hit, 'Chattanooga Choo Choo'.

11th   This is a day of celebration in Japan – to commemorate the founding of the country in 660 BC.

12th   Alexander Selkirk (the model for Defoe's Robinson Crusoe) was rescued from the uninhabited island of Juan Fernandez on this day in 1709. He had been there alone for five years.

Abraham Lincoln, sixteenth president of the United States, was born in 1809. He was responsible for the emancipation of negro slaves after the Civil War. He made the famous Gettysburg Address: 'This nation, under God, shall have a new birth of freedom; and that government of the people, by the people, and for the people, shall not perish from the earth.'

13th   On this date in 1978 Anna Ford became ITV's first female newscaster.

14th   St Valentine's Day. In the third century the Roman Emperor Claudius II passed a law against marriage because it was denuding his army of troops. A Christian priest, Valentine, continued to marry couples. He was discovered and sentenced to death. His compassion for all – including his jailer and that man's daughter – earned him sainthood. The sending of Valentine cards was probably at its peak in Britain in the nineteenth century. Postmen in London at this time felt that their task was so onerous on this day that they asked for a special meal allowance.

15th   Galileo Galilei, the astronomer, was born in 1564.

Decimal currency was introduced in Britain in 1971.

16th   Desperate unemployment in Britain in 1921 included 368,000 ex-servicemen.

Tutenkhamen's tomb and contents were discovered in Egypt in 1923.

The new synthetic fibre, nylon, was patented in New York on this date in 1937. Its name came from the two cities where work on its development had taken place: NY (New York) and LON (London).

17th   Michaelangelo Buonarotti, the Italian artist who decorated the ceiling of the Sistine Chapel, died in 1563.

In 1920 Britain's police force started to replace its horses with cars.

18th St Simon, Bishop of Jerusalem, nephew of Joseph and Mary and Christ's cousin, was crucified in 116. He was 120 years old.

Martin Luther died in 1546.

A new planet was sighted and named in 1930 – Pluto.

In 1942, to save fuel and soap during the Second World War, people in Britain were urged to take fewer baths, and to paint a 'plimsoll line' in bathtubs to regulate the amount of water put into them.

In 1949 the millionth ton of airlifted supplies reached the western sector of the beleaguered Berlin.

19th Nicholas Copernicus, the astronomer, was born in 1473.

20th Traditionally, old almanacs recommended this date as the date to sow beans. In folklore the bean is associated with ghosts and witches. In days when witches were feared it was recommended that lonely travellers carried a bean in their mouths to spit at a witch if one appeared.

Jimmy Greaves, the international footballer, was born in 1940.

21st Cardinal Newman, who wrote the hymn 'Lead, kindly light', was born in London in 1801.

In 1842 John Greenough received a patent for the sewing machine.

In 1956 the Duke of Edinburgh announced an award scheme for enterprising young people. (*Link – Assembly 40*)

22nd The first Woolworth's store opened in New York in 1879.

In 1910 X-ray machines were first used in medical treatment.

The announcement of the birth of Dolly the sheep was made on this date in 1997. Dolly was the first animal to be born using the technique of cloning.

23rd Samuel Pepys, the diarist, was born in 1632.

George Frederick Handel was born in 1685.

Dame Nellie Melba, the singer who had the 'peach melba' named after her, died in 1931.

In 1975, Laurence Stephen Lowry, the artist, died. He was born in 1887.

24th This is the feast day of St Matthias. Matthias was the apostle who took the place of Judas Iscariot after the latter committed suicide. (Bible ref: Acts 1, 23–26)

Wilhelm Karl Grimm (of the Grimm brothers' fairy tales) was born in 1786.

25th Sir Christopher Wren, the architect, died in 1723.

So important to Naples and Italy was the great opera singer, Enrico Caruso, born this day in 1873, that the world's largest candle was dedicated to his memory. It was eighteen feet high when new and is lit every year on his birthday. It is expected to last for 1,800 years.

26th Victor Hugo (author of *Les Misérables*, which contains the story of the Bishop's candlesticks, such a good assembly tale) was born in 1846.

27th This day celebrates St Thalilaeus who died in the fifth century. He is remembered for his constant weeping as penance for his sins.

In 1964 engineers in Italy pronounced the leaning tower of Pisa dangerous. They said it needed straightening by eleven feet to stop it falling over.

28th In 1912 the first parachute jump from a plane was made by Albert Berry in Missouri, USA.

In 1975 the driver and thirty-five passengers died in a London Underground train disaster at Moorgate.

29th The Leap Year tradition of women asking men to marry them was once taken so seriously in Scotland that a law was passed saying that any man who turned down such a proposal would be heavily fined.

Religious notes

Candlemas, on 2nd February, celebrates Jesus's presentation at the temple. At the time Jesus was born it was customary for every Jewish mother to go to the temple forty days after the birth of her first male child so that he could be 'presented to the Lord'. The mother was also 'blessed' on this occasion. Candles have come to celebrate this day in connection with Jesus being 'the light of the world'.

Lent is the period from Ash Wednesday to Holy Saturday – forty weekdays. During this time Christians remember the temptations of Jesus in the wilderness. It is a time for spiritual preparation for Easter.

March

The word 'March' comes from the Roman 'Martius'. It was originally the first month of the Roman calendar, named after the God of War.

1st   St David's Day. The emblem of the leek originated from soldiers wearing them in their hats to distinguish them from the Saxon enemy in battle. A great victory was won on this day and is commemorated by the same emblem.

In Switzerland cow bells 'ring out winter' on this date.

In 1976 a Road Traffic Bill was approved in the British Parliament. Its aim was to make the wearing of car seatbelts compulsory.

2nd   John Wesley, the founder of Methodism, died in 1791.

This is the feast of St Chad, a Christian missionary.

Mikhail Gorbachev was born in 1931.

In 1949 on this date the US airforce B-50 Superfortress Lucky Lady II completed the first non-stop flight round the world – 23,452 miles.

3rd   Alexander Graham Bell, inventor of the telephone, was born in 1847.

In 1937 on this date it was announced that Britain had 824 millionaires. (Link – Assembly 29)

In 1955 notice was given that London would be a 'smokeless zone' from October onwards.

In 1958 the first parking tickets were issued to British motorists.

4th   In 1824 the Royal National Lifeboat Institution was founded.

In 1927, 25,000 diggers rushed to stake their claims in the new South African diamond fields. (Link – Assembly 29)

In 1982 London's Barbican Centre was opened by the Queen.

5th   The Spitfire made its maiden flight in 1936. It was flown from Eastleigh Airport, Southampton, by Captain J Summers.

In 1942, in an effort to save pencils during wartime economies, all civil servants had their pencil sharpeners withdrawn.

6th   Davy Crockett and 86 others died when Mexican forces captured Fort Alamo in 1836.

This is the birthday of Sri Ramakrishna, the Hindu teacher, in 1833.

In 1946, when Great Britain was still suffering from food short-ages, the British food ministry issued a recipe for squirrel pie. (Link – Assembly 34)

On this date in 1947 Britain continued to suffer one of its worst ever winters when three hundred roads were blocked and fifteen towns cut off.

In 1987 the *Herald of Free Enterprise*, a Townsend Thoresen car ferry, capsized off the Belgian port of Zeebrugge at 7pm when it was setting out for Dover. It happened so quickly that there was no time to send an SOS and 193 people lost their lives.

7th   The British and Foreign Bible Society was founded in 1804. It has been responsible for translations into over 1,500 different languages.

St Perpetua's Day. She was martyred in 203 AD when she died before a crowd of thousands in the Rome amphitheatre.

The Albert Medal, for gallantry in saving life, was instituted in 1866.

In 1965 traffic jams blocked roads round Regent's Park, London, where crowds gathered to watch Goldie, a golden eagle who had escaped from London Zoo. He was recaptured on the 10th.

In 1969 the Queen opened the new London Underground line from Victoria to Walthamstow.

8th   International Women's Day.

In 1834 a Newfoundland dog called Hero saved two boys from drowning in the River Thames. As a result ten Newfoundlands were bought and trained for similar life-saving duties along the Seine in Paris. (Link – Assembly 53)

The first British pilot's licence was issued in 1910. (*Link – Assembly 50*)

On this date in 1906 the British Empire occupied one fifth of the land surface of the globe and had a population of four hundred million.

In 1925 the 'crossword craze' brought forth conflicting comments. The British Optical Association feared they would cause eye strain and headaches; the Chicago Department of Health announced that their mental stimulation was good for health and happiness. (*Link – Assembly 46*)

9th   C M Howard invented false teeth in 1827.

The French Foreign Legion was founded in 1831.

10th The first Cruft's Dog Show was held in London in 1886. (*Link – Assembly 53*)

Harriet Tubman died in 1913. She was famous for her work in helping slaves to escape during the American Civil War.

The first 'movie' was made in Hollywood in 1910. It was called *In Old California*.

11th Johnny Appleseed, the famous American apple tree planter, died in 1847.

Sir Alexander Fleming, discoverer of penicillin, died in 1955.

12th This is the feast day of St Gregory the Great, who sent St Augustine on his mission to England in 597.

In 1908 Benjamin Waugh, founder of the NSPCC, died. (*Link – Assembly 28*)

Coins replaced English £1 notes in 1983.

13th From this day onwards in 1886 British soldiers were allowed to wear beards.

The discovery of the planet Pluto was announced in 1930.

In 1918 the British school-leaving age was raised to fourteen.

14th Albert Einstein, the physicist, was born in 1879.

In 1934 it was announced that eggs in Britain had dropped to their lowest price since 1914 – 6d (2½p) per dozen.

15th Julius Caesar, Roman Emperor, was murdered in 44 BC.

The first cricket Test match was played between Australia and England at Melbourne, Australia. The Australians won by 45 runs.

In 1909 Selfridges opened in London's Oxford Street.

In 1949 clothes rationing (which had been introduced in Britain in 1941) ended.

16th   The first English FA Cup Final took place in 1872. (Wanderers beat the Royal Engineers.)

In 1917 the Czar abdicated in the face of the Russian Revolution.

In 1919 the invention of the wireless telephone enabled air pilots to talk in flight. (Link – Assembly 50)

In 1912, Lawrence Oates, thinking his death would aid the survival of his four colleagues, left the tent of Captain Scott's South Pole expedition, and walked in the snow to his death. (Link – Assembly 53)

17th   St Patrick's Day. Patrick died in 464. He was sent to Ireland by Pope Celestine to convert the heathens there. One of the ways in which he did this was to show them a shamrock – where three leaves combine to make a single plant. This he linked to the Trinity and the shamrock became a national emblem.

Feast day of St Joseph of Arimathea – who placed the body of Jesus in the tomb.

18th   John Luther Jones ('Casey Jones') stayed at the controls of his runaway train on the Chicago–New Orleans Line and died saving as many lives as he could when the train crashed. This was in 1900. The famous ballad recalls his story.

In 1945 all schools and universities were closed in Tokyo. Everyone over six years old was ordered to do war work.

19th   This is the feast day of St Joseph, Mary's husband.

Sydney Harbour Bridge was opened in 1932.

In 1962, the discovery of a 300-year-old skull was made beneath 10 Downing Street.

In 1964 the St Bernard Tunnel between Switzerland and Italy, via the Alps, was opened.

In 1967 an oil tanker, the *Torrey Canyon*, ran aground at Land's End and its cargo of oil began spilling into the sea. RAF planes later bombed it to disperse the oil which was said to be the 'greatest peacetime threat to Britain'.

20th Sir Isaac Newton died in 1727.

In 1967 Sir Francis Chichester began the last leg of his solo voyage round the world.

The landing of the first successful round the world hot air balloon flight by Bertrand Picard and Brian Jones in the Breitling Orbiter 3 on this date in 1999. The balloon covered a distance of 26,000 miles (42,197 km).

21st Feast of St Benedict. As Abbot of the monastery at Monte Cassino, he founded the order of Benedictine monks.

Johann Sebastian Bach was born in 1685.

22nd Johann Wolfgang von Goethe, the German philosopher, died in 1832. He was so clever that he could speak French, Italian, Latin and Greek by the time he was eight years old.

The English Football League was founded with twelve clubs in 1888.

23rd Roger Bannister, the first man to run a mile in under four minutes, was born in 1929.

24th Queen Elizabeth I died in 1603 after reigning for 44 years.

25th Lady Day, Feast of the Annunciation of the Virgin Mary. (Luke 1, 26–38)

Opening of London Airport, Heathrow, in 1948.

Some old English tombstones show interesting inscriptions which concern this date. In the graveyard of the parish church of St Mary, North Mymms, Hertfordshire, the tombstone of Thomas Huxley puts his death in 1695/6. This signifies the fact that until 1752 the legal New Year in Britain began on 25th March; the 'popular' New Year was 1st January. Consequently it was not unusual for gravestones recording deaths between 1st January and 24th March to show both years.

26th Ludwig van Beethoven died in 1827.

The first BBC weather forecast was broadcast on this date in 1923.

27th   The first international wireless message was sent by Marconi in 1899.

Yuri Gagarin, the Soviet cosmonaut, died in 1968.

28th   The first European use of gunpowder was at a battle between Venetians and Genoese in 1380.

The Crimean War began in 1854.

29th   The actress Sarah Bernhardt died, aged 78, on this day in 1923. (Traffic came to a halt in Paris for her funeral.)

In 1981 Dick Beardsley of the USA won the first London Marathon.

30th   Anna Sewell, the author of *Black Beauty*, was born in 1820. (*Link – Assembly 49*)

Vincent van Gogh, the artist, was born on this date in 1853. His painting 'Sunflowers' was sold at Christie's in London for £24,750,000 in 1987. (*Link – Assembly 29*)

31st   The Eiffel Tower was opened in Paris in 1889. It is 300 metres high but was not universally popular – over a hundred leading French writers, artists and composers claimed it was an affront to French taste and architecture.

In 1911 it was announced in Britain that the Government was seeking to make sixty hours the maximum working time for shop workers.

Religious notes

Purim is the Jewish festival which celebrates how the Jews of Persia were saved from the persecution of Haman. Because he hated the wise Mordecai, Haman and his followers planned a wholesale slaughter of the Jews throughout the kingdom. His plans were foiled when Esther, Mordecai's niece, was chosen by King Ahasuerus as his new queen. She revealed Haman's plot to the king. Modern celebrations at this festival are light-hearted and jolly. Much fancy dress is worn and hisses and noises greet Haman's name whenever it is mentioned. (*Link – Assembly 47*)

The same aura of colour, spectacle and jollity pervades the Hindu spring festival of Holi. On the first day of the festival a bonfire is lit, and on the second day people throw coloured water and powder over each other and exchange presents. These activities celebrate the revels of Lord Krishna.

April

Few months make such an initial impact with their first day as does April! It is also a time for obvious, and sage, advice: 'April showers bring May flowers' (*Link – Assembly 52*) ; and "Til April's dead, change not a thread.'

1st   An attempt to trace the origins of April Fools' Day is confused by its popularity in France, where an April Fools' trick is an 'April Fish' (*'un poisson d'avril'*), and by the similar goings-on at the Hindu Holi celebrations. One suggestion is that when New Year's Day used to be 25th March, 1st April presented itself as a day of levity to end the celebrations.

The Royal Air Force was founded in 1918.

2nd   Hans Andersen was born in 1805. Two of his tales which are useful for assemblies are 'The Ugly Duckling' and 'The Emperor's New Clothes'. Appropriately enough, this is also International Children's Book Day.

3rd   The Pony Express was founded on this date in 1860 when two riders set out in the USA. One was going east from San Francisco, the other west from St Joseph, Missouri. During its short life, 80 riders and 500 horses worked on the 1,900 miles of the organisation's route. (*Link – Assembly 49*)

4th   St Ambrose died on this date in 397. A great orator, he is credited with the famous phrase: 'When you are in Rome, do as they do in Rome.'

Martin Luther King, the American civil rights leader, was assassinated in Memphis in 1968. A few days later (on 9th April) over 150,000 people attended his burial in Atlanta.

5th   Robert Raikes died in 1811. He founded Sunday Schools for children throughout Britain. His first school was opened in 1780 in Gloucester, and was for poor children. (*Link – Assembly 41*)

On this date in 1955 Sir Winston Churchill resigned as Prime Minister at the age of eighty.

6th   Albrecht Dürer, the artist ('Praying Hands') died in 1528.

Houdini, the great escape artist, was born in 1874.

Robert Edwin Peary became the first man to reach the North Pole in 1909. He and his party had set out from New York by ship in July 1908.

7th   The highwayman Dick Turpin was hanged in York in 1739.

In 1832, at Carlisle, Joseph Thomson sold his wife to Henry Mears for twenty shillings and a dog.

This is World Health Day, when prayers are asked for sick and suffering people all over the world.

8th   This is the date of a Mahayana Buddhist celebration of Buddha Sakyamuni's birthday.

9th   Isambard Kingdom Brunel, the engineer, was born in 1806.

The American Civil War ended in 1865.

A letter appeared in *The Times* of London asking for a new word to describe 'progress by electric power'. Eventually the word 'motor' was chosen.

10th   William Booth, co-founder, with his wife Catherine, of the Salvation Army, was born in 1829. (Salvation Army, 101 Newington Causeway, London SE1 6BN) (*Link – Assembly 41*)

The *Titanic*, the world's largest ship, set off on its ill-fated maiden voyage from Southampton to New York on this date in 1912.

11th   St Guthlac, who died in 714, renounced his earlier career as a robber, took to living in a swamp in the English Fens and existed on only bread and water for the rest of his life.

Napoleon was exiled to Elba in 1814.

12th   The American Civil War broke out in 1861.

The Russian cosmonaut, Yuri Alekseyevich Gagarin, made the first manned space flight round the earth in 1961. His space craft was called Vostok and the orbit took 89 minutes.

13th   This is the date of Baisakhi, the festival which commemorates the founding of the Sikh Kalsa (brotherhood) by Guru Gobind Singh in 1699. The five symbols of the religion worn by the Kalsa are: the *kesh* (uncut hair), the *kanga* (a comb to hold hair under the turban); the *kara* (a bracelet), the *kirpan* (a sword), and the *kaccha* (shorts).

14th Traditionally this is the date on which the cuckoo is first heard in Britain.

Abraham Lincoln, US President, was shot by John Wilkes Booth in 1865. Booth was later killed resisting arrest.

15th Leonardo da Vinci was born in 1452.

This is traditionally Swallow Day in Britain – when swallows return for the spring and summer.

Father Damien, who gave his life treating lepers, was born in 1889.

The *Titanic* sank after hitting an iceberg in 1912 and 1,513 people were drowned.

In 1989 ninety-four people died at the Hillsborough football stadium disaster in Sheffield.

16th Wilbur Wright, the aeroplane inventor and flier, was born in 1867.

Marie Tussaud, wax modeller and founder of Madame Tussaud's Waxworks in London, died in 1850. (*See also 26th April.*)

17th Benjamin Franklin, the often-quoted American statesman and scientist, died on this date in 1790. One of his most appropriate 'sayings' was: 'Do you love life? Then don't squander time, for that is the stuff life is made of.'

This was the date, in 1492, when Columbus set sail to 'discover' the New World. He was equipped with a seal from King Ferdinand of Spain giving him the title of 'Admiral and Viceroy' over all the lands he might discover.

18th On this night in 1775, Paul Revere rode through the Massachusetts countryside to warn people that British troops were coming.

This was the date of the San Francisco earthquake in 1906. Devastation and fire caused the death of seven hundred people.

Albert Einstein, the scientist, died in 1955.

19th This is St Alphege's Day. Alphege was the Archbishop of Canterbury when captured by the Danes in the eleventh century. During his captivity he nursed sick Danes who were ill with the plague. He was executed in 1012.

Lord Byron, the poet, died in 1824. Charles Darwin, the naturalist, died in 1882. (*Link – Assembly 71*)

20th This is the date on which the cuckoo is traditionally first heard in Europe. One old belief associated with this event is that whatever you are doing when you hear its first call – you will be doing most during the rest of the year.

Adolf Hitler was born in 1889.

21st In 753 BC Romulus started to lay the foundations of a city on the banks of the River Tiber. This became Rome.

Charlotte Brontë, author of *Jane Eyre*, was born in 1816.

Mark Twain (pen name of Samuel Longhorne Clemens) died in 1910. His works included *Tom Sawyer* and *The Adventures of Huckleberry Finn*.

Manfred von Richthofen, the First World War German fighter pilot known as 'the Red Baron', was killed in 1918.

Queen Elizabeth II was born in 1926.

22nd In 1794 Edmund Bon became the first person to qualify as a veterinary surgeon in Great Britain. (*Link – Assembly 69*)

Richard Trevithick, an engineer who pioneered locomotive building in the British Isles, died in 1833.

Yehudi Menuhin, world famous violinist, was born in 1916.

23rd Today is St George's Day. ('Cry God for Harry! England and St George!' – from Shakespeare's *Henry V*). The patron saint of England supposedly saved the Libyan town of Sylene from a man-eating dragon. He did this on condition that the inhabitants of the town would be baptised.

This date is also established as Shakespeare's probable date of birth in 1564. He was baptised on the 26th, and died on 23rd April 1616.

William Wordsworth ('I wandered lonely as a cloud ... saw a crowd, a host, of golden daffodils') died in 1850.

The Pennine Way, the footpath which spans 250 miles (402km) from Derbyshire to the Borders, was opened in 1968. It was Britain's first long-distance footpath.

24th Daniel Defoe (author of *Robinson Crusoe*) died in 1731.

Joshua Slocum set out in an eleven-metre-long sloop to sail round the world from Boston, USA in 1895. His single-handed journey took three and a half years.

25th This is St Mark's Day. He died in AD 68, having served as a secretary to the disciple Peter. His writings appear in the Bible under his own name.

Oliver Cromwell was born in 1599.

Work started on the Suez Canal on this date in 1859.

In 1874 Guglielmo Marconi was born in Bologna, Italy. He invented radio telegraphy and was awarded the Nobel Prize for Physics in 1909.

26th Alfred Krupp, the German industrialist, was born in 1812.

Madame Tussaud's was opened on its current site in London in 1928.

27th Ferdinand Magellan, the Portuguese explorer, was killed on an expedition in 1521. He named the Pacific Ocean. His ship, which arrived home in Spain in 1522, had completed the first circumnavigation of the world.

Samuel Morse, inventor of the Morse Code, was born in 1791.

Henry Willis, one of Britain's greatest organ builders, was born in 1821. He was also a church organist.

The *Kon-Tiki* expedition set out on its balsawood raft in 1947.

Betty Boothroyd became the first ever woman speaker in the Houses of Parliament on this date in 1992.

28th Captain Bligh of the *Bounty*, together with eighteen men, was set adrift on the ocean in a rowing boat by mutineers led by Fletcher Christian in 1789. He survived to become Governor of New South Wales in Australia.

Lord Shaftesbury (Anthony Ashley Cooper) was born in 1801. He was a great reformer who helped poor children especially. (*Link – Assembly 68*)

29th Sir Malcolm Sargent, the orchestral conductor, was born in 1895. (*Link – Assembly 70*)

Emperor Hirohito, the 124th of Japan's 'divine' rulers, was born in 1901.

The rose 'Peace' was named on this date in 1945.

30th William Lilly was born in 1602. He was one of the first astrologers to become rich and well known for his skills.

Adolf Hitler died in 1945.

Religious notes

While not strictly religious festivals, two important modern Jewish festivals which usually fall in April or May are Yom HaShoah which commemorates the victims of the Holocaust, and Yom HaAtzmaut which celebrates Israel's independence.

The Sikh festival of Baisakhi takes place on 13th April (see the note for this date).

Although it is a movable feast, Easter often occurs in this month. The build-up to Easter is considerable. Lent is preceded by Shrove Tuesday when worshippers went to church to be 'shriven' – confess their sins. Ash Wednesday, as the first day of Lent, is a time when Christians daubed ash on their faces as a further reminder of the need to repent sins. The forty days of Lent then follow, as a spiritual preparation for Easter. It should be remembered that these forty days do not include Sundays – which always remain feast days, not fast days. Holy Week precedes Easter Sunday, which is the joyous celebration of Jesus's resurrection and which activates thoughts through the next forty days to Ascension Day.

The Jewish Pesach (Passover) festival is held to celebrate the escape of the Children of Israel from Egypt. This happened under the leadership of Moses, more than three thousand years ago. Passover occurs in the Jewish month of Nisan and lasts for eight days – the first two and the last two are full festival days.

The house is thoroughly cleaned and a meal prepared. No leaven (yeast) must be used. On the first evening of the festival, the family, dressed in their best (or new) clothes, come to the table for the Seder. Each member of the family has a cup of wine and certain food (bitter herbs, a lamb's shank bone, a roasted egg, a mixture of apples and nuts in a paste, watercress and unleavened bread). These foods are symbolic. Exodus 12 tells the story of the Passover.

May

May, named after the Roman goddess Maia, could certainly be said to be one of Northern Europe's most popular months. In Britain it is looked upon as the beginning of summer and the month of flowers.

> A trout peeped out
> From his shady nook,
> A butterfly too
> Flew lazily by,
> And the willow catkins
> Shook from on high
> Their yellow dust
> As I passed by:
> And so I know
> That summer is nigh.'
>
> (Anon.)

1st   This date is celebrated as Labour Day in many countries. Parades and other displays of human achievements are held.

The General Election of 1997 saw the election of the first Labour government for 18 years.

David Livingstone, the Scottish missionary and explorer, died in Africa in 1873.

This was the date in 1928 when footballer Dixie Dean of Everton and England scored a record number of goals in a season: sixty.

2nd   This date has an amazing number of connections with flight and flying.

Leonardo da Vinci died in 1519.

Baron von Richthofen ('the Red Baron') was born in 1892.

Robert Hewitt began America's first aeroplane passenger service in 1919.

The airship *Hindenburg* left Europe for America on this date in 1937. It exploded when about to land in America and thirty-three people were killed.

The British Overseas Airways Corporation began the first jet airline service in 1952 (England to South Africa).

The spacecraft *Pioneer X* was launched by the USA in 1972. It sent back information about the planet Jupiter.

3rd In 326 St Helena found the cross on which Jesus was crucified in Jerusalem. (*Link – Assemblies 72, 79*)

The Royal Festival Hall was opened on London's South Bank
in 1951.

Margaret Thatcher became Britain's first woman Prime
Minister in 1979.

4th In 1626 Peter Minuit, arriving with four shiploads of settlers
and their cattle, reached Manhattan Island, New York. He
'bought' it from the Indians there for some scarlet cloth and
brass buttons – valued at $24.

The first Epsom Derby horse race was run in 1780. (*Link –
Assembly 66*)

5th Napoleon Bonaparte died in 1821.

The first General Strike in Britain's history began in 1926.

Amy Johnson took off for her single-handed flight to Australia
in 1930.

Fossils and tools used by people 250,000 years ago were found
near Nairobi in Kenya on this date in 1944.

6th 'Penny Black' stamps were first put on sale on this date in
1840. Some are very valuable, but by no means all are, as
millions were printed.

Maria Montessori, the nursery school pioneer, died in 1952.
(*Link – Assemblies 78 and 80*)

On the evening of this day in 1954, at Oxford, Roger Bannister
became the first man to run a mile in less than four minutes
(3 mins 59.4 secs).

7th Nelson's flag ship, HMS *Victory*, was launched in 1765. It took
between two and three thousand oak trees to build it.

Peter Ilich Tchaikovsky, the Russian composer, was born in
1840.

The Second World War in Europe ended when Germany
surrendered at 2.41 am on this date in 1945.

In 1959 British Rail announced it was going to close two
hundred and thirty BR stations.

8th   Jean Henri Dunant was born in 1828. He founded the International Red Cross and was the first winner of the Nobel Peace Prize (shared with Frédéric Passy), in 1901. Today is World Red Cross Day. (*Link – Assembly 76*)

The Thames Barrier was officially opened in 1984.

9th   This was the date, in 1671, when Thomas Blood, disguised as a priest and with three accomplices, attempted to steal the Crown Jewels. He was captured but pardoned by King Charles II.

John Brown, leader of the anti-slavery movement in America, was born in 1800.

John Brown's body lies a-moulderin' in the grave,

But his soul goes marching on.

Tensing Norgay, the Sherpa climber who reached the summit of Mount Everest with Sir Edmund Hillary in 1953, died in 1986.

10th   An eight-day holiday from England to the French Riviera cost £8 in 1938. (Thomas Cook)

US *Triton*, a nuclear submarine, completed a submerged journey round the world in 1961.

11th   Baron Münchhausen was born in 1720. He became famous as a teller of outlandish stories.

Irving Berlin, writer of more than three thousand popular songs, was born in 1888. His compositions included 'God Bless America' and 'White Christmas'.

In 1941 London endured its worst air raid of the war. Westminster Abbey, St Paul's Cathedral and the British Museum were all damaged and 1,400 people were killed. (*Link – Assembly 59*)

12th   Florence Nightingale was born in 1820. (*Link – Assembly 63*)

A lady with a lamp I see
Pass through the glimmering doom.

(Longfellow)

In 1937 George VI was crowned king. His elder brother Edward VIII had abdicated in 1936.

This date in 1949 marked the end of the Berlin Blockade. The city had been supplied by air since June 1948.

In 1958 it was decided to establish one hundred and sixty square miles of Surrey countryside as an area of outstanding natural beauty. (*Link – Assembly 71*)

13th Fridtjof Nansen died in 1930. He was a famous Norwegian Arctic explorer who later won a Nobel Peace Prize for his welfare work after the First World War.

14th In 1796 Edward Jenner established smallpox vaccinations. (*Link – Asemblies 61, 63*)

Henry John Heinz, the American food manufacturer who created '57 varieties' of food products, died in 1919.

In 1948 the new state of Israel was proclaimed.

15th The Romans celebrated this date as the birthday of Mercury, the messenger of Zeus.

In 1970 Ann Hays and Elizabeth Holsington became the first female generals in the US army.

16th This is St Brendan's Day. An Irish saint who died in 587, Brendan is believed by some people to have been the first European to have discovered America.

The Woman's Voluntary Service (WVS) was founded in Britain in 1938. In 1966 it became the Women's Royal Voluntary Service.

In 1980 inflation in the United Kingdom reached 21.8%.

17th Paul Dukas, French composer (*The Sorcerer's Apprentice*) died in 1935.

18th This is the birthday of Karol Wojtyla – Pope John Paul II. He was born in 1920.

19th St Dunstan's Day. Dunstan was Archbishop of Canterbury, and a goldsmith, and died in 988. He is credited with devising the coronation service.

Dame Nellie Melba, the famous opera singer, was born in 1861. (*Link – Assembly 64*)

In 1980, Mount St Helens in the USA, a long dormant volcano, erupted killing eight people.

20th Albrecht Dürer, the painter, was born in 1471. (*Link – Assembly 64*)

Christopher Columbus died in 1506.

Charles Lindbergh flew *The Spirit of St Louis* from New York to Paris – the first solo non-stop flight across the Atlantic. This was in 1929.

This was the date, in 1913, of the first Chelsea Flower Show.

The BBC opened its new headquarters in Portland Place in 1932.

The Nature Conservancy Council announced in 1952 that eight areas of England and Scotland were to became nature reserves. (*Link – Assembly 71*)

21st There was an earthquake in Britain in 1382. Some churches in Kent were 'thrown down to the earth' according to *Stow's Chronicle*.

Elizabeth Fry, the prison reformer, was born in 1780.

In 1964 a BBC survey revealed that the Beatles were Britain's most popular tourist attraction.

22nd Richard Wagner, the composer, was born in 1813. (*Link – Assembly 70*)

Sir Arthur Conan Doyle was born in 1859. (*Link – Assembly 57*)

Victor Hugo died in 1885. His novel *Les Misérables* contains the story of the Bishop's candlesticks which is marvellous assembly material.

In 1959 the US state of Alabama banned a children's book because it showed a black rabbit marrying a white one.

In 1987 one of Mozart's notebooks was sold for £2.3 million at Sotheby's.

23rd John D Rockefeller, the American businessman and philan-thropist, died in 1937.

In 1956 it was announced that self-service shops, which were springing up all over Britain, had resulted in quadruple sales. (*Link – Assembly 78*)

24th Carl Linne, the Swedish naturalist, was born in 1707. He said, 'If a tree dies, plant another in its place.'

Samuel Morse sent the first message by Morse Code on this date in 1844. It was from Washington to Baltimore, USA and it said, 'What hath God wrought?'

This was the date of a great sea tragedy in 1941. The British battleship HMS *Hood* was hit by a shell from the German ship *Bismarck*. The magazine exploded and only three of the 1,421 men on board survived.

25th Captain Cook set out on his first voyage of discovery, in the seas around Australia, New Zealand and Indonesia, in 1768.

Igor Sikorsky, designer of the first helicopter in 1939, was born in 1889.

26th Samuel Pepys died in 1703. The famous diarist kept his journal from 1660 to 1669 and it encompassed three out-standing events – the Great Plague, the Fire of London and the Dutch attack on the Medway.

Petrol rationing in the UK ended on this date in 1950, five years after the end of the Second World War. (*Link – Assembly 56*)

27th This is the Feast Day of the Venerable Bede who died at Jarrow in 735. Known as the Father of the English Church, and a celebrated writer about early Christianity in England, his tomb is in Durham Cathedral. Thought to be the first person to draw up a calendar of the Christian year, he was widely revered in his day.

In 1936 the *Queen Mary* (80,773 tons) set sail from Southampton on her maiden voyage.

28th This was the birth date of Solomon in 970 BC.

Sir Francis Chichester ended his solo round-the-world voyage on his arrival in Plymouth in 1967. He had completed 15,517 miles and was later knighted by Queen Elizabeth II at Greenwich. She used the sword of Sir Francis Drake for this ceremony.

29th This is Oak Apple Day – when King Charles II rode into London on his thirtieth birthday in 1660, as newly proclaimed king. He had escaped from Cromwell's army in 1651 by hiding in an oak tree. A traditional old school jingle linked to the day was:

The twenty-ninth of May
Is Royal Oak Day;
If you cannot give us a holiday,
We'll all run away.

The summit of Mount Everest was reached for the first time on this day in 1953 by Edmund Hillary and Tensing Norgay.

In 1951 eighty-three miners died after an explosion at Easington Colliery in County Durham.

In 1977 Nigel Short (aged eleven) became the youngest ever qualifier in the UK national chess championships.

In 1985, rioting in the European Cup Final football match between Liverpool and Juventus at the Heysel Stadium in Brussels resulted in forty-one people being killed.

30th   King Arthur is said to have died in 542.

Many historians believe this was the date than Joan of Arc was burned at the stake in Rouen in 1431.

31st   This was the date, in 1678, of Lady Godiva's famous naked ride through Coventry. Her husband agreed to remit heavy taxes on the town's people if she did this.

Religious notes

In the Christian Church Ascension Day is the Thursday which is the fortieth day after Easter. This commemorates the last time the disciples saw Jesus before his ascension. This happened on the Mount of Olives and Jesus blessed his followers with the words: 'Lo, I am with you always, even unto the end of the world.' Biblical references for this event are Mark 16, 19; Luke 24–51; Acts 1, 1–11.

There then follow the ten days between Ascension and Whitsun. The latter festival, also known as Pentecost, is the fiftieth day after Easter and celebrates the giving of the Holy Spirit to the followers of Christ. ('Pentecost' comes from the Greek word meaning 'fiftieth'.) It was from this moment that these followers began to preach about Jesus, and therefore it is considered the birthday of the Christian Church. This is also the time which begins the second half of the Christian Year.

This is also the time of the Jewish festival of Shavuoth, which celebrates the giving of the Torah on Mount Sinai. Synagogues are decorated with flowers and plants.

June

June is a month of many associations, including marriage, roses, midsummer, and well dressing. Northern Europeans hope that the weather in reality matches the promise and they can agree with James Lowell's comment: 'What is so rare as a day in June.'

1st Captain Robert Falcon Scott's ill-fated expedition to the South Pole set out in 1910.

The *Queen Mary* arrived in New York in 1936 on its maiden voyage.

Helen Keller died in 1968. She was eighty-eight and had become a world-famous lecturer and writer despite being deaf and blind since the age of nineteen months. She was noted for her work with the handicapped. (*Link – Assembly 61*)

2nd Thomas Hardy, the author, was born in 1840.

Queen Elizabeth II was crowned in 1953.

3rd The game of lacrosse was introduced into Britain in 1876. A group of Canadians gave an exhibition game.

In Japan, this is the day on which a Buddhist ceremony takes place when all broken dolls are taken to priests.

Johann Strauss died in 1899.

4th In 1913 Emily Wilding Davison, a suffrage campaigner, threw herself in front of the king's horse, Anmer, in the Epsom Derby. She was killed, but her action attracted more attention to the suffrage campaign for the vote for women. (*Link – Assembly 66*)

On this date in 1940 the evacuation was completed of British troops from Dunkirk during the Second World War.

5th In 1783 Joseph and Etienne Montgolfier gave the first public demonstration of a hot air balloon. This was at Annonay, in the Languedoc in France. The balloon was airborne for ten minutes.

6th In 1930 frozen peas were sold in America for the first time. That this was possible was due to a 'quick-freeze' technique invented by Clarence Birdseye.

In 1944 the Allied troops landed on the Normandy coast in the D-Day operations.

In 1977 beacons were lit all over the country at the start of Queen Elizabeth II's jubilee celebrations – twenty five years on the throne.

7th   Robert the Bruce died in 1329.

Paul Gauguin, the artist, was born in 1848.

8th   The prophet Muhammad (pbuh) died in 632. He was the founder of Islam. (*Link – Assembly 60*)

In 1786 commercially-made ice cream was sold for the first time in New York.

In 1978 Naomi James beat Sir Francis Chichester's record for a solo round-the-world voyage by two days.

9th   This is the feast day of St Columba. He died in 597 and is considered the spreader of the gospel over the northern part of the British Isles.

George Stephenson, inventor of railways, was born in 1781.

Charles Dickens died in 1870. Queen Victoria said of him, 'He is a very great loss. He had a large and loving mind.'

In 1958 Queen Elizabeth opened the new and improved facilities at Gatwick Airport.

10th   Feast day of St Margaret (b. 1050) in England.

The first World Cup Soccer Final was played in Rome in 1934. The score was Italy 2, Czechoslovakia 1.

The 'biro', a ball point pen, was patented by Hungarian Laszlo Biro in 1943.

The 750th anniversary of the signing of the Magna Carta was celebrated in St Paul's Cathedral in 1965.

11th   This is the feast day of St Barnabas. He accompanied St Paul on his gospel-spreading journeys and is believed to have been put to death for his beliefs in Cyprus.

John Constable, the painter, was born in 1776.

Britain's first North Sea oil was pumped ashore in 1975.

In 1982 forty-two British soldiers were killed in the fighting at Fitzroy in the Falklands War.

12th Auguste and Louis Lumière showed the first newsreel film in Paris in 1895. Many among the audience were frightened by its realism.

Bryan Allen 'pedalled' across the Channel in a pedal powered aircraft in 1979. The flight took three hours.

In 1980 Billy Butlin, the founder of Britain's popular holiday camps, died aged eighty. (*Link – Assembly 78*)

13th The Virgin Mary, mother of Jesus, died in AD 40.

St Anthony, patron saint of the illiterate, died in 1231.

The MCC was founded in 1787.

Jesse Boot, Lord Trent, founder of Boots the Chemist, died in 1931.

In 1956 Real Madrid won soccer's first European Cup, beating Stade de Reims, 4–3.

14th Captain Bligh, set adrift from the *Bounty*, arrived in Timor in 1789. With the barest of supplies, he and his eighteen companions had completed a journey of 3,618 miles in an open boat.

This is Flag Day in the USA – to commemorate the adoption of the 'Stars and Stripes' as the national flag in 1777.

The first non-stop flight of the Atlantic was made by William Alcock and Arthur Whitten-Brown in 1919.

John Logie Baird, who pioneered the invention of the television, died in 1946 aged fifty-eight.

In 1961 push-button controlled pedestrian crossings were introduced into Britain. (*Link – Assembly 74*)

15th World Children's Day.

This is St Vitus's Day. This fourth-century saint and martyr is the patron of actors and dancers.

In 1215 King John signed the Magna Carta – the first documentation of human freedom. (*Link – Assembly 76*)

Benjamin Franklin proved the existence of electricity in lightning in 1752. This was done by flying a kite in a storm. It was struck by lightning and the electricity ran down it to make a spark near the ground.

223

In 1952 Anne Frank's diary was published. She had kept it from 1942 to 1944, before her family was discovered and sent to a concentration camp.

16th   Henry Ford founded the Ford Motor Company in Detroit, USA, in 1903.

General William Bramwell Booth, founder of the Salvation Army, died in 1929.

Edmund Hillary and John Hunt received knighthoods for their parts in the successful 1953 Mount Everest expedition.

In 1963 Russia put the first woman in space when Lieutenant Valentina Tereshkova circled the earth in a *Vostok* spacecraft. She was twenty-six.

17th   John Wesley, the founder of Methodism, was born in 1703. Wesley preached thousands of sermons all over the country. He travelled mainly on horseback, lived abstemiously and gave away an estimated £30,000 in his lifetime. ('Give all you can'). (*Link – Assemblies 64, 65*)

18th   The Battle of Waterloo took place in 1815. This finally ended the ambitions of Napoleon, who abdicated on 22nd June and was banished to St Helena.

19th   The French genius Blaise Pascal was born in 1623. A brilliant mathematician (he invented a digital calculator, and a syringe) he was also a very religious man and a philosopher. 'If you want people to think well of you, do not speak well of yourself.' (*Link – Assembly 73*)

James Barrie (author of *Peter Pan*) died in 1937.

In 1961 archeological evidence relating to Pontius Pilate was found a few miles from Haifa in Caesarea, Israel. A stone slab was discovered on which were two names: Pontius Pilate and Emperor Tiberius.

In 1978 Ian Botham achieved England's greatest all-round performance in a cricket test match. This was against Pakistan at Lords, when he scored a century and had bowling figures of 8–34. He was twenty-two at the time.

20th   This day in 1837 saw Queen Victoria's accession to the British throne. Her coronation was held on 28th June 1838.

The medal, the Victoria Cross, was created in 1856. The first person to be awarded it was Lieutenant Charles Lucas who threw a live bomb off a ship's deck. It exploded immediately.

21st This is the longest day of the year in the northern hemisphere (except on leap years).

22nd In 1923 runaway inflation meant that there were 622,000 German marks to the £1.

On this date in 1941 Germany invaded Russia in the Second World War.

In 1964 Francis Chichester set a new record for a solo boat crossing of the Atlantic in under thirty days.

In 1970 it was announced by the Methodist Church that women would be recognised as full ministers.

23rd In 1683 William Penn arranged the signing of a treaty between settlers and indigenous people in the State of Pennsylvania. This established peace in the state – something very different from other states in America.

24th This is John the Baptist's Day. This is unusual in that the Christian Church usually celebrates saints on the day of their death – not so in John's case. (*Link – Assembly 72*)

This is Midsummer Day.

25th This was the date of 'Custer's Last Stand' in 1876. At a battle by the Little Big Horn River in Montana Custer's force was wiped out by Sioux Indians.

The Korean War began in 1950.

26th According to legend, in 1284 the Pied Piper lured away one hundred and thirty children from the German town of Hamelin. This was because the town fathers refused to honour his fee of 1,000 guilders for ridding the town of rats. (*Link – Assembly 3*)

Delegates from fifty states met in San Francisco to sign the World Security Charter in 1945. This was to establish an international peace-keeping body called the United Nations.

27th Helen Keller was born in 1880.

28th Queen Victoria was crowned at Westminster in 1838.

Archduke Franz Ferdinand, heir to the throne of Austria-Hungary, and his wife were assassinated in Sarajevo. The assassin was a Serb called Gavrilo Princip and the act was to contribute to the outbreak of the First World War.

Prince William was born in 1982.

29th   St Peter, the disciple, was crucified in AD 68.

The Automobile Association was founded in 1905. The annual membership then was two guineas. (*Link – Assembly 56*)

In 1925 a law was passed in South Africa banning all black people from holding skilled jobs.

In 1968 Britain's first credit card – the Barclaycard – was introduced.

30th   Tower Bridge was opened by the Prince of Wales in 1894.

In 1938 a new comic appeared in the USA – *Superman*.

In 1948 this was the date the Berlin Airlift began. The beleaguered city was supplied entirely by air.

Religious notes

At the time of publication the birthday of the prophet Muhammad (pbuh) falls in June.

The Christian feast of Corpus Christi ('the body of Christ') is celebrated on the Thursday after Whit week. It commemorates the institution of the Eucharist at the Last Supper.

July

'Then came hot July, boiling like to fire'.

So said Edmund Spenser, but as well as its reputation for heat, this month has strong links with wet weather as it contains St Swithin's Day. It was Mark Antony who named the month in honour of Julius Caesar; the Anglo-Saxon name, 'Hey Monath', simply reflected the time of hay harvesting.

1st   Prince Charles became the Prince of Wales in 1969.

Louis Blériot, the French airman who made the first flight across the English Channel, was born in 1872.

Hong Kong is returned to Chinese control by Britain in 1997 after 156 years as a British colony.

Diana, Princess of Wales was born on this date in 1961. She died in a car crash in Paris on 31st August 1997; her death was mourned by many people around the world.

2nd   Nostradamus, the astrologer and prophet, died in 1566.

In 1964 the Civil Rights Act was signed in the USA. This was intended to prevent racial discrimination of any kind. (*Link – Assembly 60*)

3rd   This is the beginning of the period known to the Romans as 'the dog days' (3rd July to 11th August). The name derives from the fact that the Dog Star (Canicular) rose at this time. These days were considered the hottest of the year, when 'dogs grew mad, other animals languid and men prey to fevers, hysterics and frenzies'.

4th   This is Independence Day in the USA. The Declaration of Independence was made in 1776 and contained some memorable phrases, notably: 'We hold these truths to be self evident, that all men are created equal . . .'

Thomas Barnardo was born in 1845. It was while training to be a medical missionary in London that the Irishman discovered the orphans that led to his work with Dr Barnardo's homes. (*Link – Assembly 68*)

In 1968 Alec Rose, aged fifty-nine, completed his solo round-the-world voyage when he returned to Portsmouth. His boat was *The Lively Lady* and he had sailed her 28,500 miles in 354 days.

5th   Sir Thomas Stamford Raffles, founder of Singapore, died in 1826.

The first Thomas Cook excursion took place in 1841 (from Leicester to Loughborough). (*Link – Assemblies 56, 78*)

Phineas T. Barnum, the circus proprietor and presenter of 'The Greatest Show on Earth', was born in 1810.

In 1952 this was the last date on which trams ran in London.

6th   Sir Thomas More, Chancellor of England, was executed in 1535 because he refused to sanction the marriage of Henry VIII to Anne Boleyn. He was canonised in 1935, and the 6th is now his feast day.

Louis Armstrong, the jazz trumpeter and singer, died in 1971. His song 'Black and Blue' provides thought-provoking assembly material for top juniors.

7th   Another 'first' in Channel crossings took place on this date in 1981. Stephen Ptacek made the first solar-powered flight.

Sir Arthur Conan Doyle, creator of Sherlock Holmes, died in 1930.

8th   La Fontaine, French writer of stories and 'thoughts for the day', died in 1621. His material is still a richly rewarding source for assemblies. (*Link – Assemblies 62, 65, 67, 73, 74*)

9th   Edward Heath, the former British Prime Minister and advocate of European Union was born in 1916.

The seven-hundred-year-old York Minster was hit by a bolt of lightning in 1984. The ensuing fire caused over a million pounds worth of damage.

10th The Emperor Hadrian died in 138. Hadrian's Wall covers a distance of seventy-three miles across the north of England.

A survey in 1951 discovered that British housewives worked a seventy-five-hour week.

11th Robert the Bruce, King of Scotland, was born in 1274.

12th Julius Caesar was born in 100 BC.

George Eastman, the photographer, inventor of roll films and cheap cameras, and founder of Kodak, was born in 1854.

13th Bertrand de Guesclin, 'the founder of French chivalry', knight and statesman, died in 1380. (*Link – Assembly 58*)

14th Bastille Day. This is a national holiday in France and commemorates the storming of the Bastille Prison in 1789. It marked the beginning of the Revolution and is a symbol of the victory of democracy over aristocratic rule.

Emmeline Pankhurst, the suffrage leader who organised the Women's Social and Political Union, died in 1928.

15th Feast of St Swithin, who died in 862.

In 1945, after more than two thousand nights of official 'blackout' during the war, lights came on again all over Britain.

Officially the beginning of the Muslim age in 622. (*Link – Assembly 60*)

16th In 1439, in an effort to stop the spreading of plague germs, kissing was banned in England. (*Link – Assembly 63*)

Roald Amundsen, the Norwegian explorer and navigator who was the first man to reach the South Pole, was born in 1872.

17th St Alexius's Day. Alexius, having left home, returned in disguise to live under his father's rule as a servant as badly treated as his peers. He revealed his identity just before he died.

In 1981 Queen Elizabeth II opened the Humber Estuary Bridge – a total length of 1.37 miles.

18th WG Grace, the legendary cricketer who scored 54,896 runs, including 126 centuries, and took 2,876 first-class wickets, was born in 1848.

In 1955 Disneyland was opened in California, USA.

19th This is the feast day of St Vincent de Paul, carer for galley slaves, whose story makes very good assembly material.

The first Wimbledon Lawn Tennis Championships were held in 1877.

20th This was the date, in 1969, when men – Neil Armstrong and Edwin Aldrin – landed on the moon for the first time.

21st Ancient Egyptians believed the world was created on this day.

Daniel Lambert, recorded as England's fattest ever man, died in 1809. He weighed 739 pounds (approximately 336 kilos).

22nd The Reverend William Spooner, a nervous speaker, became famous for his 'Spoonerisms'. One example was: 'Sir, you have tasted two whole worms.' (Sir, you have wasted two whole terms.) He was born on this day in 1844 and served both as dean and later warden of New College, Oxford.

The World Health Organisation was founded in 1946. (*Link – Assembly 63*)

23rd In 1904 Charles E Menches of St Louis, USA, thought of a new way to serve ice-cream – in a cone.

24th Alexandre Dumas, author of *The Three Musketeers*, was born in 1802.

Captain Webb, the first man to swim the English Channel (in 1875), drowned while attempting to swim Niagara Falls in 1883.

25th   This is the feast day of St James, disciple of Jesus and elder brother of St John. He was martyred in 44. This is also St Christopher's Day. He is the patron saint of travellers and is symbolised by a palm-tree staff. (*Link – Assembly 79*)

The English Channel was crossed for the first time by plane in 1909 (the pilot was Louis Blériot). On the same day in 1959 the first Hovercraft crossing was made.

26th   This is the feast day of St Anne, the mother of the Virgin Mary.

John Wilmont, Earl of Rochester, a poet and wit, and leader of the court of King Charles II, said of the king: '. . . never says a foolish thing; nor ever does a wise one.'

27th   Tradition has it that this was the day Noah sent the dove out of the ark.

Jim Laker took the most wickets ever in a cricket test match. This was nineteen – for England against Australia at Old Trafford, Manchester, in 1956.

28th   Johann Sebastian Bach, the composer, died in 1750.

Hans Andersen, the Danish author, died in 1875.

In 1964 Sir Winston Churchill, then eighty-nine, made his last appearance in the House of Commons.

29th   The Spanish Armada was defeated in 1588.

William Wilberforce, the social reformer, died in 1833. One month after his death the Slavery Abolition Act was passed by Parliament. (*Link – Assembly 68*)

In 1981 Prince Charles married Lady Diana Spencer.

30th   Henry Ford, of motorcar fame, was born in 1863.

In 1966 England won the World Soccer Cup for the first time when they defeated Germany 4–2 at Wembley.

31st   This is the feast day of St Ignatius Loyola. He founded the order of the Jesuits and wrote one of the most famous prayers of all time:

> Teach us, good Lord, to serve thee as thou deservest; to give and not to count the cost; to fight and not to heed the wounds; to toil and not to seek for rest; to labour and not to ask for any reward save that of knowing that we do thy will.

230

Assemblies linked by theme

This section seeks to aid teachers who wish to present a number of assemblies linked by *themes* which are popular ones in a primary school and RE context. The assemblies are shown by their number and title.

Animals

Concern

Courage

233

Wisdom

The stories

This section classifies the stories according to source categories – *folk, original or contemporary, religious, true* – for teachers who wish to use them in groupings of this nature. The assemblies are shown by their numbers and titles.

Folk stories, myths, legends

3	I'm sorry
11	The rich and the poor
16	Not so useless
21	You go first
22	Justice is done
26	Kindness at Christmas
27	Maria
30	The prince
39	We need a king!
43	Guard my treasure
44	More!
51	Is that really what you want?
62	Getting what you deserve
65	Fair shares
67	The cooking pot
73	Six wise men?
74	Be prepared

Original or contemporary stories

1	Being different
7	At the fair
10	One autumn afternoon
18	The star
19	How can I help?
38	Pass it on
54	Don't count your chickens before they're hatched
64	The sisters
78	Enough for everybody
80	The pattern

Religious stories

13	Akiba
14	The determined friends
29	Good value?
31	St Nathalan
33	Be prepared
42	In a garden in Medina
46	The healing of the blind man
47	The idols

True stories

Resources

Addresses

SAEs are welcomed when you contact the following addresses, which are useful for specially produced material.

General
Save the Children, 17 Grove Lane, London, SE5 8RD.
www.oneworld.org/scf/

The National Society's RE Centre, 36 Causton Street, London SW1P 4AU. The centre distributes the annual journal of the SHAP Working Party on World Religions in Education, which is particularly valuable for precise annual dates of religious festivals.
www.namss.org.uk/fests.htm

Independent Publishing Company, 38 Kennington Lane, London SE11 4LS. They publish a large selection of books, posters and cards relating particularly to South East Asian countries.

Christianity
Christian Education Movement, Royal Buildings, Victoria Street, Derby DE1 1GW. By subscribing to the CEM schools receive a termly mailing of material which is always useful for RE, and sometimes specially aimed at assemblies. www.cem.org.uk

Hinduism
Hindu Centre, 7 Cedars Road, London E15 4NE.

ISKCON Educational Services, Bhaktivedanta Manor, Hilfield Lane, Aldenham, Watford, Herts WD2 8EZ. www.iskcon.org.uk

Islam
IQRA Trust, 24 Culross Street, London W1Y 3HE.
www.iqratrust.org

Muslim Educational Trust, 130 Stroud Green Road, London N4 3RZ.

Judaism
Jewish Education Bureau, 8 Westcombe Avenue, Leeds LS8 2BS.

Books and Stories

One of the difficulties of recommending books is that, particularly in recent years, titles have not only gone out of print but have also changed publishers at a bewildering rate.

The wise teacher, therefore, will seek to build up a range in two areas. The first would be the background information type of book. A Bible dictionary is a useful reference and there are many good information books on festivals and celebrations from around the world.

The second collection will consist of folk tales which often produce marvellous assembly material. New anthologies appear with great regularity and should always be examined carefully. Old favourites like *Anansi*, the *Hodja, Brer Rabbit* and Aesop's *Fables* are suitable for many re-tellings and adaptations.

Other books published by Stanley Thornes in the area of Assemblies and Religious Education include:

Join With Us Book One by Jeanne L. Jackson (a book of assembly stories covering the whole school year)

Join With Us Book Two by Jeanne L. Jackson (a book of assembly stories covering the whole school year)

Red Letter Days by Jeanne L. Jackson (the Christian year in story for primary assembly)

Stanley Thornes Infant RE by Louis Fidge and Christine Moorcroft (two teacher resource books covering Years 1 and 2 (P2–P3) and each accompanied by 12 full colour, A2-sized posters)

Stanley Thornes Junior Steps in RE by Michael Keene and Jan Keene (teacher resource books covering the four junior years and supported by a pupil book at each year)

Resources for Music

The BBC's *Come and Praise* anthologies are the source for all the hymns recommended in this book. It would be hard to better this series for primary hymns.

Festivals by Jean Gilbert (Oxford University Press, Music Department, Great Clarendon Street, Oxford OX2 6DP) is a very useful anthology with suggestions for songs and musical activities related to festivals.